Stock Market Rules

Stock Market Rules

Fourth Edition

**50 of the Most Widely Held Investment Axioms
Explained, Examined, and Exposed**

Michael D. Sheimo

New York   Chicago   San Francisco   Lisbon   London   Madrid   Mexico City
Milan   New Delhi   San Juan   Seoul   Singapore   Sydney   Toronto

1 2 3 4 5 6 7 8 9 0   DOC/DOC   1 8 7 6 5 4 3 2

ISBN: 978-0-07-180325-0
MHID: 0-07-180325-4

e-ISBN: 978-0-07-180326-7
e-MHID: 0-07-180326-2

This publication is designed to provide accurate and authoritative information in regard to the subject matter covered. It is sold with the understanding that neither the author nor the publisher is engaged in rendering legal, accounting, or other professional service. If legal advice or other expert assistance is required, the services of a competent professional person should be sought.

> —From a Declaration of Principles Jointly Adopted by a Committee of the American Bar Association and a Committee of Publishers and Associations

McGraw-Hill books are available at special quantity discounts to use as premiums and sales promotions, or for use in corporate training programs. To contact a representative, please e-mail us at bulksales@mcgraw-hill.com.

This book is printed on acid-free paper.

For Linda . . . Forever . . .

Contents

Preface

It was a dark and gloomy morning. Slowly a bell rang out. Faster and faster it rang. Louder and louder it banged. Faster still it rang and rang with a deafening clang. And then the trading day started like it does every day for every session of the New York Stock Exchange.

Analysts called 2011 the *year of the axiom*. The market has either followed or broken all the rules. The past few years have been filled with overzealous bailouts, bad crashes, and crooked scams. It's enough to make an investor wonder about putting any money in the stock market. But as the ancient bard once said, "It's all we hath."

Although filled with disappointments since 2008, the market still had its miracles. Apple Computer (APPL) sold for $72.80 in December 2008, and nearly four years later was breaking through $670 a share. So much for price doubling being easier at low prices. At that same time Exxon Mobil (XOM) did poorly, going from $70.86 to around $87. With the high prices of gasoline, you'd think it would have done better. Bookseller Amazon (AMZN) went from $48.26 in December 2008 to $193.46 just three years later. Another strong performer was Google (GOOG). It hit a low of $282 in 2008, rising to $683 nearly four years later.

Although the next few years should fare better, there are never any guarantees in the stock market, other than fluctuation. Since 2007, the market has been extra volatile. It has offered the short sellers many opportunities to make money on the down side. The problem was that those opportunities also exacerbated the down side. Market regulators claim to maintain a fair and orderly market, but there are practices that go contrary to this philosophy. Here are three changes that the stock market should undergo:

1. The U.S. Congress should not be allowed to trade on inside information. Like all inside trading it takes away the fair, orderly, level playing field the stock market needs.
2. High volume, computerized "day trading," should not be allowed or should be taxed out of existence. It is price manipulation and does nothing positive for the stock market, the economy, or the investor. It only steals money from real investors.
3. The short selling rules of uptick and zero-plus tick should be reinstated, with even stronger restrictions. Along with that, naked short selling should be prosecuted. It's against the rules, and it's against the law.

So since it's always a bull market, when can we get back to the business of investing? There's an easy answer to that question. If not before; now. Now is the time to get back to it, although a certain amount of caution is always necessary. Some ideas on how and when to be cautious can come from reading the fourth edition of *Stock Market Rules*.

List of Illustrations

List of Tables

Stock Market Rules

RESEARCH

To say that research is important to investing is like saying that air is important to breathing. The strange thing is that research is often overlooked by the amateur and the professional alike. Instead they look for today's action. What's moving now? Where's the price going? Ideally, the investor knows ahead of time what's likely to be moving, where it's going, and why. To have a relatively small group of stocks that one follows well is both wise and often fruitful. If following the current group is not fruitful, do more research, and change the makeup. Find different stocks to follow; there are thousands to choose from.

Getting the basic information before the investment is made can do absolute wonders for saving the investor money. A sudden price increase should never be the only reason to buy a stock. An increase in either price or volume might call your attention to a particular company, but you should also get the background on what has happened and what is anticipated.

Part 1 examines getting information about stocks that double in price, companies that buy their own stock, investor sentiment, and bellwethers. It won't answer all questions about getting information, but it should give some background into some of the basics and old beliefs about stock selecting.

In recent times one only need look at the lost fortunes of WorldCom or Enron to see the disaster that can befall an investor who has little or no understanding of a company. There are people who got burned on both these stocks who have very little knowledge of what the companies did and what happened to them.

Do the research before you invest, not after.

CHAPTER 1

Get Information Before You Invest

Most of the complicated aspects of our lives could be made simpler if we gathered information before we took action. Asking *why*, *how*, *where*, and *what* is important when deciding to invest in stock:

- *Why* is this stock attractive to us? Is it soaring to new highs, or has it suddenly dropped lower in a way that seems unrelated to the overall market?
- *How* is that price going to recover or keep moving up?
- Always be asking, *Where* is the new business going to come from?
- *What* has happened to create the current situation, and is it for the long term or is it just a short-term anomaly?

This approach will help you avoid a shoot-from-the-hip approach to buying stock or becoming totally dependent on the inconsistent wisdom and opinions of others.

Depending entirely on the opinions of others or shooting from the hip can lead to many misunderstandings. Misunderstandings cause bad timing and poor, ineffectual strategies. Although investment advice can be helpful, it can be even more useful as a point of reference—as a second opinion—and shouldn't be accepted as the only approach.

In the stock market, the odds of doing well are improved for the investor who becomes familiar with the current action of the market and the particular stock of interest. You can become familiar with the action by asking why:

- Why is the market making this move?
- Why is this stock an attractive purchase now?

YOU CAN DO IT

Peter Lynch, the legendary former manager of Fidelity Magellan Fund, put it very succinctly when he said, "Everyone has the brain-power to follow the stock market. If you made it through fifth-grade math, you can do it."[1]

Yes, it's the old, "Are you smarter than a fifth grader?" idea. Actually it's even a little easier than fifth-grade math. In fact, the stock market pretty much got rid of fractions (the eighths) just to make it easier.

MARKET MOVES

The stock market is a continuous auction with the same product being bought and sold every business day. If there are more buyers than sellers, the market and the prices of individual stocks rise. If there are more sellers than buyers, prices fall. It's that simple.

But if it's so simple, then why does it seem so complicated? Why are all these investors buying and selling stock? If they're investors, shouldn't they all be buying and holding stock for its investment value? Why are people surprised when the stock market drops a few hundred points? Does a severe market correction mean that the economy will take a nosedive?

The newscasters always say that the stock market forecasts the economic situation six months to a year away. So what gives?

ANTICIPATION

The most important fact to remember is that the stock market always trades on anticipation of future events, and they always change. Professional investors are looking ahead six to twelve months, but (and here's the kicker) not always. Although the market might react strongly to some negative news, it is capable of dropping severely one day and more than recovering the next day. If the Dow Jones Industrial Average is down 50 or a couple of hundred points or more, the major investors don't care about what might happen in six months. They are concerned only with what might happen in the more immediate future—that being the next ten minutes. The faster the market drops, the shorter their focus becomes.

The believers of doom and gloom busily pat themselves on the back for being correct, and those who know better take a more moderate stance. Thankfully, it usually takes more than an overcorrection in the market to cause an economic recession.

REAL, IMAGINED, AND FABRICATED FACTORS

A real factor that motivates stock market buyers and sellers is money, specifically the availability of money. Money availability changes with the movement of interest rates and the earnings of corporations. This is partly why the economy and the stock market have had some serious problems in the last few years. Problems with mortgage loan defaults caused significant reductions in the money supply. Unemployment interfered with economic cash flow, again affecting the money supply. News of unemployment often affects the entire stock market. If the news is good, the market goes up. If unemployment increases, the market drops. Obviously, higher interest rates can be another negative factor that relates to decreased money availability. Negative news on money availability can have a strong influence on the movement of the overall market. Sometimes it's short term, and other times it can last for a longer time.

An imagined factor can be the respected opinion of an economist or market analyst concerning the current strength of the stock market. Ben Bernanke, current chairman of the Federal Reserve might make a less than positive statement about the economy. This would cause the market to take a dive. If this happens, sometimes recovery comes the next day; other times it can take a few days. Although Mr. Bernanke is not the only one to influence the stock market, he is often the most important. Frequently the effect of his comments lasts only a few days, after which the market moves on to other news.

A fabricated factor is the merciless hammering of computerized sell programs. These programs are operated primarily by large hedge funds and kick in during predetermined market conditions. They have nothing to do with investing or market values. They are based on price conditions and are as close to stock market manipulation as we get. At times, the market drops straight down from the opening, bottoms out, and then runs flat or begins to rise again. At times it rises a small amount only to fall further. The rise is usually referred to as a "dead cat bounce."

The sells are often implemented with the intent of testing market strength by pushing the market down as far as possible. "As far as possible" is a point that is reached when buyers enter the scene and stop the decline; that point is called "support." Professional stock traders in large funds or hedge funds like to see volatility in the stock market so they can play both sides and make money whether the market rises or falls. Most individual investors lack the resources, knowledge, or experience to do that kind of trading.

Investors who noticed the turn in the stock market by observing the daily decline in the S&P 500 Index (see Figure 1.1) or the Dow Jones Industrial Average and who listened to the market opinions given by many analysts before March 2008 would likely have taken some protective action. Market anticipation had been fueled

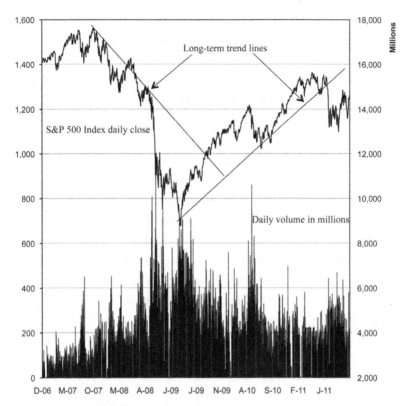

Data source: Yahoo! Finance Historical Prices

Figure 1.1   **S&P 500 Index, 2006–2011**

by a strong economy, and that was a bubble starting to burst. When the bad news came out, it became a deluge of selling. The housing bubble exploded in a tsunami of defaults on loans. And the crooks were all exposed as the tide rushed back out. The S&P 500 Index went from 1,565 in March 2007 to 676 in March 2009 (see Figure 1.1), losing more than half its value in two years.

STOCK MOVES: DOWN

Buying a car, a computer, or a new television only to see it on sale the following week can be a huge source of irritation to a consumer.

The same holds true for stocks. To pay $52 a share one day, and then hear some negative news and see a price of $42 the next week is not a pleasant experience. If your research and selection are valid, the price will probably recover and move to new highs. But the price damage on the way down can be difficult to endure. An interesting phenomenon can occur with a stock price that appears to keep on dropping.

As the price declines, investors will appear to buy up shares at perceived bargain prices. If enough of these bargain hunters appear, they can stop the price drop, but eventually the sellers can overpower them. The bottom is where the price stops declining and goes flat or begins to retrace its upward trend. The problem is that it is very difficult to see the bottom at the time it occurs. We have to observe it after the fact. In Figure 1.1 the bottom was reached on March 9, 2009, at a level of 676.53. On that day, no one knew for certain that the bottom had been reached.

ON SALE, LIMITED TIME ONLY

Many investors consider any market "dip," "pullback," "correction," or "bear market" a buying opportunity. The price is lower; the stock's on sale. The reasons for a price decline can be serious: lower earnings or estimates are predicted. The reason for a price decline might not be so serious: market correction, general profit taking, employee stock distribution, or no news-related reason at all. The investor should find out what the reason is before investing more money.

Information is easily obtained these days with the Internet news and information services:

1. Go to MSN.com, google.com, or yahoo.com and look for the "financial" section.
2. Once you're there, you can gather all sorts of information.

3. News, prices, charts, and lists of the most actively traded stocks can easily be found. Obviously news can also be obtained through other sources. Television, radio, and the newspapers are still important and available. But usually the browser finance section of the Internet will be the quickest source. The information is immediately available and can help you decide whether it's time to buy, sell, or hold a stock position.

As shown in Figure 1.2, in mid-September 2011, Netflix, a dealer in rented movie DVDs, encountered a problem. This time it wasn't earnings, but rather changes in corporate strategy:

Netflix sold off not on earnings, which were above estimates, but due to a massive loss of subscribers during the period. During its recent quarter, Netflix lost around 800,000 subscribers, a result of two major mistakes that the company made over the summer. First, it decided to raise rates on its most popular subscription plans. This definitely resulted in losing some subscribers, but Netflix assumed that the higher fees on the subscribers that remained with the company would more than make up for the lost subscribers. They were right, as evidenced by its record revenues during the quarter, but the loss of subscribers is definitely not something that Wall Street views as a positive in such a highly competitive industry.

The company's second big mistake was the decision to split up its streaming (online) and DVD rental businesses. After the decision was announced, customers were very vocal in their dislike of the idea, so much so that the company was forced to back-peddle and announce it would not be splitting the company after all. Despite the retreat, customers still fled, and for the first time in years Netflix ended a quarter with fewer subscribers than it had at the beginning.[2]

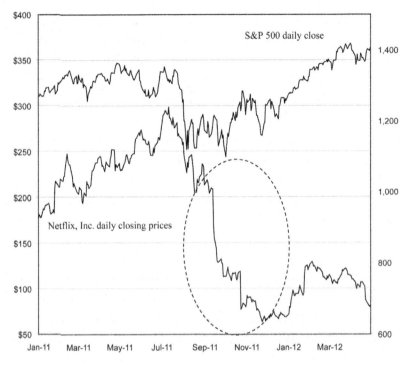

Data source: Yahoo! Finance Historical Prices

Figure 1.2   **S&P 500 Index versus Netflix (NFLX)**

Although ultimately the reason for the sell-off is almost always earnings, it can begin with other factors. These factors are believed to become a negative influence on future earnings. On this anticipation of lower earnings, Netflix fell from $216 to $77 a share. This drop was followed by further declines, as shown in Figure 1.2.

STOCK MOVES: SIDEWAYS

Again, ask questions and search for the answers. Why isn't the stock price moving? If other similar stocks and the overall market are doing well, there is a reason for a lack of movement in a given stock. Has there been bad news recently that has created a lack of investor interest, or is the stock currently a gem waiting to be rediscovered?

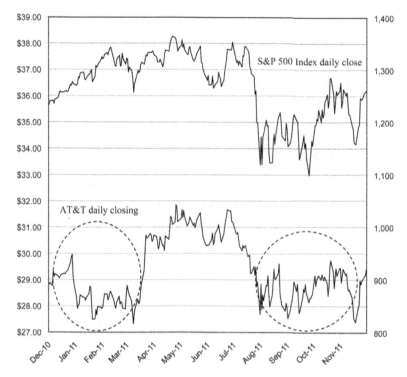

Data source: Yahoo! Finance Historical Prices

Figure 1.3   **S&P 500 Index versus AT&T, 2011**

Take a look at AT&T in Figure 1.3. Figure 1.3 shows where the price of AT&T went flat in January through March of 2011. At that time AT&T was having troubles with the Justice Department and the FCC, because of some possible antitrust violations. Obviously, the news caused a temporary lack of interest in the stock, and the price growth went on hold. The concerns appear to have abated toward the end of March, and the price improved significantly. There is another area of difficult price growth in August through November, but that is not much of a concern since it appears to be more market-driven. Notice that right above the second circle, the S&P 500 Index shows a similar pattern formation.

Although rare, undiscovered gems can experience dramatic price surges with even a small amount of publicity. Some investors follow a strategy of seeking out these gems. Sometimes they end up with well-run companies that the stock market doesn't like. The market isn't buying the stock. Often these are basically good companies with limited growth potential. The most successful investors search for companies with unlimited growth potential.

STOCK MOVES: UPWARD

Why a stock price is moving upward is important to investors who don't currently own it but would like to be in on the action. Normally when there is a sudden surge in either the stock market or an individual stock, the news appears quickly to trumpet the event.

In the middle of March 2011, Coke came out with great news:

Coke—the flagship brand of Coca-Cola (KO, Fortune 500)—is still No. 1, racking up 17 percent market share last year by selling 1.6 billion cases of soda. In second place, Diet Coke had a 9.9 percent market share. Pepsi (PEP, Fortune 500) ended the year with a 9.5 percent share, a 4.8 percent decrease in volume over the previous year. The switch marks a sea change in the industry. According to John Sicher, the editor and publisher of Beverage Digest, Pepsi has held the second position for decades.[3]

Obviously, this news plus the strong earnings and other fundamentals made Coke an attractive buy. That's exactly what happened. As shown by the first circle in Figure 1.4, the stock rose from $61 in mid-March to $66 in early April. The second circle shows Coke outperforming the stock market and advancing strongly.

OTHER IMPORTANT INFORMATION

News and price action are important, but they aren't the only important information to have when you're buying, holding, or selling stock. Other things tend to be important because they indicate how

Data source: Yahoo! Finance Historical Prices

Figure 1.4   **S&P 500 Index versus Coca Cola, 2011**

much the buyers desire the stock in question. Earnings and earnings growth are important. The amount of debt is a factor. Competition is a factor. Is the product currently marketable, or is it about to go the way of typewriters and CB radios? Additional information is readily available on the Internet and is easily checked. Some popular sites and headers are:

- Google.com, More/Finance
- MSN.com, Market Update
- Yahoo.com, Finance

There are two cautions.

1. Don't spend too much time on the intricacies of analysis. As Peter Lynch has noted, "A person infatuated with measurement, who has his head stuck in the sand of the balance sheets is not likely to succeed."[4]
2. It may look good statistically, but that doesn't necessarily make it a desirable investment.

Theoretically, the information you find on a stock is all reflected in the price action. Some investors believe this to such an extent that they don't do any research. But, it is only partly true. Add to that the mass hysteria that can quickly appear, and you have a hot stock or a disaster heading for the cliff. Either way, it is always advisable to search out the reasons behind a price move or lack of movement. To know why the stock price is acting the way it is can make all the difference.

Remember that many times the stock market is driven by professional investors who do not have the same strategies as individual investors. They are often looking for small gains on large positions and can afford to make more mistakes. Getting information and finding out why a stock is making a price move will help you make sound investment decisions—decisions to buy, sell, or hold a stock position.

CHAPTER 2

Price Doubling Is Easier at Low Prices

The most frightening thing about the idea that price doubling is easier at low prices is that those who believe it seldom consider risk. Price doubling often has nothing to do with the current price or that the lower the price, the higher the risk. If a stock has a price of $2 or $4 a share, you can often buy it, but finding someone to sell it to can be next to impossible. Such stocks are often heading for zero in short order. Even if you can put in a limit order at a doubled price, it doesn't mean that you will get an execution. There could be orders ahead of yours that are filled and the price drops before your order can be filled.

ADVICE FOR A PRICE

There are many people out there in cyberspace who will give advice or create newsletters or charting services for a substantial price. The advice or system might work for a while, but if the market changes dramatically, the advice or the system falls apart. Frankly, you would be better off going to the casino and wagering all your money on red 36 or any other number. The stakes would probably be higher and the odds better. So it's best to avoid nearly all "low-priced" stocks. And even more so, avoid the "advice sellers" promising recently discovered secrets or well-developed signal systems. They just add to the losses.

SOME 2011 LOW-PRICED STOCKS

The companies discussed below may end up being excellent in the future, and that could be the time to invest in them. The stocks were recommended on the basis of low price and insider buying. Although the buying was primarily the result of options exercises, the exercises were substantial. When you look at the price chart, it does make you wonder if people bought because they had to or they truly believed. Either way, the stock did shoot up. The trouble was that it didn't stay up for long.

Novatel Wireless, Inc. (NASDAQ: NVTL), shares were trading at $5.11 in April 2011. Novatel Wireless, Inc., and its subsidiaries provide wireless broadband access solutions for the mobile communications market worldwide. See full details at its website: http://www.novatelwireless.com.

Whatever the reason for the insider buying in April 2011, as Figure 2.1 shows, it did push the stock price higher. Things were moving along nicely until early August. On August 4, 2011, the company announced a net loss of $3.9 million, or 12 cents per share, compared with a loss of $22 million, or 70 cents per share, in the same period a year earlier. Then things changed for the worse.

The news was better than it had been earlier, but it wasn't good enough for many investors, so the price took a significant hit. Does this mean that it's even a better candidate for price doubling? Not necessarily. It does mean that the risk significantly increased, and this was the concern for the individual investor.

Idenix Pharmaceuticals, Inc. (shown in Figure 2.2), is a biopharmaceutical company that engages in the discovery and development

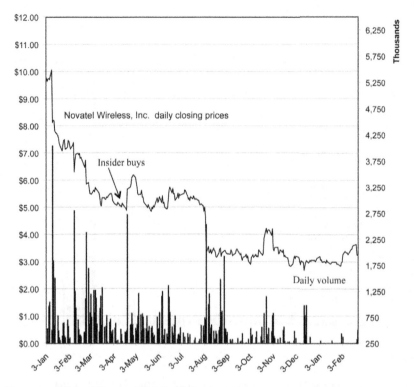

Data source: Yahoo! Finance Historical Prices

Figure 2.1   **Novatel Wireless, Inc., 2011**

of drugs for the treatment of human viral diseases in the United States and Europe. More details can be found at its website: http://www.idenix.com.

The company is described as having insider buying activity. However, the insider doing the buying is Novartis AG, a very large pharmaceutical company owning more than 10 percent of the company's stock. It isn't likely that Novartis AG is just trying to firm up the price, but rather it is making an investment.

The company had a reasonable growth year in 2011, and then in early 2012 it announced an important medical study it was

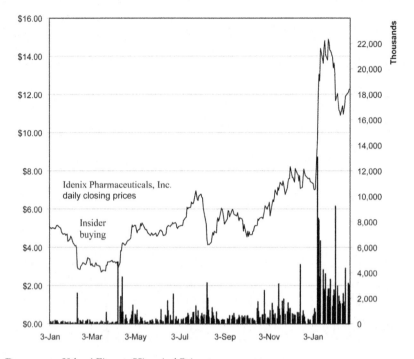

Data source: Yahoo! Finance Historical Prices

Figure 2.2   **Idenix Pharmaceuticals, Inc. (NASDAQ: IDIX), 2011–2012**

conducting. The company was not without risk. It still needs to get some positive revenues and earnings, but the interest of Novartis AG clearly made a difference. As shown in Figure 2.2, the price went from $3 a share to just under $15 a share. Not a bad move, but a risky one. So it can happen with a low-priced company, but the risk is not for everyone. Now look at some high-priced stocks.

SOME HIGHER-PRICED STOCKS

Many people erroneously believe that higher-priced stocks won't double in the near future. Although that may be true of some stocks, it is not true for them all. Many companies will see a sudden surge in business, and the price of the stock will rise accordingly. Probably

Data source: Yahoo! Finance Historical Prices

Figure 2.3 **Berkshire Hathaway, 1990–2011**

the most dramatic illustration of this is what happened to Berkshire Hathaway, Warren Buffett's company.

Back in 1990, we all could have bought one share of Berkshire Hathaway for just over $3,000 (see Figure 2.3). At the time that one share would have been considered a "round lot." Most stocks have 100 shares in a round lot. In the next 10 years that one share would have more than doubled in price at least six times. In 2012, we would have one share worth more than $100,000. So it begs the question: At what point did the stock become too high-priced to double? It never did and probably still hasn't, although the number of investors with cash available to buy that one share has decreased.

Shoulda, coulda, woulda. Yep, we should have taken that flyer with a well-known conservative investor.

Data source: Yahoo! Finance Historical Prices

Figure 2.4   **Apple Computer Corporation, 1998–February 2012**

We can't forget about Apple Computer (NASDAQ: AAPL). This stock floated in a narrow range for about 10 years and then they came out with some innovative ideas and created a whole new industry.

As shown in Figure 2.4, the price took off like a rocket. Back in 2001, you could have bought the stock for $15 to $25 a share only to see it fly to over $500 in about 10 years. That's a high-priced stock doubling and doubling again.

More high-priced stocks are shown in Table 2.1.

IS IT OVER?

According to The Associated Press on March 8, 2012:

Table 2.1   **Other High-Priced Stocks That Doubled or More**

	From	To	Time
Priceline.com, Inc. (NASDAQ: PCLN)	$176.54	$764.75	2.50 yr.
Chipotle Mexican Grill, Inc. (NYSE: CMG)	$217.74	$430.78	1.25 yr.
Autozone, Inc. (NYSE: AZO)	$198.36	$397.13	1.75 yr.

The stock market is missing you. For more than three years, ordinary investors disgusted with wild swings have pulled money out of stocks. They've missed a breathtaking bull market: The Dow Jones industrial average has almost doubled from its low point during the Great Recession on March 9, 2009.

In the meantime, corporate America has racked up double-digit profit gains. If investors valued stocks at normal historical levels based on profits, we would be celebrating Dow 15,000, not Dow 13,000.

But the profit explosion is over, and the Wall Street pros who trade stocks mostly for big institutions and the rich are getting antsy. They've been doing the buying. And if Main Street doesn't join them, the historic rally could slow or even end.

Everyday investors "are more aware of the risk of the market," says Howard Silverblatt, senior index analyst at Standard & Poor's. "They're nervous. They're scared."

The Dow closed above 13,000 last week for the first time since May 2008, four months before the financial crisis. In a sense, the milestone was disappointing: Profits are at an all-time high, yet the Dow is well below its record of 14,164, set in October 2007.

Even though profits are growing, individual investors aren't buying. That shows up in something called the multiple—the ratio of what investors are willing to pay for a company's stock, compared with its annual profits.

If a stock trades for $100 and the company has made $5 in profit per share, its multiple is a fairly high 20. A higher multiple means more confidence that profits will grow. Maybe investors believe the company will turn a bigger profit next year of $7 or $8.

These days the multiples don't show much confidence. Investors are paying a multiple of 13.5 times the past year's earnings for stocks. The typical multiple over the past 75 years is 16. If that were the multiple today, the Dow would be sitting above 15,000.

"We've built profits in the past three years," says Jim Paulsen, chief investment strategist at Wells Capital Management. "Now we need to value them differently."[1]

A PREDICTION, ANOTHER OPINION

Various bloggers and Internet newsletters will make predictions. Some are spot on and others are way off. Table 2.2 shows a list of eight stocks that are predicted to double in 2012. The article appeared in *Daily Finance* on December 23, 2011, and was written by Doug McIntyre:

It is unusual for a stock's price to double in a year, but several well-known companies' shares have done just that recently. Netflix shares doubled in 2010. Apple's shares rose 145 percent in 2009 in the midst of a climb that eventually made it the No. 1 public corporation in America based on market cap. Most stocks that move up 100 percent in a year do so for one of two reasons: either because the company is getting purchased at a premium or because of an extraordinary earnings or revenue event. The second was the case for Netflix in 2010, although the improvement in earnings reversed itself in 2011.

Table 2.2   **Price Doubling Prediction**[2]

Company	Price 12/23/11	Price 3/16/12	p/e*	Price Target
Ford Motor Co.	$10.95	$12.68	2.57	$21.90
Netflix, Inc.	$72.62	$110.30	**26.52**	$145.24
Research In Motion	$13.92	$14.70	3.34	$27.84
United Continental Holdings	$19.85	$19.90	8.81	$39.70
Groupon, Inc.	$22.84	$18.00	n/a	$45.68
Gannett Co., Inc.	$13.55	$15.18	8.03	$27.10
Sprint Nextel Corp.	$2.31	$2.87	n/a	$4.62
Bank of America Corp.	$5.60	$9.70	**30.33**	$11.22

* Price-to-earning ratio (p/e) is a ratio obtained by dividing the price by earnings of a stock. It is often used as a value measure of the stock. Higher than other stocks is risky and lower than other stocks is conservative and less risky. Ideal is usually in a range similar to other stocks. Too low can also be a lack of investor interest.

There's a mixture of price levels in the group; it will be interesting to see what December 2012 shows for final price levels. Notice that Netflix and Bank of America have rather high p/e ratios, so they could have larger obstacles to overcome. The n/a ratios for Groupon and Sprint Nextel Corp. were caused by negative earnings.

IMPORTANT POINT

Not every stock will behave in the way we discuss above. Some will take five or ten years to double in price. But the point is that it's not worth the risk involved to sock money into investments of low quality just because they have a low price. First pick a stock of decent quality based on earnings, income, debt, and future prospects. Then look at the price.

CHAPTER 3

Good Companies Buy Their Own Stock

Someday you might see a headline like this: "Johnson & Johnson Announces a Purchase of 2 Million Shares of Its Own Stock."

The stock must be a good buy if the company is willing to buy its own shares. That is still a common belief. The stockbroker tells a client, the client tells a friend, and so on, until a stock price begins to move upward. It can be one of the ways the big guys, the professional traders, end up taking money from each other and from the small investor.

Think of yourself as the CEO of a large company. The price of your stock has been advancing slower than usual. You know that there aren't any real problems; it's just that there hasn't been any great news lately. So you think and think and think. You hold some focus group meetings and ask for suggestions. Suddenly it hits you. Why not spend some of the billions of extra cash sitting around by putting it into a stock buyback program. That would get some good headlines, and the institutional investors will love it too. Stock buybacks continue to make positive news headlines.

For stocks that are included in the S&P 500 Index, stock buybacks increased 21.6 percent to $109.2 billion during the second quarter of 2011—at this point there had been eight consecutive quarterly increases in stock buybacks. The following is from a United Business Media press release dated December 21, 2011:

> Companies returned to the $100 billion quarterly buyback level in the second quarter as they continued to match and control employee options, thereby protecting their earnings per share. At this point, companies are continuing to use buybacks to prevent earnings dilution from employee options, as well as shares used for dividend reinvestment programs. Few companies are venturing outside of the box to purchase additional shares, as was the common practice from late 2005 through mid-2007, according to Howard Silverblatt, Senior Index Analyst at S&P Indices.[1]

The fourth quarter had similar news about stocks in the S&P 500 Index:

> S&P 500 Stock Buybacks Increase for Ninth Consecutive Quarter; Q3 2011
>
> Buybacks Up 48.8 Percent Over Q3 2010, Share Count Starts to Decline—Some EPS Impact Expected for Q4[2]

FACTS ABOUT BUYBACKS

Here are some facts about stock buybacks. They aren't a secret and have appeared many times in the news, especially in *The Wall Street Journal*:

1. Buybacks lower the number of shares outstanding in the active stock market. This spreads the company's future profits over a smaller base, increasing the earnings per share. Some call it earnings manipulation. However, unlike dividends, buybacks don't create tax bills for

shareholders. This makes the action more attractive to professional investors.

2. Buyback announcements can temporarily boost share prices, but companies don't always repurchase all the stocks they are authorized to buy. This makes the action seem more like a publicity stunt than anything else.

3. Since buybacks tend to increase per-share earnings and stock prices, they can be an advantage for corporate executives whose compensation often depends on achieving profit and price targets. They can also benefit employees with large holdings of stock options, ultimately representing a larger stake in the company.

4. Buybacks aren't always a great event. At best, they represent a behavior on the part of companies when they can't find profitable ways to invest shareholders' money. At worst, they are a lazy way to meet performance targets by boosting earnings per share and ultimately stock prices.

5. Buybacks haven't always been successful at resurrecting slow prices of tech stocks. Tech companies try to make the transformation from a growth stock to a mature stock using buybacks. More mature companies typically have lower price-to-earning (p/e) multiples. Sometimes valuations can fall fast enough to undermine positive aspects of a buyback program.

SOME BUYBACKS FROM 2011

Let's look at some stock buybacks from 2011:

1. "Pfizer Inc. (NYSE: PFE) added to its prior buyout plan with some $5 billion this week. Union Pacific Corporation (NYSE: UNP) announced this week that it would buy back up to 40 million shares, which comes

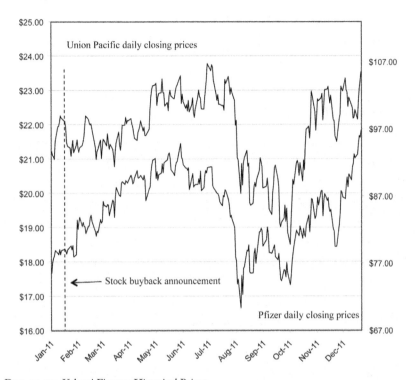

Data source: Yahoo! Finance Historical Prices

Figure 3.1   **Stock Buybacks, 2011**

to about $375 million or so versus a market cap of $46 billion."[3]

You can easily see a positive impact on Pfizer and Union Pacific prices in Figure 3.1. The price immediately jumped about a dollar a share for Pfizer and kept on rising until May, when the market started a correction. As the market recovered from the correction, so did the price of Pfizer.

2. Union Pacific jumped nearly $5 a share initially, but seemed more reluctant to follow the market upward. Obviously there are other factors affecting these stock prices. The upward surge could also be credited to what

the entire stock market was doing at the time. This is also true for the correction and secondary downtrend from July to October.

POSITIVE EVENT, MAYBE

Although a company buying large quantities of its own stock is a positive event because it at least has the cash to make the buy, always remember that the company might have ulterior motives. Those motives do not necessarily favor the individual investor. In some instances, companies will announce large stock buybacks followed by the news of massive layoffs. It's interesting to note that Pfizer had layoffs of 1,100 employees at about the time of the buyback announcement. Obviously the layoffs weren't really to save money, but rather to make the financials look better. This picture is enhanced even further with the stock buyback.

TRUE VALUE GROWTH

True value comes from the company that is growing. It doesn't come from laying off people or juggling the books to make the company look better on paper. The growth company is increasing the number of jobs and putting out more products or developing new products. These are the factors that make the balance sheet look better.

Take a look at what *The New York Times* had to say:

> What is more, share buybacks have not fulfilled their stated purpose of rewarding investors over the last decade, experts say. It's a symptom of a deeper problem, which is a lack of investment in the long term, said William W. George, a Harvard Business School professor and former chief executive of Medtronic, a medical technology company. "If we're not investing in research, innovation and entrepreneurship, we're going to be a slow-growth country for a decade."[4]

It's important for the investor to take the news of stock buy-backs with a healthy amount of skepticism rather than accepting the information as great news.

WHAT HAPPENS TO THE STOCK?

When a stock buyback is announced, invariably you'll hear some-body say, "We're buying the stock because we believe it's a fair investment price." Yeah, right. In most cases the price is at a three- or five-year high and not at a low as you'd expect.

Let's take a look at a few (see Table 3.1):

Table 3.1   **Stock Buyback Companies, 2012**

Date	Company	Symbol	Amount
2/17/12	FMC Corp.	FMC	$250 million[5]
1/26/12	Time Warner Cable	TWC	$4 billion[6]
2/17/12	Nordstrom	JWN	$800 million[7]
2/17/12	Alaska Air Group	ALK	$50 million[8]
2/15/12	Comcast	CMCSA	$6.5 billion[9]

If you look at Figure 3.2, you can easily see that all these stocks are being repurchased at three-year highs or more. So much for tim-ing the market. Why do you suppose people wait until the stock is moving to new highs? Are they trying to eat up all that extra cash?

EXPANSION AND HIRING ARE TOO LONG TERM

Companies could use all their extra cash for expansion and hiring new workers, but that's too long term a commitment. This is why companies aren't hiring, even though they have the money to do so. If they expand and hire and the economy has another setback, they look bad. Better to get rid of the money in a safe unchallengeable

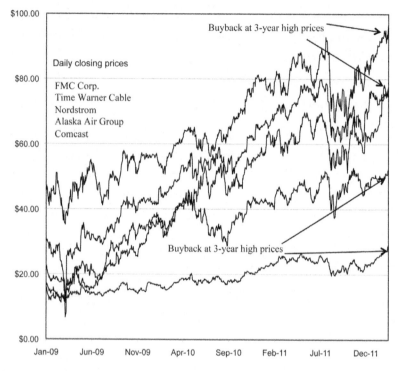

Data source: Yahoo! Finance Historical Prices

Figure 3.2   **Stock Prices, 2009–2012**

place, like the company itself. Then if they need more shares in the future, they can just do a split or issue a stock dividend. Also, buying back stock makes the company look better and helps the executives get more bloated bonuses.

WHAT HAPPENS TO THE PURCHASED STOCK?

Much of the stock that is purchased is simply retired, clearing up some of the dilution problems. Other shares are used for employee retirement programs and stock option plans. The announcement of a stock buyback should not be the only criteria used for choosing a stock. In fact a buyback could be neutral to negative. More important criteria should be based on real growth of earnings and revenues as well as growth expectations.

HAVE BUYBACKS REPLACED SPLITS?

Buybacks have probably not replaced stock splits, although for now buybacks may be more frequent. As companies need to attract new investors, they will try anything, including splits if necessary. However, it's becoming obvious that splits are currently not the favorite way to go.

It should also be noted that these are not the only companies doing stock buybacks. It's a growing trend with new announcements coming out every day. So it's a trend that will probably be with us for a while.

CHAPTER 4

Short-Term Investor Sentiment Outweighs a Lot of Arithmetic

Investor sentiment can come in different varieties. It is as basic as the investor's opinion of where the market is going in the next few months.

TWO KINDS OF INVESTORS

There are two kinds of investors: individual investors and professional investors. The differences between them can be extreme. While most individual investors prefer a slow and steady market, professional high-frequency traders prefer volatility. The high-frequency traders can set their computer algorithms to make a significant profit on a penny or less. They want to short the market on the way down, unwind their positions, and take another penny on the way up.

Individual investors want a slower pace and investments based on value with just a little speculation thrown in for extra gains. Following is information about the AAII Sentiment Survey:

The AAII Sentiment Survey measures the percentage of individuals who are bullish, bearish, and neutral about the stock market over the next six months. Originally started in 1987 as a weekly survey sent out via snail mail to a random sample of AAII members, the survey has been conducted on-line since the beginning of 2000. Members of AAII can vote once a week at the Member Surveys area of AAII.com. Results of the survey are compiled on a weekly basis (Thursdays) at the AAII Web site and are also published weekly in Barron's. The average AAII member is a male in his late-50s with a graduate degree. In addition, over half of AAII members have an investment portfolio of at least $500,000. Taking this into account, the AAII Sentiment Survey is unique among sentiment surveys in that it represents the upper echelon of active, hands-on individual investors.[1]

Here is a sample of the American Association of Individual Investors weekly survey of its 117,000 members covering where the stock market is going in the next six months. The results for January 14, 2012 are:

Bullish	48.9%
Neutral	34.0%
Bearish	17.2%

Change from Previous Week
Bullish	8.3%
Neutral	5.4%
Bearish	13.7%

Long-Term Average
Bullish	39%
Neutral	31%
Bearish	30%

It's easy to see that the sentiment of AAII members was becoming increasingly bullish in January 2012. This is the viewpoint of individual investors, not the hedge fund or pension fund professionals. This information is highly respected and used by professionals, although not necessarily in the way you might think. There's an old belief that the investing crowd is right during the trend, but wrong at the end.

Some of the high-flying professional traders will watch this sentiment information with a contrarian eye. As the sentiment becomes more extreme, they get ready for a reversal.

PROS DON'T CARE ABOUT STATISTICS ALL THE TIME

When it comes to what's happening with investor sentiment, professional traders don't care about the statistics relating to the value of their stock interest. All they care about is what's going to happen to the price or what can they make happen with the price. They put their finger on the sell button and hold their breath, hoping it's the right move.

As Figure 4.1 shows, the sell programs went into effect in the last half of July 2011. The market was hammered hard by sell programs and negative investor sentiment. Most of the bearish sentiment was caused by the U.S. debt downgrade. This did not change until the latter part of August, although the market did appear to hit bottom in early August. When August ended, buyers came out and investors started buying again. This represented a shift in investor sentiment from sell, to not sell, to buy.

When sentiment goes south, the professional traders push the button and the computerized sell programs kick in, unloading thousands of shares. Other professional traders see the action and reach for their sell buttons. All of a sudden the market is down a couple of hundred points. All this has nothing to do with the numeric value of the stocks involved. It is a created situation and usually temporary. These situations will often be heralded by announcements of the

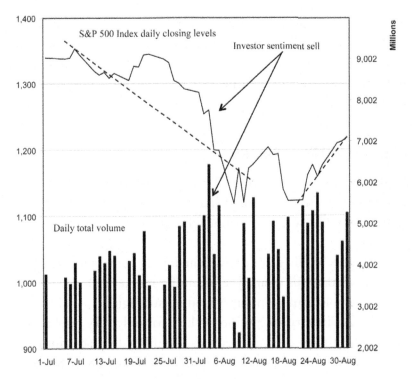

Data source: Yahoo! Finance Historical Prices

Figure 4.1   **S&P 500 Index, 2011**

weakening economy in Europe, but the so-called concern is really over the following day.

COMPUTERIZED PROGRAMS

The individual investor can buy computerized buy-and-sell programs on the Internet. They'll spin you every which way. Actually most of the web browsers have all the indicators you'll need to make your own decisions. It's just a matter of learning what they mean and practicing how to read them. Technical indicators are fine for what they are; they even work once in a while. But understanding some simple chart patterns might give you a better understanding of what might happen next. All this is mostly for the dedicated stock trader—the one who gets it right on some occasions and wrong on others. It's really not necessary for long-term investors. Understanding the company and where it's trying to go is more important to them.

HIGH-FREQUENCY TRADING

High-frequency trading (HFT) is the use of sophisticated technological tools to trade securities like stocks or options. It is typically characterized by several distinguishing features:

1. It is highly quantitative, employing computerized algorithms to analyze incoming market data and implement proprietary trading strategies.
2. An investment position is held for only very brief periods of time—even just seconds—and rapidly trades into and out of those positions, sometimes thousands or tens of thousands of times a day.
3. There is no net investment position at the end of a trading day.
4. It is mostly employed by proprietary firms or on proprietary trading desks in larger, diversified firms.
5. It is very sensitive to the processing speed of markets and of its own access to the market.

In high-frequency trading, programs analyze market data to capture trading opportunities that may open up for only a fraction of a second to several hours. To such programs, earnings or revenues are irrelevant; they trade only on the basis of price. High-frequency trading uses computer programs and sometimes specially designed hardware to hold short-term positions in equities, options, futures, exchange-traded funds (ETFs), currencies, and other financial instruments that possess electronic trading capability. High-frequency traders compete on the basis of speed with other high-frequency traders, not with long-term investors (who typically look for opportunities over a period of weeks, months, or years). They compete with one another for very small, consistent profits.[2]

Investing for them is an entirely different ballgame that takes advantage of a computerized auction system to squeeze out profits from the tiniest differences. When they are on the move, the individual investor has two choices: go along for the ride or wait on the sidelines.

Flash Crash

The "flash crash" of May 6, 2010, was believed to be caused by high-frequency trading, with computerized sell programs kicking in and forcing the Dow Jones Industrial Average to experience one of its largest one-day point losses (see Figure 4.2). The Dow Jones Industrial Average was down more than 700 points during the day, but it partly recovered by the end of the trading session.

The market quickly recovered in the next few days. This could be defined as market manipulation, except that it's not just one company, person, or computer causing the action. It's several traders taking quick action, so therefore it's not technically manipulation. Reality is a different story.

High-frequency trading is likely to be with us for a long time and will probably cause other volatile reactions in the stock market. The best advice to the individual investor is to hang on for the ride and take advantage if you are able.

Regulators Are Concerned

The following is from *The New York Times*, May 1, 2012:

> For years, high-frequency trading firms have operated in the shadows, often far from Wall Street, trading stocks at warp speed and reaping billions while criticism rose that they were damaging markets and hurting ordinary investors.

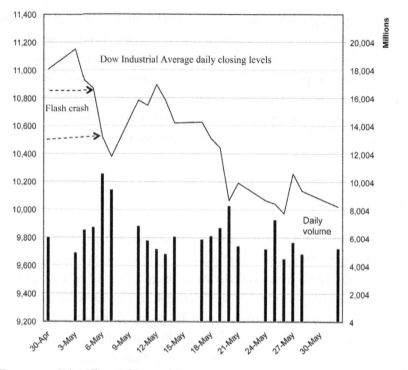

Data source: Yahoo! Finance Historical Prices

Figure 4.2   Dow Jones Industrial Average 2010 Flash Crash

Now they are stepping into the light to buff their image with regulators, the public and other investors.

After quietly growing to account for about 60 percent of the seven billion shares that change hands daily on United States stock markets, the firms are trying to stave off the regulators who are proposing to curb their activities. To make their case, the firms have formed their first industry trade group, hired former Securities and Exchange Commission staff members and spent nearly $2 million in the last few years on Washington lobbying and contributions to lawmakers. Some even want to be called "automated trading professionals" rather than high-frequency traders.[3]

Don't Overreact

The important thing to remember about sentiment whether with high-frequency trading or a slower secondary down trend is not to overreact. Let the professionals do that. They make money from overreacting. This is the time for us to keep our heads and look for opportunities.

It Should Be Stopped

Here is another quote from *The New York Times*:

> As a group, they earned $12.9 billion in profit in 2009 and 2010, according to the Tabb Group, a specialist on the markets.
>
> The S.E.C. started to think these firms needed tighter controls in early 2009 when analysts for the first time began to point to the sector's billions in profit, and critics wondered whether their technological firepower gave them an unfair advantage.[4]

High-frequency trading does nothing positive for the economy or the stock market. At the end of the day high-frequency traders own no securities. It's simply get in, hammer down the market, and get out. Effectively it is stealing money from investors. It should be controlled, stopped, or taxed out of existence. It is totally contrary to a fair and orderly market and needs some decisive control. The stock market has enough problems without having to fight technological manipulations. This is one that you as an individual investor should complain to the SEC and your congressional representatives about.

CHAPTER 5

Watch the Bellwethers

The 1960 edition of *Merriam-Webster's Collegiate Dictionary* defined a bellwether as "a leader of a thoughtless crowd."

Merriam-Webster possibly had the stock market in mind. More recent editions of the dictionary have redefined a bellwether as "one that takes the lead or initiative" or "an indicator of trends." Stock market bellwethers are individual company stocks that are believed to lead the market. If a turn in the market is coming, those who watch these stocks believe that the bellwether will turn first.

INDUSTRY BELLWETHERS

Bellwethers can relate to the entire market, to a sector, or to a smaller industry group. They might be leaders of Internet stocks or technology stocks. Someday you might read an article like the following:

> Technology stocks stabilized after Tuesday's slide on growing worries about slack demand in the computer industry. The Nasdaq composite index, which tumbled nearly 25 points on Tuesday, fell to 2988, but several computer-industry bellwethers rebounded. Intel (INTC) rose to $24.64 up $1.00, and Apple Computer (AAPL) rose $3.89 to $492.8.

Data source: Yahoo! Finance Historical Prices

Figure 5.1   **S&P 500 Index versus Apple Computer, 2009–April 2011**

The above bit lists Intel Corp. and Apple Computer as bellwethers for the computer industry. When the term *bellwether* is used
in this way, it is with a loose interpretation. In this case it is more
than a stock price that turns before the others; it is a descriptive term
synonymous with *sector, industry,* or *market leader.* But in the real
world does it work? Let's take a look. Figure 5.1 looks at the S&P
500 Index as compared to Apple Computer for the years 2009–2011.

Although you can find minor instances in which Apple acted
as a bellwether, at least two times there were more obvious leads.
Toward the end of April 2010 (A) and beginning of May, the market
wanted to correct, but Apple kept fighting the trend and went flat
with some volatility. It then rose. A similar occurrence took place

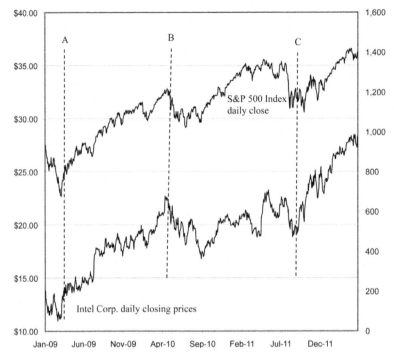

Data source: Yahoo! Finance Historical Prices

Figure 5.2   **Intel Corp. versus S&P 500 Index, 2009–2011**

in July 2011 (B) and August of 2011. And another occurrence took place in February 2012 (C).

Intel Corporation, a supplier of computer processors and other computer equipment, has also been considered a bellwether (see Figure 5.2). As with Apple, Intel Corp. shows a similar tendency to act as a bellwether. In February 2009 (A), April 2010 (B), and August 2011 (C), there were signals you might expect of a bellwether. Signals appear quickly and can change in a moment, although once they occur you can look back and see them. Probably a more important fact is not that they turn ahead of the stock market but rather that they run so close to what the market does. This means that they can be used as one more confirmation of where the stock market is going.

Following is an excerpt from an article that Hilary Kramer wrote discussing bellwethers:

> And . . . they're off. Alcoa fired the ceremonial starter's pistol for a critical earnings season last Monday, and the results were solid. The company forecast 7 percent growth in aluminum volume, an encouraging sign that global economic activity may not be as weak as many had feared.
>
> Still, while I do expect a generally positive earnings season, we're absolutely in for some surprises along the way. JPMorgan and Citigroup have already provided a couple.
>
> Here are seven companies reporting in the coming days I recommend you keep a close eye on, because they are good barometers for where this season is going:

International Business Machines	(NYSE: IBM)
Caterpillar	(NYSE: CAT)
Google	(NASDAQ: GOOG)
Intel	(NASDAQ: INTC)
3M	(NYSE: MMM)
McDonald's	(NYSE: MCD)
Whirlpool	(NYSE: WHR)[1]

This article is a good representation of news articles regarding bellwethers and the stock market. It gives good details and gives you information you can look up to confirm or add to. The bellwethers discussed can be used in the future as representative of various segments of the stock market.

Of course we must look closely at IBM in a discussion of bellwethers. For many years Big Blue has been looked at as the holy grail of bellwethers. Even today many investors will check to see what the market is doing and then check IBM to see if it confirms or diverges from the market.

A look at Figure 5.3 shows what we can expect. There are several instances in which IBM has turned or has increased at a

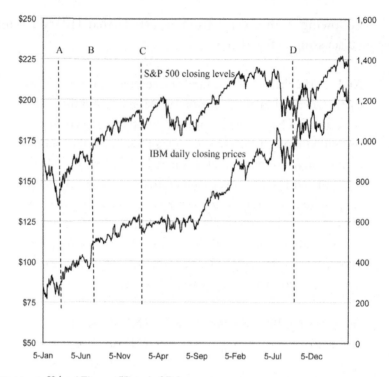

Data source: Yahoo! Finance Historical Prices

Figure 5.3   **IBM versus S&P 500 Index, 2009–April 2011**

stronger rate than the S&P 500 Index. Points A and B show areas where IBM turned only slightly before the market. Point C shows where the market rose and IBM went rather flat. The market then corrected downward. Point D shows IBM a bit stronger than the market, followed by a correction from both.

Also, IBM is a company that everyone expects to provide some direction for the economy as a whole. It has an enormous global reach, and many other businesses depend on IBM for their computer needs. No wonder IBM's earnings are always of great interest to the market. When it shows an increase in revenues and an increase in the numbers of long-term service contracts signed, this demonstrates that companies are looking forward to better times ahead. IBM's share price is positively affected, and the stock market follows suit. The following is from *International Business Times*, October 17, 2011:

> IBM, the No. 2 global technology company, reported third-quarter results that narrowly beat analyst expectations. They could be a bellwether for the entire technology sector.
>
> Operating earnings rose 15 percent to $3.28 a share, about 6 cents ahead of estimates, while revenue gained about 14 percent to $26.15 billion, slightly below estimates.
>
> Diluted earnings rose 13 percent to $3.19. IBM also boosted the full-year earnings outlook to at least $12.95 a share from $12.87.
>
> IBM shares dipped nearly 4 percent in after-hours trading to $179.79. They had closed at $186.59.
>
> IBM CFO Mark Loughridge began an investor call during which he cited "terrific revenue growth" for the company's most advanced Power servers, which operate the Watson supercomputer.[2]

It's important to note that this information on bellwethers is history. In fact it's nearly ancient history. If you want to watch bellwethers as an indicator of strength and direction, you must monitor them every trading day. No one will hold up a brightly colored sign saying that the bellwether is giving a signal. It must be observed and a judgment call made on the event. What did they do today or yesterday? What did they do last week? The historic look is more of an academic study than a useful indicator.

In Figure 5.3 going back to 2009, IBM clearly turns with the market and nearly mirrors its progress. It shows strength and weakness that are virtually identical to the S&P 500 Index. Is it a leader of the "thoughtless crowd"? Sometimes yes, sometimes no.

Although the bellwether signals exist, they can be misleading or barely existent. The fact that they confirm the market trend is most obvious. Therefore, they are one more indicator illustrating the market's strength. Like most indicators, they should not be relied on solely, but instead they should be used to confirm or deny others.

ANALYSIS

There are several ways to analyze companies and their common stock, but only one thing is important to the investor: an increase in price that is higher and faster than the more secure "fixed income" investments. This might relate to how well the business operates, but it's not always the case. There are poorly run businesses whose common stock is quite successful. Some of the successes in the banking industry or the airline industry are good examples. The opposite can also be true. There are some well-run businesses whose stock is terrible. The company or its product line might be too small to be exciting to the stock market. This is why finance professors frequently do poorly when investing. They can find good companies, but the stock market doesn't like them or buy them.

Some knowledge of trends, both of the stock market and of individual stocks, is important. Is the current primary market trend up, down, or in a secondary movement? How is the price trend of the individual stock related to the primary market trend?

In relation to trends, some knowledge of support and resistance can quickly tell you what is likely to happen in a sudden current movement. Looking back one year, three years, five years, and sometimes even ten years can provide some excellent information in terms of support and resistance levels. There is a reality to technical analysis that cannot be denied. Some people would argue that technical analysis works only because people believe it works and so it becomes a self-fulfilling prophecy. Fine. We don't care why it works, only that it does work much of the time.

Granted, there can be what appear to be false signals leading to unfulfilled expectations. At times these are all too common. This is where inexperienced day traders get in trouble. They rely too heavily on what should happen and ignore the reality of what is happening.

Part 2 looks at stock market trends, corporate management, insider trading (with some big surprises), types of orders, institutional ownership, and the professional investor ownership of companies.

CHAPTER 6

It's Always a Bull Market

In the longest of long runs, it's always a bull market. Old-time famous investor Jesse Livermore said it, modern-day Jim Cramer said it, and Warren Buffett said it. If it weren't the case, there wouldn't be anyone buying stock.

You can look at the Dow Jones Industrial Average or the S&P 500 Index (see Figure 6.1). A similar long-term bullish curve is shown. It's easy to see the constant bull market or what is also referred to as the "buying bias" of the stock market. Also, Figure 6.1 shows the volatility the market has experienced since 2000. Bear markets tend to be short term (a year or two), and bull markets are long term.

BUYING BIAS

As long as the stock market—or any stock market—remains "fair and orderly," with an essentially free trading system and an economy that continues to grow, the market will follow. There will always be a long-term buying bias to the stock market because if there isn't, the market will cease to exist.

However, although it's always a long-term bull market, some of the short-term damage can be severe. And it is not always a bull

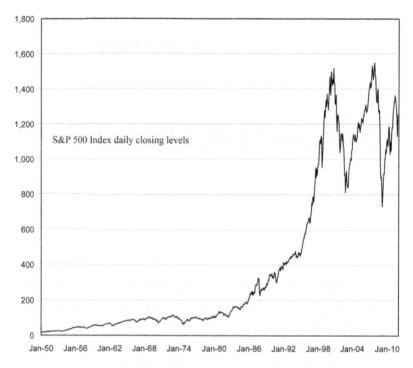

S&P 500 Index daily closing levels

Data source: Yahoo! Finance Historical Prices

Figure 6.1   S&P 500 Index, 1950–October 2010

market for every publicly traded company. Sometimes companies that have been leaders in the past lose their ability to compete in an ever-changing marketplace. Other companies are poorly managed, and still others never have much of a chance; therefore, selection is important and often difficult, but it is the essence of prudent investing. As the renowned Peter Lynch once stated: "People should at least spend as much time selecting a stock as they do when buying a new refrigerator."[1] So even though the long-term market is a bull market, a certain amount of stock analysis is wise.

THERE'S ALWAYS A BULL MARKET SOMEWHERE

Author-analyst Jim Cramer put it that way, and he further says:

Now, I know that might mean you have to do some trading. It might mean that you may have to look further and harder than your time and your inclination allow. That's okay too. What matters is that you don't simply default to what's in bear mode because you are time-constrained or intellectually lazy.[2]

Even though the market is in a bear mode, there are still good investments and good stocks to buy, stocks that might be quite cheap but that will recover nicely when the bear goes away. Even during sharp market corrections, you can still find stocks that are advancing in price. It just takes extra effort to find them. Some professionals find their best stocks during a market secondary down trend. They look for stocks that are running ahead while the market is falling.

SELECT STOCK CAREFULLY

When you are selecting stock, do it carefully. Get to know something about the companies you're considering and what they do:

- What is their core business?
- Is it a real product or a service that could go away tomorrow?
- Can you touch the product or at least see it?
- Are they an industry leader or a challenger?
- Generally the challenger has more risk than the leader. Is it a stable and viable business that will last for the next century?
- What is their debt? How does their debt compare to that of other, similar companies?
- How does their p/e ratio compare to that of similar companies?
- Where is the new business coming from?

Just answering simple questions like these can help you decide whether or not to buy stock in a particular company. There is more analysis that you can do, but the above are the core questions.

CHOOSE SIMPLE STOCK

Unless you have a personal connection to complicated stock, a connection that gives you an advantage in understanding it, pick something simple. Peter Lynch put it this way:

> Getting the story on a company is a lot easier if you understand the basic business. That's why I'd rather invest in panty hose than in communications satellites, or in motel chains than in fiber optics. The simpler it is, the better I like it. When somebody says, "Any idiot could run this joint," that's a plus as far as I'm concerned, because sooner or later any idiot probably is going to be running it.[3]

LONG-TERM APPROACH

Investing for long-term growth is always less risky than trying to make a fortune in the next couple of weeks. Losing a fortune in the next couple of weeks can be very easy. Like the old joke says, "The quick and easy way to make a million bucks in the stock market is to start with two million." Keeping risk low is best, especially when an investor is just starting out. It is important to choose stocks on the conservative side. Leave the speculation to those who can afford it or have the experience. An approach like this will save you money and keep you interested in the stock market, and it is still the most consistent moneymaker in existence.

WHEN THE MARKET FALTERS

The stock market will falter from time to time, dropping terribly. This scares many people. But hang on; don't be too quick to sell. If you can, just ride out the storm. Possibly look for buying opportunities to add to your portfolio. After all, you picked your stock carefully and know it should survive.

WHEN AN INDIVIDUAL STOCK FALTERS

If your individual stock has a problem with the market staying on course, it's time to become concerned. Then it doesn't matter what the market is doing. It's time to learn what the fundaments of your stock are doing. Find out why it's not doing well and decide whether to hold or sell.

EVEN SO . . .

Even though it's always a long-term bull market, there's always a bear market coming. Sooner or later it'll show up, sometimes when you least expect it. The good news is that it usually won't last long. The average bear market lasts about two years, while bull markets are for always, or at least one to six years or more.

CHAPTER 7

Look for Divergence in Trends

The stock market seldom has a "normal day." Up-close analysis shows that each day is unique, with its own special pattern of change. One day technology stocks will be hot and oil stocks will be out of favor. The next session might see oil stocks as the biggest gainers. One day the Dow Jones Industrial Average will be up 60 points and the outlook for business development will appear favorable. The following day has the market correcting 100 points on the Dow, with growing inflation becoming a real threat.

MARKET PREDICTIONS

Years ago it was said that when J. Pierpont Morgan was asked what the market will do, he always answered with the same word: "fluctuate." And it does fluctuate during every trading session. When stockbrokers are asked the question, "What will the market do?" they will attempt to be either positive or neutral on the subject. Many analysts will give a lengthy explanation of what the market should do and why, but it's a fact that no one knows precisely what the overall stock market will do. The best anyone can hope for is to find a few signals of strength or weakness. One way to look for these signals is to look at trends.

STOCK MARKET TRENDS

The concept of looking at stock market trends began in the late 1800s with Charles Henry Dow, one of the founding fathers of Dow Jones & Company and *The Wall Street Journal*. Charles Dow followed market trends based on the Dow Jones Industrial Average and the Dow Jones Railroad Average (now the transportation average). He followed what he called "primary," "secondary," and "tertiary" trends. The creation of the Dow averages and the definition of trends formed the basis of the technical analysis used today. The study done by Dow and later by editor William Hamilton eventually became known as the "Dow theory." Here we will look at trends in relationship to divergence, support, and resistance.

Let's examine three trends. The long-term or primary trend shows the overall direction of the stock market for an extended period of time, usually six months or more. The term *current trend* can refer to the long-term trend or to a secondary trend that is short term and shows a reaction or move in the opposite direction of the primary trend. The daily movements of the stock market, the tertiary trends, are important in the way they affect the secondary and long-term primary trends.

STOCK PRICES MOVE AS A GROUP

One concept that all analysts agree on is that stock prices tend to move as a group. Dow Jones Averages, S&P indexes, and NASDAQ indexes tend to move as a group. If they diverge from moving as a group, it can be a signal of weakness in the stock market.

The tendency of stock prices to move as a group is what makes up a trend. Divergences are changes in a trend that show stocks not moving in the direction they moved in during the recent past. It is difficult to know whether the signal means a change in a trend or the appearance of a secondary trend. However, the divergence is a technical signal of market weakness. Divergence signals can sometimes be ignored by the market. The market can correct one day and move back up the next. This is often misleading, and the change in direction frequently comes as a surprise.

S&P 500 INDEX, 2009–2011

A look at Figure 7.1 shows the change to an up trend in March 2009. The trend continues upward until late April 2010, where a correction occurs. An indecisive market goes nowhere until late August 2010, when it resumes an up trend. It stays above the trend line until late May 2011 when it becomes a somewhat indecisive up trend until the end of 2011. The primary trend is upward, with a few secondary down trends. The obvious difficulty with secondary trends is that you can't know they are secondary when they occur. It's a wait-and-see game to determine whether the primary trend continues or not.

CONFIRMING TRENDS

One way to see market strength is to look for trend confirmation. Compare two or more indexes and see whether they confirm the trend or show divergences. Figure 7.2 looks at the Dow Jones Industrial Average and the Dow Jones Transportation Average. With only a few minor divergences, it is easy to see that the transportation average indeed is confirming the primary up trend of the Dow Industrial Average. And this means they are both confirming the same up trend as the S&P 500 Index and the NASDAQ Composite Index. Again, stocks tend to move as a group. The indexes are so close that it's rather uncanny. It's almost as if all the professional traders got together on a conference call and said, "Okay, everybody buy," or, "Okay, everybody sell." With the instant data from

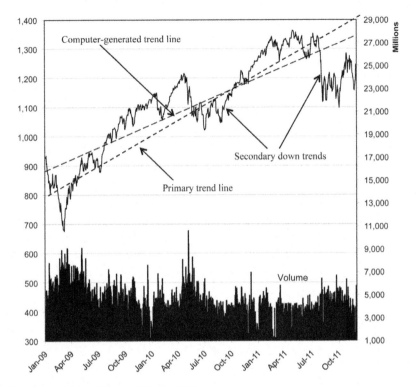

Data source: Yahoo! Finance Historical Prices

Figure 7.1   **S&P 500 Index, 2009–November 2011**

computers, people wouldn't need the phone call. The closeness of the charts also says something about investor sentiment. We can easily see where confidence comes to the scene and then wavers as the prices plummet.

SECONDARY OPPORTUNITIES

Most secondary down trends are good stock-buying opportunities. However, when the market drops more than 20 percent or is down for more than two consecutive months in three or more indexes, it is considered a bear market. The secondary down trend in April

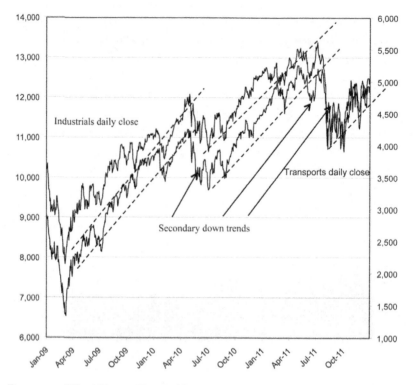

Data source: Yahoo! Finance Historical Prices

Figure 7.2   Dow Jones Industrial and Transportation Averages, 2009–2011

2010 (see Figure 7.2), although enough to make everyone nervous, was short-lived and indeed an excellent buying opportunity. Bear markets can also make good buying opportunities, but most prudent investors will wait until the primary trend stops its downward direction and turns up again.

TREND LINES

Trend lines can be computer-generated, with the most simple being the "linear trend line." It picks an average between price swings and plots the points on a line. It is accurate and unbiased and can be useful. It's not very good at showing turns in the trends. A "best fit" trend line, drawn on the underside for rising trends and the top side (peaks) for declining trends will do a much better job of showing divergences in the trend or turns in the primary trend.

DIVERGENCE INDICATOR

There is a separate technical indicator for divergence. It's called the moving average convergence divergence (MACD). The following quote is from Trading Online Markets LLC:

> The MACD also provides a good signal when the stock market trend is transitioning from a bull market to a bear market and back to a bull market. When the monthly MACD falls through its nine-month moving average, it is another sign the market is starting a downtrend. Then watch for the MACD to turn up through the nine-month moving average to give a signal that the market is starting to trend up.[1]

Information on the MACD can be found under "technical indicators" when you pull up a chart in the financial section of your web browser. You can learn more about the MACD from a simple Internet search.

TRENDS

About the only way to know where the market is headed is to check the trend. To look at the trend over a period of time—three months, six months, or a year or more—will show you where the trend is heading. The information can be invaluable as far as deciding the particulars of when to buy or sell stocks.

TREND PATTERNS

Technical traders look for trend patterns to determine strength or weakness in the stock market. We provide a brief description of some of the major patterns in the following paragraphs.

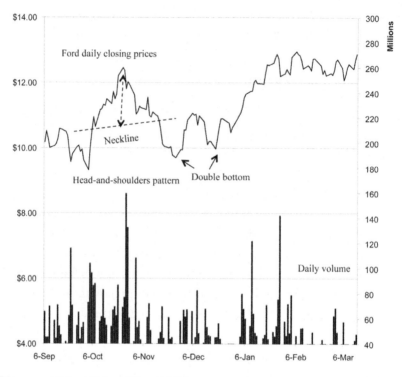

Data source: Yahoo! Finance Historical Prices

Figure 7.3   **Head-and-Shoulders Pattern, Ford Motor Co., 2011–March 2012**

Head and Shoulders

Probably the best-known and most accurate technical pattern is the head-and-shoulders pattern, in which the trading history of a major index makes an actual head-and-shoulders pattern (see Figure 7.3). It's easy to see that 2011 was a year of a lot of technical trading patterns. First look at the nice head-and-shoulders pattern that formed with Ford Motor Co. in October 2011.

Here is a practical description of some of the finer points of a head-and-shoulders trading pattern. The focus is on a stock market index movement, but of course a similar action can occur with the price patterns of individual stocks as well:

The "left shoulder" is formed at the end of a long uptrend that usually has been in place for several months or longer. Prices fall far enough to signal an end to the previous uptrend. This leaves a peak, or shoulder. Prices then rally to form another peak that is higher than the left shoulder. Prices decline from this peak and create a new short term downtrend. This forms the "head" of the pattern. Usually it takes several weeks between the peak of the left shoulder and the peak that forms the head.

The pattern cannot be fully recognised or confirmed until the right "shoulder" is formed. Again this usually takes several weeks as prices must fall, rally to a new lower peak, and then fall again. Only after the right shoulder has been confirmed can traders really recognise a head and shoulders pattern. This is a pattern that usually develops over months, not days.

This pattern confirms a high probability that the previous long uptrend has ended, and, more importantly, it sets targets below the current price for the following downtrend. These targets are set by plotting a "neckline" and then measuring the distance between the neckline and the top of the head.

The neckline joins the base of the left shoulder with the base of the right shoulder. It may slope up, down, or horizontally. The slope does not have any particular significance. The neckline provides a measurement point.[2]

The technical rule says that when a head-and-shoulders pattern forms, the market should drop the distance from the top of the head to the neckline. It can drop more, but that should be the minimum. Although head-and-shoulder patterns are a stronger signal when formed over a few months, they can form more quickly and move on. Here the rule was met. It fell that distance and then went on to form a "double bottom" which is a positive signal.

Reversed Upside-Down Pattern

The head-and-shoulders pattern can also appear upside down. This indicates a very bullish reaction.

Double Bottom

The double bottom with Ford occurred in November and December 2011 (see Figure 7.3) and signaled an upturn which followed just like it should. A double bottom marks the end of a down trend and the beginning of an up trend. Ideally the two bottoms would be about a month apart. They sometimes occur sooner but are considered weaker or are merely consolidation. The double bottom is considered confirmed when the final up leg reaches a point higher than the rest of the pattern.

Even though these pattern signals appear, they don't always work. They don't always do what they are supposed to do. Usually there is greater volume on the first bottom than the second, but this is not always the case. Occasionally you might observe several double bottoms occurring. When this happens, it is not considered a true double bottom, but rather a consolidation until the market decides on a direction.

Sometimes after a double bottom occurs, the price will drop again to test the strength of the rally. If there is not enough interest, the trend will turn down again. This did not happen with Ford, as Figure 7.3 shows.

Double Top

The double top is obviously the opposite of the double bottom. To have the most meaning, the tops should be fairly distinct and about a month apart. Anything closer can still cause a reaction but is considered weaker or a consolidation. A look at Best Buy, Inc., for November–December 2011, shows a double top occurring (see Figure 7.4).

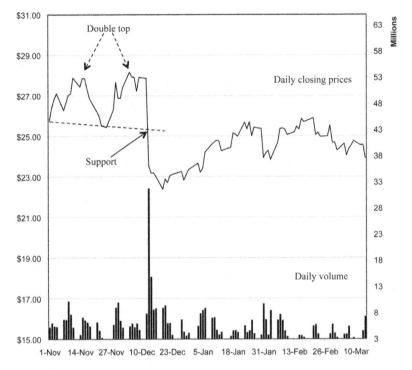

Data source: Yahoo! Finance Historical Prices

Figure 7.4   **Best Buy, Inc., November–December 2011**

The two peaks are obvious and are confirmed as a double top when the price falls through the support line. This means that there is a change in the trend. However, it was a short-term trend, lasting only to about December 19, when it turned and started up again.

Triple Top

A triple top is similar to the double top. However, it is believed by many to be a stronger negative sign of a reversal in the trend. Obviously, you have three similar tops instead of two. It shows strong resistance at the top of the peaks. With strong resistance, investors become discouraged and pull out of the stock causing the price to decline. There are also volume considerations and the price drops through the support level to be considered a true turn.

The Reverse of These Is Positive

An upside-down head and shoulders indicates a coming rise in the market. A double or triple bottom also indicates probable rises. Whether these patterns work because of how the market operates or because they become self-fulfilling prophecies doesn't really matter. What does matter is that they usually do work.

There is an entire science analyzing and understanding stock-trading patterns. Although the individual investor should be aware of them, you should also remember that, like everything else with indicators, they don't work all the time.

TECHNICAL TRADING BY PATTERNS

Technical trading by patterns is a trading strategy in itself. We have provided only superficial information here because you should be aware of these patterns. There are several books written on trading patterns. If one attempts it, one should learn much more. The bible of pattern trading is *Technical Analysis of Stock Trends* by John Magee and Robert D. Edwards.[3]

CHAPTER 8

Buy Good Management; Stick with Good People

I confess I'm not sure what makes "good management" or "good people." In business there are numerous examples of companies being run by bad managers and bad people, and yet the companies do very well. How can you determine whether the management and the people are good?

The reason I've included the axiom about good management and good people is that many columnists and financial gurus are fond of it and will frequently refer to the axiom in their investing advice. So we turn to the Internet, to see what comes up when we enter "best corporate managers for 2011."

"We come up with a list like the following compiled by Harvard's Bill George. "Bill George's Corporate 'Dream Team'." He refers to them all as CEOs, but clearly, some are not (identified in the list commentary as "*GEORGE*"):

Harvard Business School's Bill George is a best-selling author and the former CEO of Medtronic. His management strategies have made him both a popular professor and an anchor of many notable boards, including ExxonMobil

(XOM), Goldman Sachs (GS), Novartis (NVS) and Target (TGT). George says his list's strategy is simple: focus on gathering the "best of the best," seasoned CEOs who would be playing out of position to get the most out of each skill set. George is confident that, perhaps unlike the Miami Heat, these corporate stars don't need to go it alone—they can succeed as a stacked team.

1. CEO—Sam Palmisano, IBM (IBM)

   GEORGE: His track record since becoming CEO in 2002 proves my case; in 2003 he was a pioneer in introducing the first "integrated global network," buttressed by values-centered leadership and collaboration.

2. COO—Alan Mulally, Ford (F)

   GEORGE: A great operator and superb team player who gets peak performance with—like Palmisano—values-centered and collaborative leadership.

3. CFO—David Viniar, Goldman Sachs

   GEORGE: The only [sic] non-CEO on the team, he stands head and shoulders above any other CFO and could be CEO of any other Wall Street bank. He helped Goldman identify the sub-prime mortgage problem in late-2006 and guided Goldman through the 2008, meltdown and its subsequent recovery.

4. CMO—Howard Schultz, Starbucks (SBUX)

   GEORGE: Who else could sell coffee for $5? He created the customer-friendly Starbucks culture, then stepped back into leadership in 2008, and led the company to much higher levels of global success.

5. Chief Designer—Steve Jobs, Apple (AAPL)

GEORGE: His breakthrough designs have taken Apple to the top of four fields—user-friendly computers (iMac), recording devices (iPod), online music (iTunes singlehandedly wiped out the CD industry) and mobile telephone/information devices (iPhone). Then he created a new field for online information (iPads). No one in history has done this.

6. CIO—Jeff Bezos, Amazon.com (AMZN)

GEORGE: He created the greatest customer database that is user-friendly and has propelled the company to its leadership position in online merchandising.

7. Non-Exec Chair—Marilyn Carlson Nelson, Carlson Companies

GEORGE: Marilyn Carlson Nelson is the ideal non-executive chair. As chair of Mayo Clinic and Carlson Companies boards [Fortune note: Nelson is the former CEO of Carlson] and chair of governance of ExxonMobil's board, she appreciates the importance of good governance and its relationship to management.

8. General Counsel—Ken Frazier, Merck (MRK)

GEORGE: As general counsel, he saved Merck from financial disaster by successfully litigating individual cases in the Vioxx recall.

9. Chief people officer—Anne Mulcahy, Xerox (XRX)

GEORGE: She saved Xerox from pending bankruptcy by rebuilding employee trust and passion for restoring the company well beyond its former greatness.

10. Chief of research—Daniel Vasella, MD, Novartis (NVS)

   GEORGE: A medical doctor, he guided Novartis to the top of the health care industry by inventing more new drugs than any pharma or biotech company in the past decade.[1]

SO NOW WHAT?

So, there's the list. Now what happens?

Do you just make a list of stocks to buy from the companies these people work for? You could do that and probably be okay. But, it might be even better to look more closely at the people and their backgrounds. Then take a good hard look at the company to see how it has done and where it is heading in the next few years, if you can figure out a way to do all that.

Most of what business people say about managers being good or bad is a bunch of baloney. What is said is generalizations and compliments or criticisms that are mostly undeserved. Basically you can judge the effectiveness of management only by results you can measure. You can measure earnings, revenue growth, dividends, debt, and price growth. Those should be your measurement of management. They are not perfect, but they are mostly reliable.

LOOK OUT FOR GOOD OLE BOYS

Never forget that lists such as the one above can easily become lists of "good ole boys" who are friends or business associates of the person creating the list. As far as I know, Harvard never tells you about these possible situations. So take the information with a grain of salt and proceed with caution.

YOU CAN CHECK ON MANAGERS

Look up a company's quote on your browser, go to "profile" which gives information about the company, including its website. Then click on the website and go to the "about us" area which should list all or most of the company's senior managers. Normally information on the managers' background is listed, but with the most positive spin likely. Take their names and search the Internet for more information about the managers. Sometimes you'll find a lot of information; other times not much. At best you will find some analyst's opinion of the manager, and that can be helpful.

For example, suppose you are interested in checking the management of Monsanto Corporation (NYSE: MON). On the financial page of the web browser enter the trading symbol MON. The basic quote page will appear. On the left side you will see the word "profile." Clicking on it will get you information on what the company does for a living. With Monsanto you'll see that the corporate address in St. Louis, Missouri. You'll also see the word "website." A click on the website will take you to Monsanto's corporate website. Toward the top of the homepage you will see the words "Who We Are." Holding your mouse pointer over these words will give you a list of items including "company leadership." A mouse click on this item will give you a list of Monsanto's managers, including Mr. Hugh Grant the CEO. A click on his name will give you his background.

Copy his name and paste it into web search. This it will bring up information on Hugh Grant, the actor. If you add the words "of Monsanto" to the search, it will provide several articles about Mr. Grant, but still some articles on the actor of the same name (that's just a weakness of the Internet). The articles about the CEO of Monsanto Corp. can provide valuable information about him as a manager and be well worth the time. You can mostly ignore the information on the actor unless you are interested.

IT CAN BE HELPFUL

It can definitely be helpful to find out some information about the management of companies in which you invest. Sometimes you will learn that managers just left or are about to leave a company. How to use this information is sometimes difficult; other times it hits you over the head with a definite yes or no concerning buying or selling the stock. Just remember that EMCOM and Enron had well-respected managers when they hit the skids. Also don't forget the very long list, according to *The Wall Street Journal*'s special tracking page of bank failures, 386 banks, savings banks, and thrift organizations failed between January 2008 and August 2011.[2] Also, several brokerage firms in the past five years. If they had one good thing, it was management. That's why they got paid all those millions as they were pushed out the door.

So yes, it can be helpful to learn about management. Just don't count on that information to reflect the total quality of the company. It would be better to go by what managers do rather than by what they say or what they say they are.

CHAPTER 9

Look for Insider Trading

Insiders of a corporation are the decision makers and strategy formulators. They are the directors, the officers, and the high-level line personnel. If anyone knows what's going on in a company, it is the managers who are directly involved in the upper-level decision-making process.

ILLEGAL VERSUS LEGAL

In a broad sense, it is illegal for anyone in the United States to buy or sell shares of stock based on information not yet available to the public. Examples of *insider trading* cases that have been brought by the SEC are cases against:

- Corporate officers, directors, and employees who traded the corporation's securities after learning of significant, confidential corporate developments.
- Friends, business associates, family members and other "tippees" of such officers, directors, and employees, who traded the securities after receiving such information.

- Employees of law, banking, brokerage, and printing firms who were given such information to provide services to the corporation whose securities they traded.
- Government employees who learned of such information because of their employment by the government. It is interesting to note that in 2011, it became public knowledge that this apparently does *not* apply to members of the U.S. Congress and who can get advantageous information from their work and use it for investing. Hopefully this will be changed soon.
- Other persons who misappropriated and took advantage of confidential information from their employees.

The idea is to keep the stock market fair and orderly. Trading on inside information erodes confidence in the market.

The Securities and Exchange Commission (SEC) adopted rules 10b5-1 and 10b5-2 to resolve two insider trading issues where the courts have disagreed. Rule 10b5-1 provides that a person trades on the basis of material nonpublic information if a trader is "aware" of the material nonpublic information when making a purchase or sale. The rule also sets forth several affirmative defenses or exceptions to liability. The rule permits persons to trade under certain specified circumstances where it is clear that the information they are aware of is not a factor in the decision to trade, such as pursuant to a preexisting plan, contract, or instruction that was made in good faith.

Rule 10b5-2 clarifies how the misappropriation theory applies to certain nonbusiness relationships. This rule provides that a person receiving confidential information under circumstances specified in the rule would owe a duty, trust, or confidence and thus could be liable under the misappropriation theory.

A lot of this is legal-speak, but the idea is simple. If a person has important information about a company that will influence the price of a company's shares, the law is broken if that person uses the information for buying or selling securities related to the company. It is also illegal for people trading on the information (or even on the act), even if they do not have a direct connection with the company. In other words, if a stockbroker observes a CEO selling stock and then makes a similar transaction, the broker could be guilty of insider trading.

FAIR AND ORDERLY MARKET

Disallowing trades based on inside information is important. It is part of the *fair and orderly* market concept now being adhered to by all the stock exchanges in the world. If such activities were allowed or ignored by the authorities, the public securities market would lack integrity, without which it could not function. Why trade stocks or other securities if insiders and others have a distinct advantage? Stock market prices are driven by anticipation based on information. Making trades based on privileged information, ahead of the public, amounts to fraud. Individual investors need to have the same information as the professional investors in order for the public markets to be a level playing field.

ILLEGAL INSIDER TRADING IS STILL A PROBLEM

Insider selling was on the rise late in October 2011, in sharp contrast to the near record lows of the preceding August and September, as Hibah Yousef notes in a report for *CNN Money*.[1] Furthermore, insider trading that is illegal is still going on. Almost every day there is another story in the news about insider traders being arrested. Read the following from March 15, 2012:

> (Reuters)—The U.S. government announced civil and criminal charges against a Chicago-based consultant on Thursday for allegedly trading on confidential information about private-equity firm Carlyle Group's planned acquisition of vitamin company NBTY Inc.
>
> The U.S. Securities and Exchange Commission said Sherif Mityas has agreed to settle the civil insider-trading

charges and pay a $78,000 fine for allegedly purchasing NBTY stock and tipping off a relative ahead of Carlyle's acquisition. He and the relative later made a $38,000 profit, the SEC said.[2]

INSIDERS MUST REPORT

At times corporate employees are privy to inside information, and they want to legitimately buy and sell their company's stock. For various reasons, such information cannot be immediately released to the public. In fairness, the insiders are allowed to trade, but they must report transactions, holdings, and other information to the Securities and Exchange Commission. A sense of fairness is maintained because the public is able to view and assess such transactions.

SEC Insider Forms 3, 4, and 144

According to the Securities Exchange Act of 1934, an insider is defined as an officer or director of a public company or an individual or entity owning 10 percent or more of any class of a company's shares. The definition in all its legalese is given in Section 16 of the 1934 act; there are further words on how to more specifically define an "officer" and a "beneficial owner" (i.e., the one who benefits from the transaction) in Rule 16a-1 of the Code of Federal Regulations.

For all the legal definitions of *titles* and *share owners*, what the rule says is that anyone involved in the inner workings of a publicly traded company is an insider. The concern is that this person could gain an unfair advantage over the public when trading company shares. Therefore, an insider must register by making a statement of holding (*SEC Form 3*) within 10 days of a transaction. Changes in ownership must be filed by the tenth day of the month following the transaction (*SEC Form 4*).

At the end of the fiscal year, an insider or former insider must file Form 5 within 45 days. Its intent is to prevent people from moving in and out of insider status. Obviously, Form 4 gives the most useful information to investors. It answers the question of what the insiders are doing—buying or selling—as well as their current holdings in the company. Information on insider trades, available on the Internet and through several newsletters, is usually based on this SEC form.

SEC Form 144, used by the SEC to track insider information, is for those currently holding securities that are not registered. This form is the last step, allowing the shares to be sold on the open market and be publicly traded. It allows the shares to be sold but ensures that the number is relatively small and that the seller isn't an underwriter bringing a new issue to market.

The form dictates how many shares will be sold within the following three months. If they are not sold, the form must be amended. In the real world, by the time the investor sees the Form 144 information, the shares have been sold. Many will file Form 144 and Form 4 at the same time.

RISE IN NUMBER OF INSIDER BUYS

Some people view an increase in the number of insider buys as an additional reason to buy a stock. They believe that a sudden flurry of insider buys is a positive statement of growth potential for the company. It is important to keep in mind, however, that sometimes companies lend money to their employees to buy stock with the intention of having the public see the buys. Such corporate strategies suggest a manipulation of public interest; therefore, it is important to view the presence of insider trades in relation to other information about a company.

Take a look at Harsco Corp. (NYSE: HSC) in Figure 9.1. There was an insider buy of 5,000 shares on January 30, 2011. Obviously

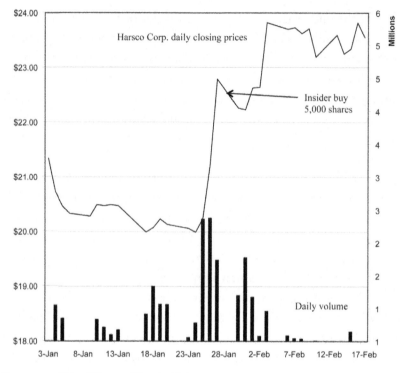

Data source: Yahoo! Finance Historical Prices

Figure 9.1   **Insider Buying, 2011–2012**

somebody was paying attention as the stock dropped the next day and then skyrocketed by 79 cents in the next couple of days. There was not a whole lot of impact on this one buy. But this is typical. You may see one, two, or maybe even three buys but seldom much action resulting from them.

MEDIA ATTENTION

If the insider's trading has been significant enough to be discussed in the financial media, it calls additional attention to that activity. The extra attention can affect the stock's price. However, the impact follows right on the heels of the announcement. If investors plan to take action based on the news, they must do so quickly. Waiting even a day or two can be too late, but it usually won't make much difference.

PART OF THE PICTURE

Obviously, an investor can follow insider trading as an investment strategy in and of itself. However, investment professionals recommend the use of additional analysis to form a conclusion before taking action. Corporate insiders can have any one of several reasons or motives for buying and selling their company's stock. Therefore, it is prudent to use information on insider trades as *part* of the picture of a company rather than as a sole indicator.

SELLS VERSUS BUYS

Unless there are several insiders selling the same stock, sells are usually not meaningful as an indicator. Insiders are often selling stocks to raise cash to purchase items other than the company's stock. A new BMW, a new yacht, or a down payment on a beach house can be motivators for the selling insiders. Also important is the strength of the individual sector or the entire stock market. If a market sell-off is in progress, it would not be particularly meaningful to see company insiders selling stock.

BUYS CAN HAVE MORE SIGNIFICANCE

Buys can have more significance than sales, although they should never be the only consideration for selecting a stock. Are buys more significant? The answer is mixed, but one can find evidence of successful situations based on insider buys. One of the difficulties with buys is that companies encourage their employees to buy stock. As previously stated, they might even lend their employees money to do so. It puts the company in a good light and is encouraging to the employees.

Corporate selling can be a signal of approaching weakness in the stock's price. The idea behind it is that if the corporate executives are selling the stock there must be a negative reason. Many professional traders believe that it's the buying of shares that is most significant in forecasting good times ahead. Witness the following:

> "Historically, when company executives sell their shares, the stock tends to underperform the market by more than 5 percent over the next year," writes University of Michigan professor Nejat Seyhun in his book, *Investment Intelligence from Insider Trading*. "Meanwhile, stocks purchased by company insiders typically outperform the market by almost 9 percent over the following 12 months," he said.[3]

Most people would say that it's a flurry (meaning lots) of insider buying or selling that has the most meaning. Notice that the above quote doesn't mention anything about quantities. Although it's easy to find many articles on the Internet about insider buying and selling, it's hard to find consensus. Each article will say that the sky is falling and it's time to sell or things are great because insiders are buying. Actually, neither is true.

On October 25, 26, 27, and 28 of 2011, Bill Gates sold 5 million shares of Microsoft each day for a total of 20 million shares. On November 15, 2011, the price of Microsoft plummeted from $26.74 a share to $24.30 a share. Coincidence? Most likely.

Figure 9.2 reveals that the short-term decline was most likely a result of the stock market and not caused by Mr. Gates's sale of stock.

FINDING INFORMATION

Insider buys and sells can easily be found in any of the major browsers. Just go to the finance section of the browser (e.g., MSN, Google, Yahoo!), enter a stock symbol, and then look in the left column for

Data source: Yahoo! Finance Historical Prices

Figure 9.2   **Microsoft Corp. versus S&P 500 Index, 2011**

"Insider Trades." Information on quantity comparisons can be found just by searching the news articles for insider trading news.

WHAT ABOUT CONGRESS?

Another important exception to trading on "inside information" has recently come to light. Members of the U.S. Senate and House of Representatives are allowed to make trades on information they might have gotten as a result of legislative activities. This is information that might affect a specific industry or a specific company. This is often information not available to the public. Such activities do have a negative impact on the "level playing field" of a free market system and should be stopped. Much of this congressional advantage was well documented in a *60 Minutes* program aired in November 2011. The script of "Insiders," which aired on November 13, 2011, is still available online, as of this writing. Steve Kroft was correspondent; Ira Rosen and Gabrielle Schonder were the producers. Now is the time for the SEC to step up and say that no more of this will be allowed.

It is a serious problem facing individual and professional investors: This is only the section of the interviews that dealt primarily with insider trading of stock. Other investments were discussed later in the interview.

Washington, D.C. is a town that runs on inside information—but should our elected officials be able to use that information to pad their own pockets? As Steve Kroft reports, members of Congress and their aides have regular access to powerful political intelligence, and many have made well-timed stock market trades in the very industries they regulate. For now, the practice is perfectly legal, but some say it's time for the law to change.

The following consists of excerpts of the script of "Insiders," which aired on November 13, 2011.

60 Minutes Overtime

The next national election is now less than a year away and congressmen and senators are expending much of their time and their energy raising the millions of dollars in campaign funds they'll need just to hold onto a job that pays $174,000 a year.

Few of them are doing it for the salary, and all of them will say they are doing it to serve the public. But there are other benefits: power, prestige, and the opportunity to become a Washington insider with access to information and connections that no one else has, in an environment of privilege where the rules that govern the rest of the country don't always apply.

Most former congressmen and senators manage to leave Washington—if they ever leave Washington—with more money in their pockets than they had when they arrived, and as you are about to see, the biggest challenge is often avoiding temptation.

PETER SCHWEIZER: *This is a venture opportunity. This is an opportunity to leverage your position in public service and use that position to enrich yourself, your friends, and your family.*

Peter Schweizer is a fellow at the Hoover Institution, a conservative think tank at Stanford University. A year ago he began working on a book about soft corruption in Washington with a team of eight student researchers, who reviewed financial disclosure records. It became a jumping-off point for our own story, and we have independently verified the material we've used.

Schweizer says he wanted to know why some congressmen and senators managed to accumulate significant wealth beyond their salaries, and proved particularly adept at buying and selling stocks.

SCHWEIZER: *There are all sorts of forms of honest grafts that congressmen engage in that allow them to become very, very wealthy. So it's not illegal, but I think it's highly unethical, I think it's highly offensive, and wrong.*

STEVE KROFT: *What do you mean "honest graft"?*

SCHWEIZER: *For example insider trading on the stock market. If you are a member of Congress, those laws are deemed not to apply.*

KROFT: *So congressmen get a pass on insider trading?*

SCHWEIZER: *They do. The fact is, if you sit on a healthcare committee and you know that Medicare, for example, is—is considering not reimbursing for a certain drug that's market moving information. And if you can trade stock on/off of that information and do so legally, that's a great profit-making opportunity. And that sort of behavior goes on.*

KROFT: *Why does Congress get a pass on this?*

SCHWEIZER: *It's really the way the rules have been defined. And the people who make the rules are the political class in Washington. And they've conveniently written them in such a way that they don't apply to themselves.*

The buying and selling of stock by corporate insiders who have access to nonpublic information that could affect the stock price can be a criminal offense. Just ask hedge fund manager Raj Rajaratnam, who recently got 11 years in prison for doing it. But congressional lawmakers have no corporate responsibilities and have long been considered exempt from insider trading laws, even though they have daily access to nonpublic information and plenty of opportunities to trade on it.

SCHWEIZER: *We know that during the healthcare debate people were trading health care stocks. We know that during the financial crisis of 2008 they were getting out of the market before the rest of America really knew what was going on.*

In mid-September 2008 with the Dow Jones Industrial Average still above ten thousand, Treasury Secretary Hank Paulson and Federal Reserve Chairman Ben Bernanke were holding closed-door briefings with congressional leaders and privately warning them that a global financial meltdown could occur within a few days. One of those attending was Alabama Representative Spencer Bachus, then the ranking Republican member on the House Financial Services Committee and now its chairman.

SCHWEIZER: *These meetings were so sensitive, that they would actually confiscate cell phones and Blackberries going into [them]. What we know is that those meetings were held one day and literally the next day Congressman Bachus would engage in buying stock options based on apocalyptic briefings he had the day before from the Fed chairman and treasury secretary. I mean, talk about a stock tip.*

While Congressman Bachus was publicly trying to keep the economy from cratering, he was privately betting that it would, buying option funds that would go up in value if the market went down. He would make a variety of trades and profited at a time when most Americans were losing their shirts.

Congressman Bachus declined to talk to us, so we went to his office and ran into his press secretary, Tim Johnson.

KROFT: *Look, we're not alleging that Congressman Bachus has violated any laws. All . . . the only thing we're interested in talking to him is about his trades.*

TIM JOHNSON: *Okay . . . okay, that's a fair-enough request.*

What we got was a statement from Congressman Bachus' office that he never trades on nonpublic information or financial services stock. However, his financial disclosure forms seem to indicate otherwise. Bachus made money trading General Electric stock during the crisis, and a third of GE's business is in financial services.

During the healthcare debate of 2009, members of Congress were trading healthcare stocks, including House Minority Leader John Boehner, who led the opposition against the so-called public option, government funded insurance that would compete with private companies. Just days before the provision was finally killed off, Boehner bought health insurance stocks, all of which went up. Now speaker of the House, Congressman Boehner also declined to be interviewed, so we tracked him down at his weekly press conference.

KROFT: *You made a number of trades going back to the health-care debate. You bought some insurance stock. Did you make those trades based on nonpublic information?*

JOHN BOEHNER: *I have not made any decisions on day-to-day trading activities in my account. And haven't for years. I don't—I do not do it, haven't done it, and wouldn't do it.*

Later Boehner's spokesman told us that the healthcare trades were made by the speaker's financial adviser, with whom he only consults about once a year.

[SCHWEIZER: *We need to find out whether they're part of a blind trust or not.*]

Schweizer thinks the timing is suspicious, and believes congressional leaders should have their stock funds in blind trusts.

SCHWEIZER: *Whether it's, uh, $15,000 or $150,000, the principle in my mind is that it's simply wrong, and it shouldn't take place.*[4,5]

The Securities and Exchange Commission does not have the authority to hold employees of Congress or the executive branch liable for using nonpublic information gained from official proceedings for insider trading. Under current law, "insider trading" is defined as the buying or selling of securities or commodities based on nonpublic information in violation of confidentiality—either to the issuing company or the source of information. Most federal officials and employees do not owe a duty of confidentiality to the federal government and thus are not liable for insider trading.[6]

Of course, members of Congress do owe a duty of confidentiality to the citizenry by whom they were elected. That's why congressional ethics rules specifically state that "members must not use privileged information gleaned during the course of their duties for personal gain."[7] But the rule is just a rule; it is not legally binding, and the SEC has never brought an enforcement action against any member of the Senate or the House.

It's easy to see what a serious problem this is for the entire world of investing. It totally destroys the idea of a fair and stable market. It takes away the level playing field and makes it one of haves and have-nots. It must be stopped soon.

Insider trades, the legal kind, can be useful as one small part of stock analysis. They must not be relied upon for the only indicator. They can be deceptive with executives buying to give a good impression on the state of the company. The sells can often have no meaning except it was time to pay off the cabin at the lake. In other words, the sells aren't necessarily due to coming misfortunes of the company.

CHAPTER 10

Know the Best
Type of Order

There are many different types of stock orders an investor can place. Some are of debatable value and are seldom used. This chapter provides simplified descriptions of some of the basic types of orders.

MARKET ORDER

If you're looking for an order at the best available price, a *market order* should be filled as soon as possible. For example, an investor calls a broker and learns that shares for XYZ Corp. are trading at $55.25 to $55.75 and that the last buy was at $55.75. The investor says, "I want to place a 'market order' to buy 200 shares of XYZ. Computers make this order easy to enter and easy to fill. In all likelihood the investor can get an oral confirmation of the order execution while still on the phone. The broker comes back to the phone and says, "Confirming a buy of 200 shares of XYZ at the market. The order was filled at $55.50. The settlement is *regular way*." That means the current trade date plus three days, or T + 3.

The main advantage of this type of order is that it's placed and filled immediately. That is a big advantage. Some investors wilt on the vine waiting-waiting-waiting for their orders to be filled. It's usually best to place the order and buy or sell the stock immediately. Waiting is unpleasant and can ruin focus. It can also result in lost opportunities. The disadvantage is that it's impossible to know the price ahead of time, although in most trades it will be very close to the current trading range.

LIMIT ORDER

A *limit order* is an order at a specific acceptable price. It should be filled when the trade can be completed at the order price or better. If the order cannot be filled, it remains a limit order until it is cancelled. It can be entered as a one-day-only order or as a *good-till-canceled* (GTC) order. For example, "Buy 200 XYZ at a limit price of $55, good for today only." The order is entered by the broker. If 200 XYZ can be purchased at $55 a share or better, the order is executed. If the limit is not activated, the order is automatically canceled at the end of the trading session. A limit order can be fully filled, partly filled, or not filled at all.

A note about the good-till-canceled order: brokerage firms can cancel these after a period of time, usually 30 days, and sometimes at the end of the current month. Check with your broker for the GTC rules.

BUY STOP ORDER

A *buy stop order* is an order at the best available price once the stop price is traded on or through. "Buy 200 XYZ with a buy stop at $59. Put the order in good till canceled." The buy stop is placed above the current trading price. The investor wants to buy the stock only if the price is moving up. The order to buy 200 shares will become a market order if XYZ stock trades at $59 a share or higher. If the order is not executed within a time specified by the brokerage firm, usually the end of the month or 30 days, it is canceled.

SELL STOP ORDER

Be careful with sell stop orders. If they are too close to the current price, the specialist will come after them. A sell stop is a price at which the investor wants to sell the stock if the price is dropping. It is intended to stop a loss by selling the stock. It becomes a market sell order if the price trades at or through the set stop price. Some investors make the mistake of placing stop orders within 10 percent of the current price. Many times the result of this strategy is to doom their portfolio to a 10 percent loss.

Another thing that can happen is that when computerized, sell programs kick in and the market temporarily drops. Some people refer to this as "kicking out the stops." Professional traders know there are stop orders at certain levels which will help them out if they start selling or selling short. They can knock a stock price down a few dollars and pick it back up the following day. Meanwhile the frustrated individual investor sold the stock and has to decide whether to buy it back or not. This is one of the ways you get sudden and unexpected volatility in today's stock market.

The sell stop is placed below the current market price. It is an order that you prefer not be filled. The price should be selected by checking a chart of price movements. The sell stop is considered a defensive strategy—selling the stock if a sharp decline occurs. Many would say if you truly believe a stock's price will drop, why not just sell it and consider buying it back later?

STOP LIMIT ORDER

A *stop limit order* is an order placed at a specific, acceptable price, once the stop price is traded on or through. The limit price can be placed at the same price as the stop or at an entirely different price from the stop price. If the order cannot be filled, it remains a limit order until it is canceled.

"Sell 200 shares of XYZ at a stop of $48, with a limit of $46, good till canceled." The stop will be triggered when the price of XYZ Corp. trades at or through $48 and will sell if and only if the order can be executed at $46 a share or better. Again, the unexecuted order will remain in the system for a length of time designated by the brokerage firm, unless the order is canceled.

TRAILING STOP ORDER

The *trailing stop order* is similar to the stop limit order, but you use it to protect a profit, rather than to protect against a loss. If you have a profit in a stock, you can use the trailing stop order to follow it up. You enter the trailing stop order as a percentage of the market price. If the market price declines by that percentage, the trailing stop becomes a market order, and your broker sells the stock. If the stock continues to rise, the trailing stop follows it up since it is a percentage of the market price. This protects your additional gains. For example here is how the trailing stop works:

> Imagine you purchased 500 shares of Hershey Chocolate at $50 per share; the current price is $57. You want to lock-in at least $5 of the per share profit you've made but wish to continue holding the stock, hoping to benefit from any further increases. To meet your objective, you could place a trailing stop order with a stop value of $2 per share.
>
> In practical terms, here's what happens: Your order will sit on your broker's books and automatically adjust upwards as the price of Hershey's common stock increases. At the time your trailing stop order was placed, your broker knows to sell HSY if the price falls below $55 ($57 current market price – $2 trailing stop loss = $55 sale price). Imagine Hershey

increases steadily to $62 per share; now, your trailing stop order has automatically kept pace and will guarantee at least a $60 sale price ($62 current stock price – $2 trailing stop value = $60 per share sale price). In other words, the trailing stop order will increase in your favor and lock in any gains you've made in the interim. If Hershey were to fall to $60, your trailing stop order would convert to a market order for execution, your shares would be sold, and should result in a capital gain of $10 per share.[1]

MARKET IF TOUCHED

Market if touched (MIT) is an order qualifier for buy orders placed below the current trading price and sell orders placed above the current price. It is executed if the security trades at or through the current price. Effectively, MITs are the opposite of stop orders in terms of dynamics. They are used extensively with futures trading.

MARKET ON OPEN

Market on open, or *market on the open*, is an order that specifies the market opening as an activator. This order does not guarantee the opening price. Obviously, it must be placed before the market opens.

MARKET ON CLOSE

Market on close, or *market on the close*, is an instruction to a stock exchange floor broker to execute the trade at the best available price during the last 30 seconds of the trading sessions. There are no guarantees that the order will be filled or that it will be filled at the final trading price. Essentially the trading day is over if the order isn't filled.

MARKET ORDER IS USUALLY BEST

Time and opportunity are often lost while investors are messing around with order qualifiers, especially limits. It's usually best to go with a market order and get a fast execution. Then move on to the next strategy.

CHAPTER 11

Institutions Show Where the Action Is Now

Any stock in too many institutional portfolios or the
subject of excess advisory bullishness should be suspect.
Someday a majority will want to take profits.[1]

—GERALD M. LOEB

Who was Gerald M. Loeb? He had an impressive-sounding name.
He was a founding partner of E. F. Hutton (now part of Citigroup), a formerly respected name in the brokerage business. Supposedly he made it through the crash of 1929 without experiencing
any major harm to his portfolio and went on to fame and fortune.
His statement refers to two issues: institutional ownership and advisory bullishness.

Institutional ownership brings up two considerations. First,
can the individual investor compete with the big money managers?
And second, should an individual select or avoid stock owned by
large institutional investors? Advisory bullishness is simply defined
as a stockbroker's positive attitude and selling enthusiasm. It is

hardly worth a detailed discussion. Institutional ownership will be discussed at this point.

DAVID AND GOLIATH

Institutional investors are professional money managers for corporations, pension funds, mutual funds, hedge funds, and other investment companies. Their strategies may be long term, short term, or both. They implement their strategies by moving the market when buying and selling stock. Fund managers might do their own analysis or hire others to do the basic analysis for them. Every business day they deal with large amounts of money. Obviously, they have advantages not available to individual investors. Possibly the biggest advantage to professional investors is the large amount of money available to them. Because of this, they can make larger trades, thereby profiting from small price moves, and they can afford to make more mistakes than individual investors can.

When it comes to analysis, the only real advantage held by the institutions is experience. According to securities laws, information is made available to everyone at the same time. The only exceptions are corporate insiders who were involved in a decision-making process. However, they must report any transactions to the Securities and Exchange Commission, or they will be charged for illegal insider trading.

PROFESSIONAL TRADERS

Institutional stock traders are the professionals of the market. They are involved with stock trading on a constant basis—some would even say 24/7. Many of them not only remember what happened yesterday, but last week as well. These are important differences between them and the individual investor who might have $10,000 or $100,000 to invest, and who sweats bullets to make the right investment. Professional investors might have $3 million or $500 million to invest in the next 15 minutes. When that's done, they take on the next challenge. They are usually not too worried about one or two stocks; they worry more about world economics for the next six months. More importantly, they worry most about how emotionally the stock market will react to the news of world and nation events.

Institutional stock traders aren't always right. In fact, they are frequently wrong. Peter Lynch, the former respected manager of Fidelity's Magellan Fund, refers to them as the "blundering herd."

Lynch knows much about institutional investors and the things they do to make money through investing. Professional institutional investors now dominate the investing markets. Lynch believes this fact often leads people to think (incorrectly) that the individual has no chance in the stock market. In reality, amateur investors now have improved chances for success in the market if they do their homework and know their companies well.

As Peter Lynch puts it in *One Up on Wall Street*:

> He or she can take an independent tact by zigging when the herd zags and buying stocks that the herd has overlooked, and especially the ones that the herd has recently trampled. What holds them back is the inferiority complex they've gotten from mistaking the cattle drive for the Atlanta Braves.[2]

This is reminiscent of stock trader Jessie Livermore's philosophy of winning big when you know you're right, as described in Chapter 20. The thundering herd analogy refers to the earlier days of the United States, when cattle drives were used to deliver beef to market. Drovers would work hard to keep the herd calm and quiet. Large groups of cattle tend to excite easily and stampede mindlessly off in one direction, just like investors who panic and sell.

Lynch likes the Atlanta Braves. As a professional baseball team, they know what they're doing. It's the panicked and directionless cattle that represent the actions of institutional investors when the stock market goes crazy. Thanks to good public relations work, many individuals believe that the professionals know what they're doing all the time. The fact is that the professionals don't always know. They do make mistakes—big ones. The belief still exists, however, and according to Lynch, causes many individual investors to develop an "inferiority complex."

The inferiority complex can cause investors to do three self-destructive things:

1. Imitate the professionals, buying "hot stocks" or trying to "catch the turn" in IBM or other stocks
2. Become "sophisticated" and invest in futures, options, or options on futures
3. Buy what they've heard has been recommended by a magazine or by one of the popular financial programs

Information on what the pros think is so readily available that the celebrity tip has replaced the old-fashioned tip from Uncle Harry as the most compelling reason to invest in a company.

Catching the gain with any stock means that you are competing with professionals. They can be profitable for a 25 cent gain or less and can afford to take a loss if they are wrong. Futures, options, and so on can be an even faster spin with which to lose money. As for stock tips, some are good, some are bad, but most are old, and the situation could have changed by the time the individual takes action. Such tips should never be the only reason for selecting a stock.

THE INDIVIDUAL'S EDGE

Instead of becoming self-destructive, take advantage of special investing edges that individuals have. Two kinds of edges are too often overlooked by investors.

First, there's the "on-the-job edge," in which one has a working relationship with either an industry or the related companies with whom the investor conducts business. Second, there's the "consumer's edge." Individual investors can capitalize on their experiences in, for example, restaurants, airports, and shopping malls.

Thus individuals can derive advantages from what they do for a living and for fun, such as shopping as a consumer. Investing in the stock of an employer or a competitor makes sense. Often, the competitor is the better selection, and there is less chance of being too forgiving if things don't turn out as expected.

As a first rough screen, going shopping can provide a whole list of possible investment opportunities. Which stores have great products and great service? Do they look as though they plan to be around for awhile? Do the stores have several customers? Are the customers browsing or buying? These observations should be just the beginning.

Make a list of the best stores, and then do the important background research. The research is extremely important, so the investor doesn't just buy the glitzy presentation of a particular business. Select companies with good-looking fundamentals, a reasonable price, and a great-looking future. Buy the stock and watch the new developments.

SOME THINGS ARE CHANGING

It used to be that professional investors (mutual funds, hedge funds, pension funds, etc.) would avoid owning more than 5 percent of the stock of any one company. That was because owning that much stock required certain restrictions and that reports be filed with the SEC. Nowadays they are starting to ignore that problem; they buy the stock and do the paperwork. This will probably be a growing trend in the future. It means that these fund managers have more control over the companies whose stock they own and they can place demands on those companies. They can influence who's on the board of directors and whether the CEO or other high-level officers go or stay. They can also have an influence on the direction of the company. If the managers don't like the way things are working out, they just sell the shares and move on to another company.

MATTEL

Let's take a look at Mattel, the toy manufacturer. Mattel's motto used to be "Mattel, That's Swell." Here we have a breakdown of the stock ownership and some of the ownership changes.

Table 11.1 Mattel Corp.

Ownership Information:[3]	
Shares outstanding	339.00 mil
Institutional ownership	91.03%
Top 10 institutions	41.80%
Mutual fund ownership	1.44%
5% insider ownership	1.00%
Float	99.00%

Ownership Activity:		
Description	No. of Holders	Shares
Total positions	474	308,602,944
New positions	47	0
Sold out positions	170	0
Net position change	−128	−32,227,436
Buyers	227	33,713,512
Sellers	355	−65,940,948

It's interesting that Mattel shows 91.03 percent institutional ownership. Sure that's a lot, but both Apple Computer and IBM have better than 63 percent institutional ownership. Google, Inc., shows nearly 80 percent institutional ownership, and Amazon is close to 70 percent. So these days it might be more prudent to be concerned about a lack of institutional ownership in a particular stock, rather than be nervous about too much.

Let's take a look at Mattel's price movement for 2011, as shown in Figure 11.1. The primary price trend has a nice upward direction with a few secondary down trends. Assuming that the growth factors remain steady, the strong institutional ownership is a recommendation for the future of Mattel.

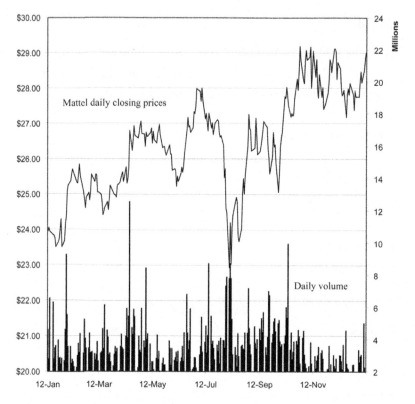

Data source: Yahoo! Finance Historical Prices

Figure 11.1   **Mattel, Inc., 2011–January 2012**

INSTITUTIONAL OWNERSHIP SIGNIFICANCE

Rather than trying to figure out whether the amount of institutional ownership is too high or too low, it's a better use of your time to learn why the institutions like or dislike a stock. Search for online articles on the subject. It's an easy thing to do. Why do they like Amazon or Google? Why are they selling out of Yahoo? This type of analysis will give a better idea of what gets professional investors excited. Understanding the information can help with stock selection and timing.

CHAPTER 12

It Depends on Support and Resistance

Understanding the basic concept of technical support and resistance informs the investor of the significance of stock market moves. This concept can send a signal of strength or weakness related to a specific move. Support can show the likelihood of a halt in a market decline, and resistance can show where an advance might have trouble continuing.

THE DOW THEORY

The idea of market support and resistance goes back to the Dow theory, which was originated by Charles Dow and further developed by an editor of *The Wall Street Journal*, William Hamilton.

The Dow theory is based on the movement of stock market indicators in the form of two indexes: the Dow Jones Industrial Average and the Dow Railroad Average (now known as the Dow Transportation Average). Each is a list of stocks selected because they were believed to represent the stock market. According to Dow theory, the market movement was strong when the two averages confirmed each other's direction and weak when they diverged.

Support and resistance also played an important role in understanding the indicators.

SUPPORT IS USUALLY UNDERNEATH CURRENT PRICES

Support is a point in a declining stock market at which buyers start buying. *Resistance* is the point in an advance where the sellers start selling. When a market declines, analysts look lower for the next area of support on a chart of historic prices. The strength of an area of support is determined by how many times the level stopped previous declines. If it stopped only once before, it is weak support and will likely drop further.

Looking for support zones, rather than precise points, can help prevent overreactions:

> Support levels are usually below the current price, but it is not uncommon for a security to trade at or near support. Technical analysis is not an exact science and it is sometimes difficult to set exact support levels. In addition, price movements can be volatile and dip below support briefly. Sometimes it does not seem logical to consider a support level broken if the price closes 1/8 below the established support level. For this reason, some traders and investors establish support zones.[1]

RESISTANCE IS WHERE SELLERS APPEAR

Resistance, the opposite of support, is a level where stock market advances stopped in the past, where stock buyers stopped buying. If advances were stopped only once or twice, it is weak resistance. If several advances were stopped, it is strong resistance. When the market breaks through resistance, it tends to rise much higher. Sometimes support or resistance levels are at precisely the same point. Other times they are not so even but rather are a considerable range between support and resistance:

Resistance and support are too precise for some analysts; it is easier and more effective to see support and resistance in zones. This helps to prevent overreacting to a minor event. Here's another way to look at the situation.

Resistance levels are usually above the current price, but it is not uncommon for a security to trade at or near resistance. In addition, price movements can be volatile and rise above resistance briefly. Sometimes it does not seem logical to consider a resistance level broken if the price closes $1/8$ above the established resistance level. For this reason, some traders and investors establish resistance zones.[2]

ONE BECOMES THE OTHER

Resistance becomes support, and support becomes resistance. The two conditions of support and resistance switch roles. When resistance is penetrated, it becomes support. When the market falls through support, it then becomes the new resistance. As Figure 12.1 shows, there are several examples of resistance turning into support and support becoming resistance. Looking back at these levels can help indicate the market's next move should it correct or advance. If it corrects, there is a good likelihood that it will fall to previous support levels. If it is down and begins to advance, it could well be halted at previous resistance levels.

SUPPORT AND RESISTANCE CHANGES

In the old days, areas of support and resistance were heavily analyzed and relied upon for trading. Now, rather than split hairs and nitpick over the details of whether a point or even a line is support or resistance, there is an approach in today's market that cuts through the confusion and picks areas of support and resistance (see Figure 12.2). For most analysis this is just fine. Some day traders might be pickier but that's okay. Just find an area where the market went a little flat; if it's higher than the market is now, the area is "resistance." If the area

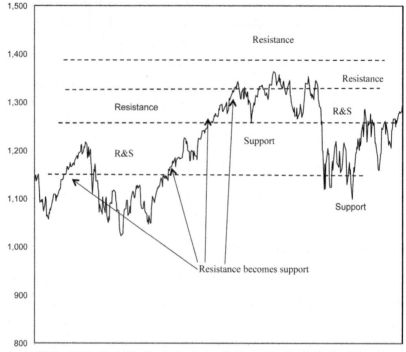

Data source: Yahoo! Finance Historical Prices

Figure 12.1   **S&P 500 Index, 2010–2011**

is lower than where the market is now, it's "support." The length of the particular area in question refers to strength, such as a longer area or an often repeated area being "strong resistance." The shorter area is "weaker resistance." In Figure 12.2, the A, B, and C areas are all fairly short, but they are repeated several times thus making the 1,200 area a level of strong support. If the S&P 500 Index falls below the 1,200 area, they will become strong resistance.

As a stock market index or stock price fluctuates up and down, support and resistance change roles. Resistance will become the new support level and in a falling market when support is broken through it will become the new resistance. Put another way:

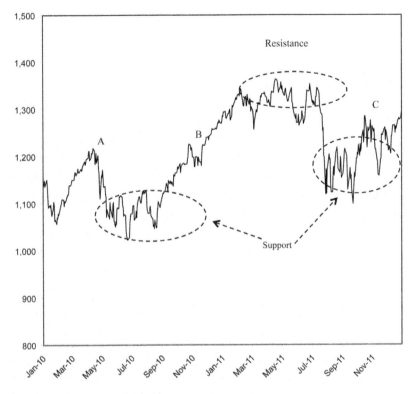

Data source: Yahoo! Finance Historical Prices

Figure 12.2   **S&P 500 Index, 2010–2011**

Another principle of technical analysis stipulates that support can turn into resistance and vice versa. Once the price breaks below a support level, the broken support level can turn into resistance. The break of support signals that the forces of supply have overcome the forces of demand. Therefore, if the price returns to this level, there is likely to be an increase in supply, and hence resistance.

The other turn of the coin is resistance turning into support. As the price advances above resistance, it signals changes in supply and demand. The breakout above resistance proves that the forces of demand have overwhelmed the forces of supply.

If the price returns to this level, there is likely to be an increase in demand and support will be found.[3]

IMPERFECT PREDICTORS

Support and resistance do not really predict what will happen next. All they do is indicate what happened in the past and what could happen again. The anticipation and subsequent actions of buyers and sellers will determine what happens. However, the knowledge of support and resistance can give the investor an indication of the strength of the current market movement.

STOCK PRICES

A similar situation exists for individual stock prices. They also follow patterns of support and resistance. The levels are a key element in technical analysis and are frequently observed by the fundamental analyst for relative strength. Essentially, the idea of support and resistance has the same meaning whether you're looking short term or long term, although the strength requires a more long-term look. There is a diminishing return of meaning as the long-term look is extended. The market trades mostly on information from here and now, rather than on five or ten years ago.

GOOGLE

Google, Inc., an Internet service provider and search engine, came out in 2004 at about $100 a share. It has been a hot stock ever since. It has a tendency to follow the rest of the market and sometimes takes a lead position. Figure 12.3 shows the price and volume action for 2011. There is clearly strong support at the $500 to $550 area (dashed circle), but there is also good support higher at the $600 to $625 area. At the time this chart was made, Google's price was sitting at this support area. It's also easy to see that this area was resistance but became support in December 2011 as the stock price broke through and moved higher.

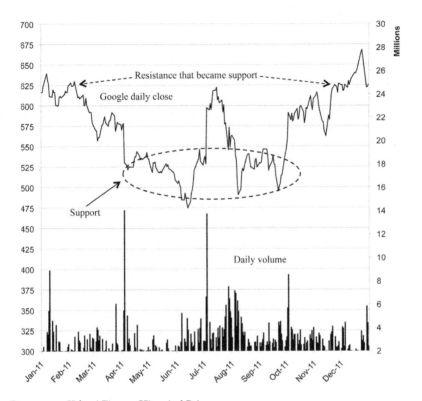

Data source: Yahoo! Finance Historical Prices

Figure 12.3 **Google, Inc., 2011**

What does this mean? It means that if some selling starts with Google, there is a good chance it will stop at the first level of support. If it doesn't, investors look to the next level of support and so on. In this manner they can select possible buy points to add to their portfolios, or they can select sell points if they become too afraid that the decline won't stop anytime soon.

THEY ARE IMPORTANT

An understanding of resistance and support, both at the broad market level and at the individual stock price level, is important to seeing what a price is likely to do. Remember that when a support or resistance level is penetrated, more of the same can be expected, usually (but not always) at the next level of support or resistance. When a market index or stock price falls through support, it can easily fall to the next support level. When it breaks through resistance on the up side, it can keep on going until a new resistance level is reached. These are the technical indicators of the stock market, and they often have nothing to do with fundamentals.

CHAPTER 13

There Is a Bear Market Coming

Yes, of course there's a bear market coming. There is always the specter of a bear market on the economic horizon. It's as true as the fact that some investors believe that the Dow Jones Industrial Average will drop below 2,000 again—although, hopefully not in our lifetime. Many people who believe that the bear is hiding around the corner don't even have a clear definition of what makes a bear market.

WHAT IS A BEAR MARKET?

There is more than one definition of a bear market. The classic definition of a bear market is a time when stock prices steadily decline for a period of weeks, months, and sometimes years.

Trader Vic's Bear Market

Victor Sperandeo is a trader, index developer, author, and financial commentator. He was originally based in Dallas, Texas. He says that a bear market is a long-term down trend (a down trend lasting months to years) in any market, especially the stock market and is characterized by lower intermediate lows (those established in a time frame of weeks to months) interrupted by lower intermediate highs.

Marty Zweig's Bear Market

Marty Zweig is an American stock investor, investment advisor, author, and financial analyst. He is, according to *Forbes Magazine*, renowned for his "eccentric and lavish lifestyle" as well as having the most expensive residence in the United States. It was listed on the New York City real estate market a few years ago for $70 million. His particular investing methodology is based on selecting growth stocks that also have certain value characteristics, through a system that uses both fundamental analysis and market timing.[1]

A bear market is a decline of at least 15 percent in each of three important stock averages: the Dow Jones Industrials, the S&P 500 Index, and the Value Line Index.

Another Classic

A bear market is a decline in the Dow Jones Industrial Average of 20 percent more. It can also be a time when the Dow Jones Industrial Average is down (from previously established highs) for more than two consecutive months.

Keep in mind that newscasters and analysts will talk of "bearish" moves in the stock market. They do not necessarily mean that the stock market has become a bear market. Virtually all corrections or secondary market down trends are referred to as "bearish."

WHAT'S THE TREND?

A bear market represents a downturn in the long-term trend. Most of these trends are short-lived. They might last from three to six months. Only a few last more than a year, the most famous being the bear market from October 1929 to July 1932.

One of the problems with the crash of 1929 was the fact that many companies went out of business, either because of the bear market or the economic climate that followed. By 2012, we have seen worse crashes, but none quite so extended. We have had many economic problems in the past few years. The housing bubble burst, mortgages went bad, financial and manufacturing institutions have gone under, and unemployment has been high.

A WORD OF CAUTION

It's hard to say exactly what caused the crash of 2008. The banking and mortgage problems were certainly a large part of it. Bernard Madoff and a bunch of other crooks didn't help the situation. This brings up an interesting point. If there's a positive side to market crashes, other than the buying opportunities they provide, a lot of the crooks are forced into the open. Although hints of Madoff's problems appeared earlier, it was in early December 2008 when he finally revealed what had been happening. He couldn't afford to pay the redemptions to his customers.

So this may be a good reason to have a deep bear market occasionally—to shake out the crooks. And a bear market could stimulate buying good stocks for the recovery.

As Figure 13.1 shows, the primary trend turned in early 2008 and became a bear market. It didn't start back up until March 2009. Officially, it became a primary up trend in May 2009, which continued to July 2011. A short, quick secondary down trend and the primary up trend continues.

STOCKS TO SELL IN A BEAR MARKET

Although the general rule is to ride out a bear market and look for good buying opportunities, there are a few stocks that should probably be gotten rid of because of the risk involved.

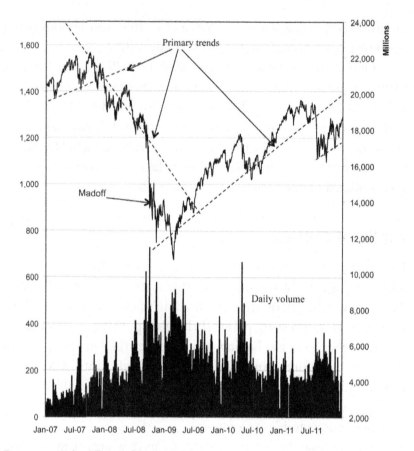

Data source: Yahoo! Finance Historical Prices

Figure 13.1   **S&P 500 Index, 2007–2011**

- *Margined stock:* The margin calls can be devastating.
- *Highly speculative stock:* It might not survive the hard times ahead.
- *Stocks involved with the crash:* These resemble the financial stocks that were involved in the 2008 crisis.
- *Poor performing stocks:* Stocks you had been thinking of selling because of poor performance. It could get worse.

So, it's time to clean up your portfolio and look for buying opportunities. Keep the stocks that are still basically good. Those are the positions you want to build.

DOOM AND GLOOM IN 2012

Even at the end of 2011, the doom and gloomers were nervous about a new bear market in 2012. The primary concern at that time was the debt problems in Europe. A collapse in the efforts to resolve those problems would have worldwide implications, dropping the S&P 500 Index by 20 percent or more. The following is from "What If There's a Bear Market in 2012?" by Robert Holmes:

> Still, a 20% drop next year would be the worst performance since 2008, when the global financial crisis struck. It would take a cataclysmic event—such as the unraveling of Europe, a recession in key emerging markets or war—for stocks to fall into a bear market. After all, corporate profit margins are big and borrowing costs at record lows, conditions that are ripe for earnings growth.[2]

It appears that not all is bad. If corporate margins are big and the cost of borrowing is down, the U.S. economy should be engaged in growth and recovery. But here's the concern:

> Tom Villalta, chief investment officer with Austin, Texas-based Jones Villalta Asset Management, says that a 20% drop would have to be predicated on unemployment rising and some sort of bank run in Europe. "There is credence to this negative feedback loop idea," he adds. "The market is not running on fundamentals of companies. It's running on a macro, psychological aspect. The volatility increases in those situations."[3]

Doom and gloomers tend to be contrarians on the economy. If they always predict that the economy will fall into a hole, eventually they'll be right. Granted the potential for a weakness in the economy is always present. Sometimes it's obvious, and other times we get blindsided.

BEAR MARKETS EQUAL BUYING OPPORTUNITIES

Bear markets have certainly presented buying opportunities in the past with a few notable exceptions. The 1929 bear saw several companies go out of business. In more recent years Enron, Lehman Brothers, and even Merrill Lynch disappeared. The way to avoid such difficulties is to choose stocks carefully and wait for some signs of stability. Of course, diversity in a stock portfolio also helps. However, a wait can be difficult because of the speed with which the market can recover. Waiting too long leads to missed opportunities.

So build your stock portfolio during a bear market. Just do it with extra care and caution. Select companies with good analysis and research. All of the risk cannot be removed from investing, but it can be at least partly mitigated.

Part 3

STRATEGY

The most important part of strategy is setting investment objectives. Each investor should have a well-defined general objective as well as a specific objective for each individual investment. To say, "I want to make a lot of money in the stock market," cannot be considered an objective. It's a dream, a wish without definition.

An investment objective must:

- Be specific
- Be reasonable in expectations
- Consider risk
- Have a time frame
- Be measurable

Setting these kinds of objectives allows the investor to know what is to be achieved, by when, and by how much. The objective can be analyzed periodically to see if it is possible to achieve it. If it is not possible, a new objective can be established.

If you sell the losers, how do you determine which stocks are losers? Is it weak fundamentals or weak price or both?

How do you determine which stocks to buy high and sell higher? What's high? What's low?

What is the trend and how do you figure which way the market is really going?

How do you make "winners win big"?

Where do you find out about rumors? Should you act on them or ignore them? Should you buy a stock that just announced a 2-to-1 split, or is that bad?

Sell in May and go away. Sometimes referred to as the October effect (because that is when you buy the stock back), this strategy is looked at closely. Is it always a good strategy or is it unpredictable? What are its shortcomings?

Is it truly cheaper to buy stock using "dollar cost averaging," or are you better off buying all at once and taking the risk?

Just what is a perfect hedge, and how can an investor take advantage of it on a regular basis?

Other fine points of strategy are also examined in this part: selling short, selling short against the box, and deciding which stocks to sell. Diversification as a strategy is also examined. Diversification is limited in what it can do and often doesn't offer as much protection as many people think. The fact is that if the market is in a down trend, diversification offers little or no protection.

CHAPTER 14

Invest According
to Objectives

"I want to make a lot of money in the stock market, but I don't want to take any risk."

Is this a wish or an objective? The general statement is assuredly a wish. However, a wish can be redefined as an objective.

ESTABLISHING A GOOD OBJECTIVE

Often such things as retirement, children's college education, a house, or a new car are stated as objectives for investing. Even these are quite general, although they're more specific than "a lot of money." What about a set time for reaching the objective? Retirement and children's education have built-in time periods; however, it's a good idea to break these large (10–20-year) blocks of time into smaller segments, like 1 to 5 years. Having a short time to reach your objective helps to ensure that the investor evaluates performance and makes changes along the way.

DECISIONS NEED TO BE MADE

In order to meet an investment objective, certain questions must be answered:

- What specifically will be done?
- What performance is acceptable?
- What kind of stocks or other investments will be purchased?
- How much diversification is necessary to moderate the risk?
- What time frame should be used?
- How will success be measured?

Once you've decided on the answers, write them down.

An objective should have the following characteristics:

- *Be specific:* What will you do to help you decide on what kind of investments to make?
- *Have reasonable expectations:* Base expectations on observable performance.
- *Consider risk:* Select stocks and diversify to a comfort level (five or six companies).
- *Have a time frame:* One year, two years, five years, and so on.
- *Be measurable:* Performance needs to be measured in order to be evaluated on a regular basis.

CATEGORIES OF STOCK

When brokers open new accounts, they are required by Rule 405 of the New York Stock Exchange to know their customers. This means they need to know details about the investors' investing experience, financial status, and, most importantly, their investment objectives. In order to standardize objectives into mutually understood concepts, the broker and the customer usually refer to a list of categories of stock:

- *Income:* Investments that generate income from dividends or interest payments
- *Growth:* Investments that demonstrate price growth—usually newer companies that pay no dividends
- *Total return:* Investments that will see both price growth and income from dividends
- *Speculation:* Investments for short-term trades that result in quick profits (e.g., new companies, companies in rapid growth areas, turnarounds, and other speculative situations)

Income, growth, total return, or speculation. All financial investments fit into one or more of these categories.

INCOME STOCK

Traditionally, income stocks are most often utilities, especially electrical utilities. They are usually conservative investments with steady streams of income and are typically financially stable. Although there is always risk involved with common stock investing, income stocks should have some of the lowest risk. Sometimes they are colorfully referred to as the "widow and orphan stocks," meaning that these are investments for those people who can't afford to lose money. Isn't that all of us?

Obviously, dividends are a priority when an investor's objective is income. Dividend growth and dividend stability are likewise important. Looking at the average annual growth of dividends over a five-year period can give the investor some idea of how much growth to expect in the future. In order for a company to pay out dividends, the growth of revenues and income is important.

The primary sources of income can be a concern. The Detroit area might have trouble if the automotive industry is in a slump. The

Silicon Valley area of California might have trouble when the computer industry is slow. The source of income is part of risk—more specifically, the risk of slower growth.

Matching the General Objective

With income as a general objective, we narrow the focus to electric utility companies that have a good current yield (say 4 percent or better). In the old days we would use U.S. Treasury 10-year notes as a benchmark, but Treasury yields are quite low in 2012. Therefore, it's better to take some risk for a better yield. Keep in mind that we are also looking at dividend growth history. This means that we need to find companies that have had consistent growth in revenues and earnings.

With an income objective and electric utilities as the target, we look at three possible selections, beginning with Dominion Resources (NYSE: D):

> Dominion Resources, Inc., together with its subsidiaries, engages in producing and transporting energy in the United States. It operates in three segments: DVP, Dominion Generation, and Dominion Energy. The DVP segment includes regulated electric transmission and distribution operations that serve residential, commercial, industrial, and governmental customers in Virginia and North Carolina. This segment also involves nonregulated retail energy marketing of electricity and natural gas. The Dominion Generation segment includes the electricity generation through coal, nuclear, gas, oil, and renewables; and related energy supply operations. It also comprises generation operations of the company's merchant fleet and energy marketing, and price risk management activities for these assets. The Dominion Energy segment includes the company's Ohio and West Virginia regulated natural gas distribution companies, regulated gas transmission pipeline and storage operations,

natural gas gathering and by-products extraction activities, and regulated LNG import and storage operations. It also provides producer services, which aggregates natural gas supply; engages in natural gas trading and marketing activities; and is involved in natural gas supply management. The company's portfolio of assets includes approximately 27,615 MW of generation; 6,100 miles of electric transmission lines; 56,800 miles of electric distribution lines; 11,000 miles of natural gas transmission, gathering, and storage pipeline; and 21,800 miles of gas distribution pipeline. Dominion Resources, Inc., also owns approximately 947 bcf of storage capacity of natural gas and serves retail energy customers in 14 states. In addition, it sells electricity at wholesale prices to rural electric cooperatives, municipalities, and into wholesale electricity markets. The company was founded in 1909 and is headquartered in Richmond, Virginia.[1]

Dominion pays an annual dividend rate of $2.11 per share for an annual yield of 4.16 percent. Its five-year annual dividend rate is 4 percent annually. It is considered a "clean utility" and is rated a "buy" according to the analysts at Deutsche Bank.

For an income objective the most important information is the current dividend yield of 4.16 percent. If the shares are purchased at the current price of $50.47 each, you will be receiving that yield for as long as you own the stock. That yield will increase when and if the dividends are increased, but it cannot go down unless the dividend itself is lowered.

Figure 14.1 shows the dividend growth for Dominion Resources from 2007–2011. It's easy to see a rather steady growth for the dividends as well as consistency of payment. In that same time period the price of the stock grew from $40.26 a share to $50.47. Although price growth isn't our objective, it is a positive event.

The statistics for dividend history came directly from Dominion Resources. A longer period of time can be viewed, but a longer period usually isn't meaningful for the present situation.

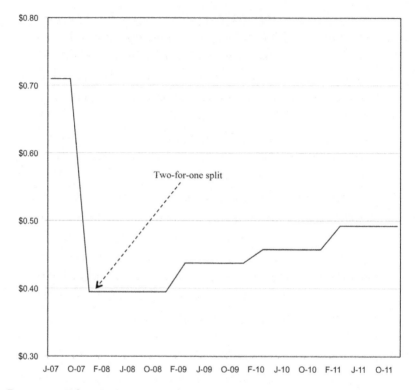

Data source: Yahoo! Finance Historical Prices

Figure 14.1   **Dominion Resoures Dividends, 2007–2011**

Twelve-month sales growth is up 2.70 percent, and earnings for the same period are up 135 percent. So, this appears to be an excellent possibility for an income stock.

Hawaiian Electric Industries (NYSE: HE) is another income stock:

> Hawaiian Electric Industries, Inc., through its subsidiaries, primarily engages in electric utility and banking businesses primarily in Hawaii. Its Electric Utility business engages in the production, purchase, transmission, distribution, and sale of electricity from renewable energy sources, such as wind, solar, photovoltaic, geothermal, wave, hydroelectric,

sugarcane waste, municipal waste, and other bio-fuels, as well as from fuel oil. It distributes and sells electricity on the islands of Oahu, Hawaii, Maui, Lanai, and Molokai, as well as serves suburban communities, resorts, the U.S. armed forces installations, and agricultural operations. The company's Banking business engages in accepting savings accounts, checking accounts, money market accounts, and certificate of deposits; and providing residential and commercial real estate, residential mortgage, construction and development, multifamily residential and commercial real estate, consumer, and commercial loans. As of December 31, 2010, it owned 138 automated teller machines. The company was founded in 1891, and is based in Honolulu, Hawaii.[2]

Hawaiian Electric Industries is a power company in Hawaii. It has been around since 1891 and appears to be a stable company. The company pays $1.24 as an annual dividend with a current yield of 4.8 percent based on a current price of $25.75. The dividend doesn't show any growth for the past several years. The price of the stock hasn't grown much either. Obviously, one of the main problems is where the new growth will come from for a company that's in the middle of the Pacific Ocean. Although the yield is within our parameters, the growth should be a serious concern.

Southern Company (NYSE: SO) is yet another income stock to consider:

Southern Company, through its subsidiaries, operates as a utility company that provides electric service in the southeastern United States. The company generates, transmits, and distributes electricity through coal, nuclear, oil and gas, and hydro resources. It offers electric service primarily in Alabama, Georgia, Florida, and Mississippi; and serves approximately 4.4 million retail customers with approximately 42,000 megawatts of generating capacity. Southern Company also constructs, acquires, owns, and manages

generation assets and sells electricity in the wholesale market. Its transmission assets include 27,000 miles of transmission lines and 3,700 substations. The company also provides
digital wireless communications, such as push to talk, cel-
lular service, text messaging, wireless Internet access, and
wireless data in the southeast; and wholesale fiber optic
solutions to telecommunication providers under the name
Southern Telecom. Southern Company was founded in
1945, and is headquartered in Atlanta, Georgia.[3]

Southern Company pays an annual dividend of $1.87 a share for
a current yield of 4.2 percent based on a current price of $45.27 per
share. The sales growth for the past 12 months is 10.9 percent, and
the earnings growth for the same time is up 20.20 percent. Southern
Company could be an excellent candidate for income stock. The
dividend has also shown steady growth (see Figure 14.2).

Stock analysis can be much more thorough than what has been
shown here. It depends on how deeply the investor wants to dig
into a company's financial situation. Debt, new projects, and future
sources of revenue can also be examined.

With electric utilities, nuclear and coal issues can be an important area of examination. However, companies that have been consistent in the past will likely continue to be consistent in the future,
unless something unusual arises.

Objective

For purposes of dividend income, let's say that we've invested
$100,000 in the stock of at least three electric utility companies.
The expected annual yield will be 4 percent with at least a 2 percent
annual growth rate in the dividend. Risk is determined by evaluating
the consistency of the growth in revenues, earnings, and dividends.
Performance is evaluated at least on an annual basis, with changes
made as necessary.

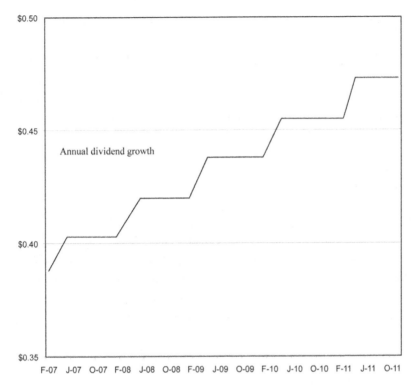

Data source: Yahoo! Finance Historical Prices

Figure 14.2 **Southern Company Dividends, 2007–2011**

Current Yield

An important point to make about current yield is that it is locked into the price you pay for the stock. It will remain the same unless the dividend is increased or decreased. It can also change if you buy more shares with a different current yield. Obviously your total yield would be a calculated average of the different purchase prices.

Evaluation

When an objective is precisely detailed, evaluation is simple. Either the objective is being met or it is not. If not, learn the reason why not and make a decision to hold your position or sell the stock for a better-performing candidate.

Price growth is not part of the objective. It's the income that's important. Any price growth is just an extra benefit if the investor chooses to sell some or all of the stock. The price growth is often why income investors will choose stock rather than safer U.S. securities.

A Short Analysis

The analysis used in this chapter is a brief form of fundamental analysis, which examines the revenues, earnings, dividends, and price growth of a company. Even a short analysis tells a lot about a company and its consistent growth. The purpose of this chapter is not to explain analysis, but to illustrate how an analysis can be made based on information readily available to investors.

GROWTH STOCK

Investors looking for growth should consider revenue and earnings growth as a higher priority than dividends. Price growth over the past three to five years essentially replaces dividend growth as a focal point. Growth companies are generally small to midsized, and they are leaders or are becoming leaders in their industry niche. A benchmark for performance can be an index such as the Russell 2000 Index, the Wilshire 5000 Index, or the S&P indexes. However, because of the influence of growth stocks on the entire stock market, the investor should also look at the stock's performance within the Dow Jones Industrial Average and the S&P 500 Index for growth comparisons.

The price to earnings ratios (p/e ratio equals the price divided by earnings) can be an important part of determining risk in growth stocks, but the ratios should not be examined alone. A current p/e ratio in comparison to a company's five-year average p/e ratio can show whether a stock is currently more or less attractive. Although it's an oversimplification, a higher-than-average p/e ratio indicates more risk; a lower-than-average p/e ratio indicates less risk. It is essential to look at the information behind the p/e ratio and then ask why the ratio is high or low. Comparing the company's p/e ratio to that of other companies in the same industry can also be helpful in determining risk and market appeal.

For growth stock objectives, look at:

- Price growth
- Revenue growth
- Earnings growth
- P/E ratio
- Analyst opinion (why will the growth continue?)

Many analysts would also look at cash on hand and cash flow to determine stability in growth stocks. Tables 14.1 and 14.2 look at some possible selections for growth stock; they include some of the primary financials.

All these companies look good—some excellent growth over the past three years, not much debt, and reasonable volatility. They are all good candidates. The negative earnings on Western Digital

Table 14.1 Growth Stock Targets[4]

Company Name	Symbol	Price	3-Yr. Growth	P/E[*]	Sales[†]	Income[†]
Western Digital Corp.	WDC	$39.68	100%	9.25	−3.30%	−47.50%
KLA-Tencor Group	KLAC	$50.19	102%	11.33	74.40%	274.20%
Starbucks Corp.	SBUX	$54.48	354%	31.52	9.30%	31.70%
Jabil Circuit Inc.	JBL	$21.01	200%	14.70	23.20%	125.70%
Hurco Companies Inc.	HURC	$24.07	72%	11.01	70.40%	293.73%

[*] Price-earnings ratio.
[†] Last 12 months, as of May 9, 2012.

Table 14.2 Growth Stock Targets (Additional Information)

Company Name	Symbol	Rate	Institu-tion	D/E*	Beta	Dividend
Western Digital Corp.	WDC	8	96.73%	0.04	1.35	n/a
KLA-Tencor Group	KLAC	7	94.76%	.025	1.70	1.40
Starbucks Corp.	SBUX	10	77.02%	.012	1.10	0.68
Jabil Circuit Inc.	JBL	7	86.40%	0.63	2.07	0.32
Hurco Companies Inc.	HURC	6	65.99%	0.01	1.53	n/a

* D/E is the debt-to-equity ratio; the amount of debt divided by the amount of ownership.

could well be a turnaround situation and make it a good year for the stock. All the companies have strong market position, although an investor would be wise to dig a bit deeper to find out where the growth will come from.

Considering the price growth these companies have shown in the past three years, it would not be unreasonable to expect a 15 to 20 percent annual growth rate over the next five years. That could be too much for 2012, but could catch up in 2013 and in the future.

Growth Objective

Your growth objective is to invest $100,000 in five to ten growth stocks for the next five years for a minimum 10 percent annual return. The risk level will be moderate to moderately high. Results will be evaluated at least every six months, with changes made to the portfolio as necessary.

TOTAL RETURN STOCK

Total return stocks are dividend-paying stocks that also have good price growth. The focus with these stocks is usually on industry leaders, the "stalwarts" that also pay dividends. The list would

Table 14.3   **Total Return Stocks**[5]

Company Name	Symbol	Price	3-Yr. Growth	Div. %
Bristol-Meyers Squibb Co.	BMY	$32.91	63%	4.10%
Deere & Company	DE	$79.22	106%	2.28%
General Electric Co.	GE	$20.16	34%	3.53%

include the so-called blue-chip stocks like General Electric, 3M, and IBM. They are considered lower-risk stocks because they are well-established companies and because every time a dividend is paid out, the risk is lowered by the amount of the dividend.

Analysis of total return stocks is similar to the analysis for growth stocks, but it would obviously include dividends and dividend growth. The objective statement needs to include both price and dividend growth.

Total return objectives can be evaluated annually, quarterly, or monthly. Just be careful with sell decisions. Don't sell out too quickly when the whole market declines. Often that is the best time to buy more stock.

As Table 14.3 shows, with total return we are looking for price growth and dividend growth.

Objective

Your objective is to invest $50,000 in a portfolio of at least three to five different total return stocks to expect an 8 to 10 percent total return annually for the next five years. The risk level will be low to moderate. The portfolio will be analyzed quarterly, and underperforming stocks will be sold and replaced.

SPECULATION

The speculation category of investments covers everything else. It can be the act of investing with "wild abandon," or it can include some analysis to moderate risk. Although there is a belief among many people that higher risk brings higher rewards, this is not usually what happens. Higher risk can also bring higher losses.

Rather than approach speculative investing with wild abandon, why not just move the objective to a higher level. If the S&P 500 Index is growing at 10 percent, set the objective at 20 or 30 percent, or use a shorter time period for achieving your objective. Use basic fundamental analysis to find companies that either have or are working toward strong revenues and earnings. Technical analysis is also used for short-term speculative investing, and the risk can be moderated by learning some basics about the company.

No matter what type of analysis is used for speculative investing, the greatest difficulty is keeping up with the rapidly changing market. Opportunities appear suddenly and are gone within minutes. The individual investor can have problems trying to keep up with the professionals who watch the market change tick by tick. Evaluation of speculative trading is often done on a trade-by-trade basis.

WHAT AN OBJECTIVE DOES

Setting a well-defined objective makes investing easier for the individual investor. Decisions to buy or sell stock are easier because it is necessary to determine if the stock fits the objective or is achieving the objective. If a stock doesn't fit, don't buy it. If performance is below standard, with recovery unlikely, sell it.

REVIEW

An objective should have the following characteristics:

- Be specific
- Have reasonable expectations
- Consider risk
- Have a time frame
- Be measurable

CHAPTER 15

Sell the Losers, and Let the Winners Run

The title of this chapter is one of the oldest sayings in the stock market. In the late 1800s, Daniel Drew had a slightly different version: "Cut your losses, and let your profits run."

The concept is sound; in fact, it is one of the most important things an investor must understand about the stock market. It is prudent for an investor to sell stocks that are losing money—stocks that could continue to drop in price as they drop in value. It makes equally good sense to stay with stocks that show significant gains as long as they remain fundamentally strong.

But just what is a loser? Is it any price drop from the high? Is a stock a loser only if the investor is actually in a loss position—that is, when the current price is below the original purchase price?

Any price drop is a losing situation. Price drops cost the investor money. They are a loss of profits. In some circumstances the investor should sell, but in other situations the investor should take a close look before reaching a sell decision. The determination of whether a stock is still a winner depends on the cause of the price decline. If a price drop occurs because of a weakness in the overall market or is the result of a "normal" daily fluctuation of the stock price, it can still be a winner.

If, however, the cause of the drop has long-term implications, it could be time to take the loss and move on to another stock. Long-term implications could be any of the following:

- Declining sales
- Big tax difficulties
- Giant legal problems
- An emerging bear market (maybe)
- Higher interest rates (maybe)
- Huge negative impacts on future earnings

Any event that has a negative impact on the long-term prospects for earnings or earnings growth can quickly turn a stock into a loser. Many long- and short-term investors will sell out their positions and move on to a potential winner.

SELLING LOSERS IS DIFFICULT

The following is from Forbes.com, Intelligent Investing Panel:

> Selling a loser is hard. It is one of the most challenging decisions you make as an investor. There are many excuses for holding on to losers, such as: "It's only a paper loss," or "It will rebound if I'm patient." Not selling losers is a common practice called Loss Aversion. Underlying this behavioral tendency is the desire to avoid the regret that can accompany turning a paper loss into a realized one. Realizing losses may have the unintended effect of making you feel like a loser . . . and that is a feeling understandably avoided.[1]

So it's understandable that selling is a difficult decision to make, but it must be done and done in a timely fashion.

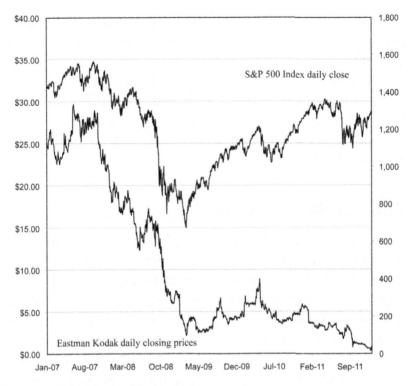

Data source: Yahoo! Finance Historical Prices

Figure 15.1   Eastman Kodak versus S&P 500 Index, 2007–2011

Eastman Kodak

Let's take a look at Eastman Kodak. What do you do when you've controlled a large part of the camera and film market for decades, and suddenly film becomes obsolete? You adapt quickly or die! As the market fell, so did Eastman Kodak (see Figure 15.1). Keep in mind that the stock had already fallen from $90 a share back in 1985. When the market started to recover, obviously Eastman Kodak did not.

Twelve-month sales growth in early 2012 was a minus 5.50 percent. Income growth at a minus 189.70 percent. Could it become a turnaround? Sure. Stranger things have happened. But at this point it is most definitely a loser that should be removed from most portfolios.[2]

One interesting point about the stock, even as bad as it looks, is that it still has 44.55 percent institutional ownership. Either somebody has faith in it, or the speculators are looking for a "dead cat bounce." That would be a short-term profit made on a small upturn at the end.

VALUE IN EARNINGS GROWTH

Value, in terms of growth potential, is based on earnings and earnings growth. Analysis of earnings and news about a company can give some insight into the quality of earnings. If management has increased earnings by firing half the company's personnel or the increase is derived from closing several facilities or a share buyback program, the quality of increase is not as valuable as it would be if it reflected improved sales and revenues. Slash-and-burn strategies can lead to a further decline in productivity, resulting in additional weakness in earnings and eventually lower prices for the stock. On the positive side, drastic cuts can force companies to become more efficient, thereby increasing the quality of earnings, which may lead to higher stock prices.

The investor should analyze the company's growth and observe the stock price in action. From the analysis the investor can determine whether the value of a stock is more likely to increase, remain flat, or begin to decline. The analysis can be difficult at times because a winner can temporarily take on the appearance of a loser.

Three situations—daily price fluctuations, market declines, and price advances followed by price weaknesses—can make a winner appear to look weak, but they are not necessarily a signal to begin selling. These are usually temporary situations and are therefore exceptions to the sell-the-losers rule.

Exception 1: Daily Price Fluctuations

Stock prices fluctuate up or down in day-to-day trading. A glance at any daily price chart will show what may be considered normal daily fluctuations—the short-term look. Stock prices also move from one trading range to another. For example, a stock price could have a daily fluctuation of $30 to $35 but could occasionally move to $40 and then drop back to the $30 to $35 range. The trading range would be considered $30 to $40. When the stock moves up and begins fluctuating between $40 and $55, it is obviously trading in a new higher range.

Johnson & Johnson

Let's take a look at Johnson & Johnson for 2011. Figure 15.2 shows some basic day-to-day fluctuations. Most of the time these movements are not meaningful. Even the sharp drop from November 15 to November 25 quickly moves back up to the trading range. The upward move toward the end of the year could become meaningful if it establishes a new trading range.

Exception 2: Market Decline

A market decline does not necessarily make a loser. Toward the end of 2007 and the beginning of 2008, the stock market became nervous. It started a decline that became very serious in early May. From May 2008 until March 2009, the market took the down elevator, and most stocks fell right along with it. The market can make a lot of stocks look like losers, but does that mean it's time to sell? Not usually. Sure, selling out and buying back at a lower price can be a valid strategy. Just keep in mind that at the time it's happening, you never know how far it will drop or how long it will stay down. This can make it very difficult determining when to buy the stock back.

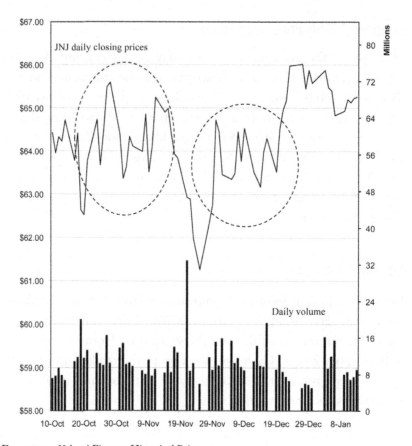

Data source: Yahoo! Finance Historical Prices

Figure 15.2   **Johnson & Johnson, October 2011–January 2012**

Many investors will get lucky once or twice, but most often they will miss the best opportunities.

As we have seen in the last few decades, the stock market can drop several hundred points and make an amazing recovery in a short period of time. Look at Figure 15.3. If we were lucky enough to buy Google at $413 a share in March 2008, we would be worried by early October because it dropped through $400 a share and kept falling.

Figure 15.3 shows the market pushing down the price of Google. It isn't really a reason to sell Google, if the fundamentals

S&P 500 Index daily close

Google, Inc. daily closing prices

Data source: Yahoo! Finance Historical Prices

Figure 15.3   **S&P 500 Index versus Google, Inc., 2007–2011**

remain strong, which they did. Also, if you sold out, where and when would you buy back? Keep in mind that you can't see the price movement until after it happens.

The decline of 2008 had some special situations: some of the financial institutions were drowning in underwater mortgages while the market was plummeting. The U.S. government selectively bailed out some and let others drown. It will forever be debated whether the bailouts should have happened or not. Many people agree that far too much of the bailout money went to line the pockets of those who had caused the problem in the first place. Perhaps if tighter strings had been attached, it would have been better. But, we cannot change that now. So what about the people who owned stock in

Lehman Brothers or Merrill Lynch? Yes, they should have sold, but when and at what price? It's not an easy answer. It's also the main reason to have diversification in a stock portfolio.

If the market correction is sudden and appears to stabilize in just few days or weeks, it may be best to hold a position and get ready to buy more. Sure, it's okay to sell if it gets worse, but just remember that it's more the market situation than a problem with the individual stock, and you'll have to figure out where and when to buy the stock back. Most investors will just hold on and look for buying opportunities rather than selling.

Exception 3: Price Advance Followed by Weakness

A significant upward move to a new trading range followed by some price weakness is a normal occurrence. As a stock price makes major upward movement, many professional investors will begin to take profits. Although there is nothing wrong with taking profits, the upward price movement might have only just started. Even so, it is inevitable that some profit taking will occur and that the stock price that has risen to new highs will show some downward price correction.

A signal is given if a stock begins to fall lower than its daily trading range and the overall market is unchanged or advancing. If a stock price that normally trades between $45 and $50 a share drops to $43 and then to $40, it is time to be concerned. It's the concept that is important here, not necessarily these actual prices. The signal is even stronger if the stocks of comparable companies are not showing a similar weakness. It is a signal to either sell the stock or better yet find out the reason for the decline.

CONSISTENT GROWTH

Winners are the stock of those companies showing consistent growth in revenues, earnings, and price. They are the leaders in their industry and have continual new product developments for new or existing markets. Their products are not passing fads.

Even though a product may have created a tremendous demand, how likely is it that this demand will remain strong in the next three to five years? Pet Rocks, Wall Walkers, and Cabbage Patch dolls can have a strong market for a year or two, but seldom can this type of product build enduring demand. Although faddish products can be earnings boosters for well-established companies, they are usually not a firm enough foundation on which to build an entire company.

FUNDAMENTALS

Winners should be held until the fundamentals that make them winners begin to weaken or until the price runs too far ahead of the earnings causing a decline in value. Stocks trade on the anticipation of future growth. At times the anticipation is vastly greater than the growth and even the growth potential. Add the news of weaker earnings to that anticipation and the stock price gets hammered down hard. The winner stock becomes a loser.

Losers take money from investors and should be sold and forgotten until they stabilize and rebuild the fundamental strength necessary to become winners again.

END-OF-THE-YEAR SELLING

The best time to sell your underperforming stocks is near the end of the current year, because of tax loss selling. The following is from the Internet, "retirebyforty," November 2011:

> Today, let's look at the other year end portfolio fixing task—selling your losers to get the capital loss tax deduction. Tax deduction? You may think I don't have to worry about tax until April. However, you have to take action now before the year is over to get the tax deduction for 2011. If you wait

until 2012, then you won't get the tax deduction until April 2013. That's why the end of the year is a great time to *sell some of the losers in your portfolio.*[3]

When you have some losers, especially ones that you are uncertain about, the year end can be an excellent time to reevaluate and do some tax loss selling. Take the money you have left and look for some new winners that will fit better into your portfolio objective. You don't have to wait till the end of the year; you can sell losers sooner if the situation seems appropriate.

CHAPTER 16

Buy Low, Sell High

B ack in the early days of Wall Street, it was stated; "Buy that which is cheap, and sell that which is dear."

Charles Dow, one of the founding fathers of Dow Jones and the first managing editor of *The Wall Street Journal*, might have put it this way; "Buy a stock that has value in earnings and dividends paid out. As this stock rises in price and the value of earnings and dividends declines, sell the stock."

Although the methods of evaluating stocks "of value" may have changed, the basic idea is still around. The anticipation of value and value growth are what make a stock price rise. The value is not the price alone. However, it is one of the factors in determining value. Another important factor is earnings past and earnings forecast. Stock prices move in anticipation of future earnings and their growth.

AN OLD IDEA

The idea of buy low, sell high is as old as trading ownership of properties. It is the basis of all business. Buy a property at one price, and sell it at a higher price. Making a profit is the reason to buy and sell stock.

It is the one axiom almost everyone understands but many have trouble following. An investor hears that Company ABC is buying out XYZ Company. The stock had been trading at $24.50 a share, but the buyout is expected to be $28.00 a share. The investor knows that there is some risk involved and decides to think about buying 200 shares. The following afternoon the investor calls the broker and learns that XYZ is now trading at $30.00 a share. A feeling of panic overcomes the investor because the price is above the buyout price already. Better place that buy order. An order to buy 200 shares of XYZ Company is placed and filled at $29.50.

The following week the investor calls the broker to check on XYZ and learns that it is trading at $25.50. That's a $4.00 loss per share—more than 15 percent. Trying to restrain the feeling of panic, the investor gives the broker instructions to sell the 200 shares of XYZ Company at the market. The order is entered and executed at $25.50.

A few weeks later the investor decides to look at the price quote and is shocked to learn that the stock closed yesterday at $28.00 a share. The investor feels disappointed and exasperated about stock investing.

Situations like this happen every day in the stock market. Many times there aren't takeover rumors involved but rather just some good news that brings the company's name to the public.

WHAT WENT WRONG?

Several things went wrong. By the time the investor first heard about the takeover, it was already late in the game for making a stock play. Thinking for a day or two about buying or selling can be disastrous. The investor both bought and sold the position without learning the details.

Once a strategy is put in play, an investor should not be quick to change. The investor should have checked the background on the two companies. The 10 or 15 percent loss strategy is just that, a 10 to

15 percent loss. It has nothing to do with how a price will perform in the next few days. Some professional investors look for stocks that are down 10 to 15 percent and consider them buying opportunities. They know that the 10 percenters have "weak hands" and will be bailing out thereby making the stock prices even better bargains. These professional investors will allow a 10, 15, or even 20 percent drop (sometimes more) because the majority of buyers did not buy right at the top.

PRICES CAN BE VOLATILE

If investors are going to speculate on takeovers, it is important that they realize that the prices will tend to be volatile until the actual takeover occurs. The reason for this is that the professional speculators run the price up and test the resolve of the other shareholders. They have the money to play with, and they have experience. They often know what they are doing. The individual usually cannot outguess them, but with some understanding and patience might be able to go along for the ride.

WHY NOT THE CYCLICALS?

If an investor wants to buy low and sell high on the same stock, why not go to the cyclicals, such as automobile stocks? These stocks are supposed to follow the ups and downs of the economic cycles. The one big problem with this strategy is that the cyclicals aren't very cyclical anymore.

Take a look at Ford Motor Company. Figure 16.1 is a monthly chart going from 1977 to early 2012. It once had some cycles, which we can safely assume were tied to the economic cycles, but doesn't appear to be the case anymore. In truth it's hard to find a stock with a cyclical price trend. If you do, how do you test its reliability for the future?

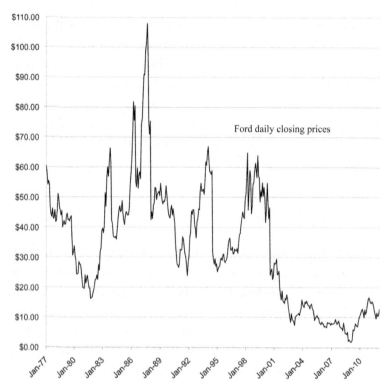

Data source: Yahoo! Finance Historical Prices

Figure 16.1   **Ford Motor Company, 1977–January 2012**

BUY LOW, AND SELL HIGH

Yes, the idea is to buy low and sell high, but don't be too quick to sell. Stock should be sold for only two reasons:

1. You need the money.
2. The fundaments have weakened and the company's prospects for the future have changed.

If you are able to sell at a much higher price than you bought, you held onto the right stock. This is related to Chapter 15, Sell the Losers, and Let the Winners Run. As long as the fundamentals are holding up, there is no reason to sell a winning stock. If you have set dollar objectives for the stock that have been surpassed, fine. Consider yourself brilliant and set new price objectives. But do not be too quick to sell.

CHAPTER 17

Buy High, Sell Higher

Many individuals are attempting to "buy high and sell higher" when they buy a stock that is on the move. In fact, professional traders frequently use this strategy. Soaring prices are attractive to investors who believe that the prices will keep moving. As long as the momentum of the price swing attracts new buyers, the stock price will continue to climb. It might run up for a couple of days, weeks, and sometimes months. Eventually, however, there is a hesitation followed by a turn as the profit taking begins. The last buyers not only have the smallest gains from the run up, but they will obviously also have the biggest losses if they don't sell quickly. It's somewhat like a pyramid scheme where the losers are the last ones to join.

A severe market decline creates lower prices and large cash positions even though the earnings of stocks can remain unchanged (meaning that their value is increasing as prices decline). The bargains can be resisted for only a limited time. In a severe market decline, the climb back to former levels could take a few months or longer, but the recovery will come.

WHERE ARE THE PLAYS?

Individual investors can seek out stocks that are either in play or are likely to come into play. Often they are stocks with strong fundamentals in earnings and revenues and are found in industries with good growth potential. In the first decade of the new millennium, technology and medical products were very hot. Some Internet stocks have been exciting. Sometimes older products companies with strong growth records also do well.

Google

Google is an Internet Search Engine known for its high speed and other services. When Google (NASDAQ: GOOG) first went public in August 2004, it came out at a whopping $100 a share. That was actually a bargain, since it hardly ever looked back on its way to $732.94 a share. An investor would still be comfortable even if the buy was at $200, $300, or even higher. On the graph in Figure 17.1,

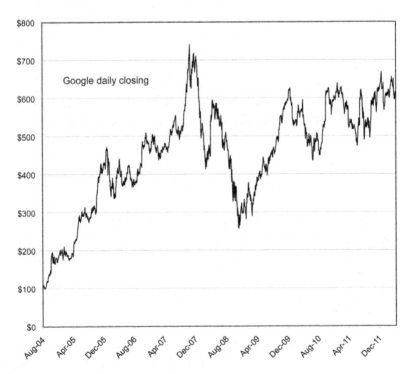

Data source: Yahoo! Finance Historical Prices

Figure 17.1   **Google, Inc., 2004–2011**

the $300 level appears to be the lowest strong support. There is also good support between the $500 and $600 levels.

Assuming that the growth continues at Google, it's an excellent example of buy high and sell higher.

ENHANCEMENTS

The strategy of buy high, sell higher can be enhanced by anticipated increases in earnings or by corporate takeover situations. Although anticipation of higher earnings creates unusually high p/e ratios, when the earnings do increase, the ratios return to normal levels. If the earnings do not return to former levels, sellers will eventually force the return. This is sometimes referred to as an "overbought" situation. As the price drops from selling, so does the p/e ratio.

BUY STOP

Some aggressive investors will make use of a buy stop order where they believe a stock price will rise but don't know when. Unlike the sell stop which is an order you prefer not to fill, the buy stop is one you want filled. You buy the stock when it starts its move upward and hang on for the ride. The buy stop order is activated and executed when the buy stop price is traded on or through. Effectively it becomes a market order, so you might end up paying a different price from where the order is set.

It's an interesting technique, but many investors would say that if you believe the stock price is going up, buy the stock and don't pay the extra money caused by the buy stop order.

TAKEOVERS

Corporate takeovers create a different situation. Professional arbitrageurs go on search missions looking for companies likely to be bought out by some other company. Takeover and merger announcements frequently appear in the news. They tend to drive prices up, sometimes for both companies. If defensive moves are made, they often have a negative effect on stock prices. Many takeovers fail to materialize for one reason or another, but many others are accomplished.

LONG-TERM INTENTION

Buying high and selling higher can be a viable way to make money in the stock market, but it is not without risk. The strategy usually calls for the intention of a long-term hold. When the earnings cannot catch up with the price or if a takeover deal never occurs, the price can have a downturn. Although it is possible to trade in and out during volatile times, the whipsaw effects can be devastating. Obviously, timing is everything.

BUY ONLY STOCKS YOU KNOW OR HAVE LEARNED ABOUT

A conservative approach would be to buy only stocks you know. Have a group of stocks (five or ten) that you are watching as possible portfolio candidates and become familiar with how they react to bad news or good news. If one stock in the group becomes a takeover target, you are in a good position to decide whether or not it is a buy opportunity.

CHAPTER 18

Sell High, Buy Low

Sell short at a high price and buy back at a lower price. Wonderful! An investor can make money in a falling market. If XYZ Corporation has trouble breaking through price resistance at $50 a share, chances are that many speculators are going to be selling short between $45 and $49; higher if possible. If the price falls back to $36 and the investor who sold short at $49 buys back, that's a profit of $13 a share. The strategy can be profitable in the right situation; however, there are considerations to be aware of to protect a short position.

LIMITED GAIN

A short position can profit only to the amount that a price drops, and it can't drop below zero. But in a short position, there is virtually unlimited risk because there is no limit to how high a stock price can go. Eventually, the shares must be bought back or, if the investor currently owns the shares, delivered against the short position. The potential problem arises when the price doesn't fall. It might rise higher than the investor can afford to pay. Perhaps a verse attributed to old-time investor Daniel Drew in the 1800s says it best: "He who sells what isn't his'n, buys it back or goes to prison."

MARGIN CALL

All short selling must be done in a "margin account." That is why you can't sell short in an IRA or other retirement account. A *margin call* is a brokerage firm's request for money or other marginable securities to be deposited in the account immediately. The call helps to control the risk for the investor and the brokerage firm. Risk can be seriously escalated if a takeover announcement appears relating to the company in a short position.

Since a short seller of stock has an obligation to buy back the stock at some point, the broker does not normally permit the short seller to withdraw the proceeds from the short sale. In fact, the brokerage firm could require the short seller to deposit an additional sum of money or marginable securities in case the stock price rises and additional funds are needed to buy back the stock. All this is determined by the situation existing in the investor's margin account.

BORROWED STOCK

Shorted stock has to be "borrowed." What borrowed means is that stock sold short must be matched up with actual shares existing somewhere in the stock market. The purpose of this rule is to prevent a situation in which there are more shares sold short than actually exist. Although the shares are borrowed, they are never delivered. It's an accounting function. If shorted shares can't be borrowed from within the brokerage firm, the firm looks to other firms to borrow the stock. Sometimes there are not enough shares, and the short seller cannot make the trade.

Lenders of stock for short positions can call back the stock at any time. If stock cannot be borrowed elsewhere, the position can be closed out by the brokerage firm no matter what the current profit or loss situation looks like. The short seller is notified, though not necessarily before the stock is repurchased. The borrowing situation means that it is good to select a stock candidate with a fairly large number of outstanding shares.

Although shares for borrowing can become scarce with any company, the more shares that are outstanding, the more shares there are available for borrowing.

PRICE IMPLICATIONS

All short selling, except "short against the box" (where the investor owns the same stock being sold short), is considered high-risk speculation. There are usually more forces at work trying to push the price higher than lower. It becomes very high speculation with low-priced stock. Although the lower prices attract many investors, the risk is often much higher than the potential reward. A stock price can drop only to zero, so a $5 or even $10 price doesn't have much room to drop. Even though the volatility is often higher in the low-priced stocks, the return potential is very limited. Also, it can be difficult to find stock to borrow.

It makes sense, especially for someone new to selling short, to start with a stock that has a price with some room to fall, although the price will depend on the investor's funds available to meet the margin account requirements.

NAKED SHORT SELLING

According to the Securities and Exchange Commission (SEC):

> Naked short selling, or naked shorting, is the practice of short-selling a financial instrument without first borrowing the security or ensuring that the security can be borrowed, as is conventionally done in a short sale. When the seller does not obtain the shares within the required time frame, the result is known as a "fail to deliver". The transaction

generally remains open until the shares are acquired by the seller, or the seller's broker settles the trade. Short selling is used to anticipate a price fall, but exposes the seller to the risk of a price rise. Abusive naked short selling has been illegal in the United States since 2008, as well as some other jurisdictions, as a method of driving down share prices. Failing to deliver shares is legal under certain circumstances, and naked short selling is not *per se* illegal. In the United States, naked short selling is covered by various SEC regulations which prohibit the practice. Critics, including Overstock.com's Patrick M. Byrne, have advocated for stricter regulations against naked short selling. In 2005, "Regulation SHO" was enacted; requiring that broker-dealers have grounds to believe that shares will be available for a given stock transaction, and requiring that delivery take place within a limited time period.[1]

Even though it's restricted and not approved, naked short selling does happen and can cause some problems in the stock market.

United Technologies Corp.

As shown in Figure 18.1, on July 15, 2011, the short interest (number of shares sold short) for United Technologies Corp. was 7,657,299. By August 15, there were 8,392,995 shares sold short, and by September 15, there were 12,097,993 shares sold short. A lot of short sellers held out until the end of the year, and on December 30, 2011, there were still 9,086,000 shares sold short.[2] There were other short sales during this time period. The dates given here are just some selected days. Knowing the amount of short selling on a stock can help you understand why the price volatility is occurring. The up-and-down movement of the stock price would be partly a result of closing shorts by buying back and partly due to new sell shorts.

Data source: Yahoo! Finance Historical Prices

Figure 18.1   **United Technologies Corp., 2011**

SHORT INTEREST ON THE INTERNET

Information on the number of shares sold short can be readily found on the Internet. Using a search browser, just enter in the words "short interest," and a number of resources will appear with special interactive tables to show short interest and other information. Also an interesting figure called the "short interest ratio" can be found. It is the amount of short interest divided by the average number of shares being traded daily. It comes up with a number believed to be the number of days it would take to cover those shorts. A low number like one, two, or three days is considered bullish, whereas a higher number is bearish.

Knowing if a stock is being heavily shorted can be helpful in timing the buy of a stock, especially if there is a bearish signal, although heavy short interest can change quickly if unexpected good news appears on a stock.

SHORT SQUEEZE

Sometimes a high amount of short activity can attract large buyers. Buyers know that the short positions will be covered if the stock price rises enough so that the covering will push the price even higher. Such actions are commonly referred to as a "short squeeze." If they happen, it's more often by accident than intent. Intentional short squeezes are considered a form of price manipulation and are technically illegal, but it is difficult to prove such intent in a bull market.

THE UPTICK RULE

Stock exchanges had a rule that short sales could be executed only on a price uptick or a zero-plus tick (where the price is the same as the preceding price and the preceding price was an uptick). That rule was halted in 2007, but there has been much debate about returning it in order to halt some of the price hammering that can occur from selling short in a volatile market.

CHAPTER 19

Never Short the Trend

Shorting the trend refers to selling short when a new high is reached in the stock market or by an individual stock price when the trend has been definitely upward. When investors short the trend, they are making a large gamble that the market or the stock has peaked and will decline.

LOOK FOR THE TURN

Stock prices tend to move as a group, and trends continue until they turn. Just like buying stock at the bottom, shorting a stock at the "top" is generally an exercise in futility and can become costly if an up trend continues. For individual stocks, a top might be the beginning of a takeover that will push the price even higher. Although it is not a good idea to short the trend, *shorting the turn* can be profitable.

Sure, the professional traders will short the trend; they love to be contrarian just to see what will happen. They love to see if the other shareholders have "weak hands" meaning that they will sell easily. They'll start selling short just to see how serious everyone else is about the recent advances. But they have the experience and the resources to take that risk. They'll be in and out for a dime profit or less.

Boeing Company

As trend lines A and C in Figure 19.1 show, the best time to short the stock of Boeing Co. during 2011, was when the trend was penetrated by a down turn, especially where the price fell through support. Starting in early May 2011 and lasting into August, the trend was down. In mid-August, the price started an up trend lasting into

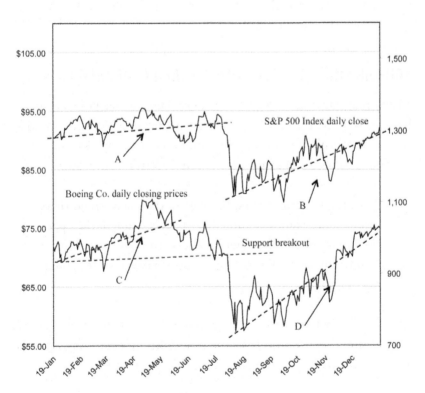

Data source: Yahoo! Finance Historical Prices

Figure 19.1   **Boeing Co. versus S&P 500 Index, 2011**

2012. The figure also shows that there weren't really any good short opportunities during the four up trends.

NEVER SHORT THE TREND; SHORT AFTER THE TURN

Figure 19.1 clearly shows that the best short selling opportunity is after the turn. Selling short is a risky way of investing. It should be approached with caution and with knowledge of the company with its price trend. Buy stop orders can be used for upside protection, but they cannot substitute for vigilance in study and observation. Short selling is most often pursued on a short-term basis, before the stock drops low enough to become attractive to buyers or another company with takeover plans.

YOU CAN SHORT THE SECONDARY TURN IN THE TREND

In any major up trend, there are times when the market hiccups and has a short-term down trend. This can be shorted but should be watched carefully because they often don't last long. As soon as the economic news gets better, the primary up trend continues:

> The trend is your friend, but within the major trend there can be opportunities riding mini-trends going in the opposite direction. Just don't get greedy on those plays; the major trend will eventually consume most smaller counter-trending plays.[1]

So a short position in a secondary trend must be watched closely, and this position runs the possibility of becoming a turn in the primary trend just to complicate things further.

THE HARD PART

Obviously the hard part is figuring out the turn. Is it a turn in the primary trend, or is it a secondary down trend? In a way it doesn't matter, because you can short the turn even if it is secondary. Just be ready to close the short quickly.

It takes bad news to cause the primary trend to turn. More bad news, followed by even more bad news is usually a sign that the primary has or will turn.

SOMETHING TO REMEMBER

Short sales are all done in margin accounts. Therefore, investors must follow all margin requirements, including some rules for the sale:

> There are also margin rule requirements for a short sale in which 150% of the value of the shares shorted needs to be initially held in the account. Therefore, if the value is $25,000, the initial margin requirement is $37,500 (which includes the $25,000 of proceeds from the short sale). This prevents the proceeds from the sale from being used to purchase other shares before the borrowed shares are returned.[2]

Since the short sale must be in a margin account, it cannot be done in an IRA or in any other retirement account. Regular mutual funds cannot be sold short.

Also remember that selling short is a speculative strategy that can lead to substantial losses. It should be approached with a great deal of caution.

CHAPTER 20

Make Winners Win Big

I t was Jesse Livermore, known for his aggressive investing at the turn of the century, who indicated the importance of winning big. When the investor's conclusions, based on analysis, are correct, it's time to win big. Livermore demonstrated this when he sold short shares of Union Pacific Railroad just before the 1906 San Francisco earthquake. At first, the price did not drop. The company was strong, and the price held. After all, it was one of the best companies on Wall Street. Livermore believed it would take a few weeks for the news to spread and the implications of the news to be realized. He put his fortune on the line. Eventually he was proven right and his fortune multiplied significantly. He believed in winning big when he knew he was right.

VALUE

Winning stocks are a special situation. Although it is prudent to establish a price objective for a winning stock, value also needs to be considered before selling. Just because you set a price objective doesn't mean that you have to sell out when that objective is reached or passed. *Value* is the price appreciation in relation to earnings and revenue growth. The momentum of anticipation can cause a company's stock price to run ahead of earnings potential. Sometimes the earning potential makes up for the price growth, and sometimes it doesn't.

INVESTMENT ADVISOR—BAD ADVICE

More than one investment advisor is guilty of saying, "When you make 100 percent or 200 percent on a stock, sell and take the profit. Leave something for the next investor." Livermore didn't believe in such a strategy. Institutional investors surely do not follow this practice, and it's a cinch that Warren Buffett doesn't sell because of the amount of profit in a stock. So why should anyone else sell just when the price action gets interesting? If the fundamentals remain strong and you make 100 percent on a stock, go for 200 percent. Let the other investors buy their own stock.

PROFITS LEFT ON THE TABLE

Any sustained bull market will give examples of stock that should not have been sold even though the price may have doubled, tripled, or even quadrupled. Significant profits are too frequently "left on the table" as a misguided investor sells to take profits too soon. Forget the other investors. Let them find their own profitable stocks.

Say you were lucky enough to buy Apple Computer back in March 2009 (see Figure 20.1) for $87.94 a share. Your investment would have doubled by September of the same year. That's 100 percent gain in less than a year. Is that a reason to sell? I don't think so. Should you leave all that remaining gain for the next investor? Nope. Again, let the next investors by their own stock.

So you hang onto the stock, and by February 2011 it doubles again to a price of $351.76 a share. Sell now? No reason to. And by January 2012 the stock is up to $427.75 a share with virtually no debt and a p/e ratio of 15.23 when the S&P 500 Index has an average p/e of about 20. There may be a reason to sell in the future, but for

Data source: Yahoo! Finance Historical Prices

Figure 20.1   **Apple Computer, 2009–January 2012**

right now forget about it. Hang on and count your profits. The profit on only 100 shares would be $33,981 not counting commissions or taxes. Not bad for a three-year investment.

HERE WERE SOME WINNING STOCKS IN 2012

4 Stocks Hitting 52-Week Highs:
MSFT, NKE, MAT, BWLD

NEW YORK (TheStreet)—Shares of the following stocks hit 52-week highs on Thursday: Microsoft (NASDAQ: MSFT), Nike (NYSE: NKE), Mattel (NYSE: MAT) and Buffalo Wild Wings (NASDAQ: BWLD).[1]

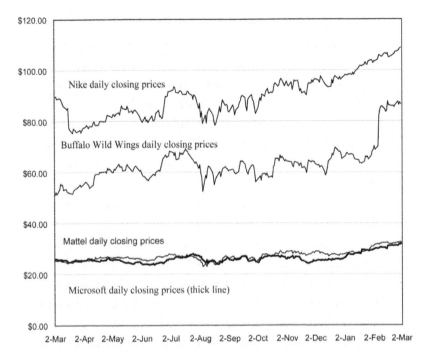

Data source: Yahoo! Finance Historical Prices

Figure 20.2   **Four Winning Stocks, March 2, 2011–March 2, 2012**

The author of the above-quoted article believes that these are winning stocks, even though they are trading at 52-week highs. Looking at Figure 20.2, you can see that the prices are indeed at one-year highs.

In fact, considering the economic difficulties of 2011, these four stocks have done very well in the past 52 weeks.

The judgment of "winner" wasn't based only on being at 52-week highs, but also took into consideration some of the fundamentals. The following was the analysis for Microsoft Corp.

The software company gave a preview of its Windows 8 operating system test version this week.

"In the mid- to long-term, we believe that the market has not only meaningfully undervalued Microsoft's ability to expand operating margins for the next several years (given the increased focus on cost control), but also the sustainable revenue growth and defensive competitive characteristics of Microsoft's dominant market positions with respect to its client operating system and office productivity suites," Credit Suisse analysts wrote in a February 29 report.

Shares of Microsoft hit a 52-week high of $32.39 on Thursday. The stock's 52-week low of $23.65 was set on June 16.

Microsoft has an estimated price-to-earnings ratio for next year of 10.74; the average for software companies is 28.5. For comparison, both Oracle (ORCL) and Intuit (INTU) have higher forward P/Es of 11.63 and 17.42, respectively.

Twenty-five of the 39 analysts who cover Microsoft rate it at buy. Thirteen analysts give it a hold rating and one analyst rated it sell.

TheStreet Ratings gives Microsoft an A grade with a buy rating and $36.23 price target. The stock has risen 24.5% year to date.[2]

The fact that these four stocks are at their 52-week highs doesn't stop the analysts from recommending a buy. This brings up an interesting point. When selecting stock to follow or buy, don't eliminate stocks trading at highs. They might become your best buys.

LET IT WIN BIG

When a stock is winning, let it win as big as it can. Avoid chopping the legs out from under it by selling too soon to take profits. It's the losers you want to sell, not the winners. If you're in business, you don't fire your best employees, and if you're an investor, don't sell your best stocks.

CHAPTER 21

Buy on the Rumor;
Sell on the News

An old saying that usually accompanies the buy high, sell higher strategy is to, "Buy on the rumor; sell on the news." This can be an effective strategy, but the investor must be aware of the circumstances. For instance, the rumor might have been fabricated with the intent of pushing up the stock price.

Financial consultants, advisors, or stockbrokers tend to discourage those who would buy any stock based on rumor. False rumors frequently appear regarding corporate takeover situations. The share prices advance but then suddenly retreat to former levels. In most situations it is best to leave the rumor alone. In fact, buying "on the news" can be appealing at times.

THINGS CHANGE

Back in the 1980s the tire company Firestone had a takeover offer at $40 a share, which was later sweetened to $70 a share by a new suitor. Such large increases are rare and have not occurred recently.

It was definitely a case in which selling on the first news was not a good idea. You would have missed out on $30 a share.

Back in September 2009, news of a rumored takeover of Symantec Corp. by Microsoft appeared. The company is primarily a provider of computer storage systems and other services on an international level. A possible price target of $19 to $20 a share was discussed in the news. But the takeover never happened. A look at Figure 21.1 shows what happened to the price.

Even though the news did not appear until September 2009, the price became active several months earlier in May. The price advanced above $17 a share. As Figure 21.1 shows, it then dropped

Data source: Yahoo! Finance Historical Prices

Figure 21.1   **Symantec Corp. and S&P 500 Index, 2009–2011**

back to $15 a share and started a new advance in September. It followed a market correction down to just over $12 a share and then ran up to just over $20 a share in 2011. It is interesting to note that the rate of institutional ownership in January 2012 was 91.68 percent, so you wonder what they knew or thought they knew.

TARGET PRICE

When takeover details are announced, the market price of the target company will usually rise to or close to the new market value, which is the value of the acquisition. Many investors sell their holdings at this point instead of waiting for the actual takeover. Although they might not receive the full acquisition value, their assets aren't tied up while they're waiting for the deal to be completed. Also, they don't lose out if the acquisition fails to materialize.

NOT JUST INDIVIDUAL STOCKS

"Buy on the rumor" doesn't necessarily refer to only individual stocks. It can also refer to the entire market, what you might call market sentiment. Investors sometimes sell on the news with the market also. This is at least partly why you will see wild gyrations from one day to the next. On one day the headlines will indicate a sell-off resulting from debt problems in Greece. The following day the news will be that the debt problems weren't as bad as was thought, or that a partial solution is in the works. At times it gets so convoluted that investors are buying on the rumor of a rumor. The buying part is great. The selling is not so great, but hopefully there is a net gain with all those transactions.

YOU CAN ALSO DO OPTIONS

Obviously, the easy play would be to buy calls. You would have less cash at risk than if you buy the stock and just sell the calls if the price goes up. Here's some advice from an options trader:

The best bet for most investors is ignoring takeover rumors. If you own options on a takeover stock, sell them, and book the profits. How much better can it get? When rumors become facts, or fail to become facts, implied volatility declines. If you must trade takeover rumors, buy inexpensive out-of-the-money calls that expire in three months or less. If the deal emerges, you'll make money, and not lose much if nothing happens. To be sure, institutional investors who own dud stocks, or who want to create profits where none exist spread rumors to drive options and stock prices higher to attract unsophisticated investors.[1]

So, the best advice is don't get caught in the big boys trap.

HOW WILL THE NEWS OR RUMOR AFFECT OTHER COMPANIES?

You could ask about what changes might occur to other related companies when you're looking for a play in stock trading. If a large company is going into bankruptcy, how will it change the business of its vendors? All of a sudden the vendors have lost one of their key accounts. It's gotta have an impact. Competitors' businesses will probably increase to take up the slack.

If there's a huge merger, the price of both companies will likely rise, but what about their suppliers? If the business shifts to the company doing the takeover, its suppliers will benefit; therefore, their shares will also experience a positive change. On the other hand, the suppliers of the company being taken over will likely falter, unless the same suppliers are involved with both companies.

This is the perfect situation for those who work at one of the companies involved. They will know who the suppliers are and be able to take advantage of the situation. Such information would not be considered insider information because anyone who wants to can research and find the information.

NOT ALL RUMORS ARE POSITIVE

Sometimes rumors are inexplicable even though they might rate an article in the big-time press, like the following from *The Wall Street Journal*:

> Forget trying to read any logical explanation into the stock movement of Sears Holdings, the owner of Kmart and Sears stores. Just forget it right now, and step away from the E*Trade account.
>
> Shares are up more than 11% today for no apparent reason. Yes, there has been some chatter about a hedge fund or two falling in love with Sears, or the company going private. Heck, who doesn't want to throw some hard-earned money at stores selling stuff people don't want on the fringes of ugly malls?
>
> The fact is, no one really knows anything about Sears, and it's becoming very dangerous to read anything into the stock price gyrations.[2]

This isn't so much negative as cautionary. When rumors start to fly, surprising things can happen. If the rumors don't come to fruition, they disappear like the wind, leaving damage in their wake. The interesting thing with the one about Sears is that apparently no one knows exactly what the rumor is, just that there is one. Trades are being made based on nothing, not even a solid rumor, just that there might be a rumor.

SPECULATIVE STRATEGY

Buying on rumor and selling on or after the news is high speculation. Things change, and takeovers can fail to occur. Bad news affecting the economic situation comes one day and disappears the next.

Rumors usually reach the news media after the action has started. Often, it is too late for the individual investor to take advantage of the situation. It is more prudent to look for positive situations and companies that might become attractive takeover candidates and have other desirable growth traits. Then, if these companies are not taken over, the investor still has a quality stock at a good price.

CHAPTER 22

Buy the Stock That Splits

The sound of a happy investor: "This stock split two-for-one at $40 a share and ran up to $40 again, all within six months. It's just incredible how fast this company is growing. The stock is now at $42 a share, and there's talk of another two-for-one split. It would be great to have more stocks like this one."

Stock splits are looked upon as being good news because it is believed that the price will continue to increase. However, even though many stock splits are positive, sadly, this is not always the case. Many times the price will soar for the split, only to fall back to previous price levels, adjusted for the split. If the price does keep climbing, it's usually caused by something other than a split.

MECHANICS OF A SPLIT

Stock dividends and splits have basically three events:

1. Announcement date
2. Record date
3. Payment date

To qualify for the split, the investor must be the owner on the record date (similar to the ex-date for dividends—by settling on or after that date, the investor gets the stock for the split price). There-fore, the stock must be purchased at the appropriate time before the record date to qualify (three days prior).

Announcement Date

The announcement date can be considered the most important date because it tends to have the greatest positive impact on a stock's price. Even companies that do not react well to a split tend to move initially higher on the announcement. Rumors of a split sometimes leak ahead of the announcement date which also tends to push the price higher.

Stock split and stock dividend announcements are given to the media on the announcement date. The company provides all the important details of the split and often a brief history of the company's previous stock splits, which it sends out in the form of a press release. The company considers a forward stock split a positive event and wants to get as much free media publicity as possible.

Record Date (Date of Record)

Buy the stock on or after the recond date and you will not participate in the split. However, you will get the price adjusted for the split.

Payment Date

The payment date is the date when the new stock is actually credited to your account in a forward split or taken from your account in a reverse split.

PRICE WEAKNESS

It's not unusual to see some price weakness either after a split announcement or shortly after a payment date. Any number of things can cause a price to drop. For example, speculators could be exiting and taking profits, especially if the price has been flat for a time. Some investors might fear that the price action is over and expect a drop, and they would rather sell too soon than too late. Obviously, others see this price weakness as a buying opportunity, and they are the investors who drive the price upward.

Cabot Oil and Gas Company announced a two-for-one stock split for January 26, 2012. A look at Cabot's history shows an interesting trend. Back in early April 2005, Cabot had a three-for-two stock split, and that was followed by a two-for-one stock split in April 2007. Although that's all very interesting, look at the price history following the two splits (see Figure 22.1).

Data source: Yahoo! Finance Historical Prices

Figure 22.1   **Cabot Oil and Gas Corp. versus S&P 500 Index, 2005–January 2012**

The price plummeted soon after the split and then slowly rose back to its former level. The price plummeted again when the market dropped in 2008 and then rose to new heights. In February 2008, the price of Cabot rose while the market was starting to fall. It reached a new high in mid-June of 2008 and fell with the stock market.

On January 26, 2012, Cabot did another two-for-one stock split. Makes you wonder how far the price is going to drop. It is interesting that sales and revenues were down just before this third stock split.

WHY DO COMPANIES HAVE STOCK SPLITS?

Usually the reason given for a stock split is to make the stock more affordable for a larger number of investors. The logic is that more people will buy the stock at $30 a share than at $60 a share.

While a $120 price might be too high for many people, a $60 or even $30 price will get them to buy the stock. However, there is no assurance that the stock will continue to rise in price after the split. Often, a stock price declines after a split, which can be true particularly if a stock splits more than once in a year.

Another reason for a company to have a stock split is to make more shares available, thereby broadening its stockholder base. The stock becomes more marketable and liquid. Somehow, positive publicity also fits into the stock split scenario. A company might use a stock split announcement to soften the blow of some negative news.

NOT ALWAYS TWO-FOR-ONE

Not all stocks split two-for-one. Some other ratios for stock splits are three-for-one, three-for-two, and five-for-four. However, regardless of the ratio used, the stock price will decline, and the number of shares outstanding will increase directly in proportion to the amount of the split. Splits do not give the investor something for nothing in terms of financial gain. Splits do not make a company any better or more financially sound.

WHY DOES THE PRICE RISE?

A price can rise for many reasons resulting from pressure from one factor or several factors combined. There are still novice investors who don't realize that the price is adjusted for the split. Brokers often hear the confused and complaining phone calls asking what made the price drop so suddenly, especially with a three-for-one split. Though the group is small, it's part of the picture.

Speculators buy either before or soon after an announcement because they believe the price will rise. These short-term traders pick an early point at which they will take profits. Their actions account for much of the price weakness that appears shortly after many splits, when they sell. Investors in general still believe the publicity of a stock split is good news for a company. Although the stock does become more affordable for the individual investor, a split does nothing to add real value to a company.

REVERSE STOCK SPLIT

One of the main reasons for the forward split of a stock is to lower the price. The opposite of a forward split, the reverse split, is to raise the price of the stock. Companies believe that raising a price will make the stock more attractive for trading. Commonly, reverse splits are one-for-three, one-for-ten, or one-for-twenty, but they can be for any quantity. In the one-for-ten situation, one share of stock is received by the shareholder for every 10 shares owned. Instead of having the original 100 shares, an investor ends up with 10 shares, but the new price is 10 times higher.

Reverse splits used to be considered a death announcement for a company, but that is not always the case. Some companies reorganize and pull themselves together to become successful.

New research indicates that reverse stock splits are usually good for investors.

> According to a new report by Cleve Rueckert, Birinyi Associates senior equity strategist, there have been 14 stocks in the S&P 500 since 2000 that have undergone a reverse stock split. Of those fourteen stocks, twelve were higher one year after the effective date of the reverse split, two were lower. The average gain was a gigantic 62.55 percent.[1]

One of the major difficulties is the selling by disappointed investors. Even though the reverse split significantly increases the market price, active selling frequently hammers it back down. To counteract this tendency, companies will sometimes try to time a reverse split announcement to coincide with good news. A positive earnings report followed by an, "Oh by the way, we're reverse splitting one-for-three," can stop some shareholders from leaving.

STOCK SPLIT INVESTING

Over the past several years various studies have gone to great lengths to show that forward stock splits are positive events in about 50 percent of the cases. Looking ahead, about half the companies do well for the following 6-to-12-month period. More recently, studies are showing that forward stock splits are positive for good companies. Of course, a strong economy and a bull market will help. The main problem with any study concerning the effects of a stock split is that it's impossible to determine how much of price growth is the result of the split, how much is the result of growth, and how much is the result of a strong market. All these factors work together to increase the stock's market price.

BE PRUDENT; BE NEUTRAL

The prudent approach is to treat forward splits as neutral events. If the company is a good investment and the lower price after a split makes it a viable candidate for your portfolio, buy the stock. If a price weakness appears after the stock splits, then don't buy the stock, but wait and see what happens in the next couple of weeks or so.

CHAPTER 23

"Our Favorite Holding Period Is Forever"

The rather famous quote, "Our favorite holding period is forever," is usually attributed to Warren Buffett, the illustrious portfolio manager for the Berkshire Hathaway stock funds. It is important to note upfront that he is not saying buy any stock and hold on forever. What he is indicating is that before you buy the stock, know it well. Learn its strengths and weaknesses. Know what is likely to happen in a market reversal or a period of earnings weakness. Learn how much the market likes the stock and how quickly it can turn against the company.

Note that Buffett said "favorite holding period," not "holding period for every stock." It's possible to structure a portfolio of stock so that you can maintain a forever holding period. Just set your objective to include stocks that are likely to maintain their steady growth and not be too badly damaged by market reverses—the stocks that are able to maintain a stable financial situation.

FOREVER STOCKS

It's easy to find candidates for forever stocks. Just go to an Internet browser and enter "Forever Stocks." Several lists from various analysts will suddenly appear. Here are some examples:

1. Philip Morris International Inc. (NYSE: PM), through its subsidiaries, manufactures and sells cigarettes and other tobacco products in markets outside the United States. This company has raised dividends every year since it was spun-off from Altria (MO) in 2008. The following information was obtained on May 3, 2012:

   Current price, $89.78
   Current p/e ratio, 18.46
   Debt/equity ratio, 186.08 (high)
   Dividend rate, $3.08
   Dividend yield, 3.41%

   (Note: Because this company carries a lot of debt, one would wonder about the security of the dividend. Also, tobacco going out of favor might be negative for this stock.)

2. McDonald's Corporation (MCD), together with its subsidiaries, operates as a worldwide food service retailer. McDonald's has raised dividends for 34 consecutive years. (Note: McDonald's may not be the first fast-food chain, but it is one of the oldest. It appears to be in good shape and had market position.) The following information was obtained on May 3, 2012:

   Current price, $97.07
   Current p/e ratio, 18.15
   Debt/equity ratio, 86.97
   Dividend rate, $2.80
   Dividend yield, 2.87%

3. Walmart Stores, Inc. (NYSE: WMT), operates retail stores in various formats worldwide. This company has raised dividends for 37 years in a row. (Note: Walmart has been legendary in its rise over the past 30 years. It is a well-established business phenomenon.) The following information was obtained on May 3, 2012:

   Current price, $58.97

> Current p/e ratio, 13.00
> Debt/equity ratio, .75
> Dividend rate, $1.59
> Dividend yield, 2.69%

4. Colgate-Palmolive Company (NYSE: CL), together with its subsidiaries, manufactures and markets consumer products worldwide. The company has raised distributions for 48 years in a row:

> Current price, $100.20
> Current p/e ratio, 20.00
> Debt/equity ratio, 2.17
> Dividend rate, $2.48
> Dividend yield, 2.47%

5. The Procter & Gamble Company (NYSE: PG) provides consumer packaged goods in the United States and internationally. The company has raised dividends for 54 years in a row. (Note: P&G is a good example of an old stalwart company, surviving and growing through many economic cycles.)

> Current price, $64.44
> Current p/e ratio, 19.77
> Debt/equity ratio, .51
> Dividend rate, $2.25
> Dividend yield, 3.51%

6. The Coca-Cola Company (NYSE: KO) manufactures, distributes, and markets nonalcoholic beverage concentrates and syrups worldwide. The company has paid investors higher dividends for 49 consecutive years.[1] (Note: Another old stalwart company, Coke has been able to keep its market consistently for many years.)

> Current price, $77.41
> Current p/e ratio, 20.58
> Debt/equity ratio, 0.95
> Dividend rate, $2.04
> Dividend yield, 2.64%

It is important to remember that factors such as a dividend cut could cause a stock to be marked as a sell. Given the strong earnings power of the above companies, however, this should not be an immediate issue for long-term investors. These could be forever stocks.

Another "Forever Stock" search (on May 3, 2012) came up with the following information.[2]

1. Eaton Corp. (NYSE: ETN), $46.52
2. FedEx Corp. (NYSE: FDX), $89.36
3. Gilead Sciences, Inc. (NASDAQ: GILD), $51.39
4. Hasbro, Inc. (NASDAQ: HAS), $36.96
5. Illinois Toolworks, Inc. (NYSE: ITW), $57.53

Although further analysis should be done, these are good initial candidates for "forever stocks."

IF YOU HAD BOUGHT . . .

On January 2, 1970, the first trading day of the year, you bought 100 shares of McDonald's stock at the closing price of $44.25 a share, for a total cost of $4,425 plus commission (see Figure 23.1). Not a bad trade. If you held MCD until May 3, 2012, and then sold, you would have received $97.07 a share; however, you would have been selling not 100 shares, but 1,200 shares because of stock splits along the way. See Table 23.1.

Not too shabby. That's the kind of winner we like to win big with.

SELLING

Warren Buffett sells stock. He sells the not forever stocks or the stocks that were forever but have lost their luster (fundamental strength). Building a forever portfolio is a process. No one can

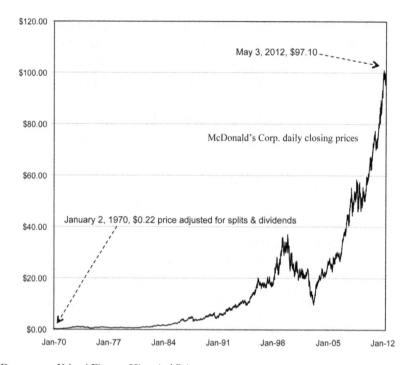

Data source: Yahoo! Finance Historical Prices

Figure 23.1   McDonald's Corp., 1970–January 2012

Table 23.1   McDonald's Corp.

McDonald's Corp. 1/2/70	Cost per Share	Total Cost
Buy 100 shares	$44.25	$4,425
McDonald's Splits	**Total Number of Shares**	**Cost Basis/Share**
1987, 3 for 2	150	
1989, 2 for 1	300	
1994, 2 for 1	600	
1999, 2 for 1	1,200	$0.22*
McDonald's Corp. 5/3/12	**Price per Share**	**Total Proceeds†**
Sell 1,200 shares	$97.07	$116,484

* Includes dividends paid 1970–2012
† Total proceeds do not include dividends.
Data source: msn/money.com.

hit it right the first time with every stock. But if you proceed with patience and understanding of the companies and their ability to handle tough times, it can be done. If you are a long-term conservative investor, before you buy the stock ask yourself, do I want to hold this stock forever? If not, a reassessment is in order.

CHAPTER 24

It's Better to Average Up Than Down

Price averaging is a prudent strategy with the right stock and in the right situation. There are two ways to lower the average cost of a stock purchase. One is averaging up, and the other is averaging down. When faced with a dropping share price while the longer-term outlook is believed favorable, it can be worthwhile to hold the current shares and let the price hit bottom. When the price turns and begins to increase, begin a program of buying at various price levels.

Averaging down, though frequently suggested, is usually not the best course of action. It can work in some situations, but it doesn't fit well into most investment plans. Many people describe this aggressive strategy as, "throwing good money after bad," or, "taking the down escalator." The problem with averaging down is that it is impossible to know at what point the price will stop falling.

ARE YOU INVESTING IN STOCK OR INVESTING IN A COMPANY?

There is a big difference between investing in a stock and investing in a company. It also depends on whether your investing is long term or short term. Short term involves more trading, so selling at the first sign of trouble makes sense. Here's the way some would describe the difference:

If you are investing in a stock, you look for buy and sell signals based on a number of indicators. Your goal is to make money on the trade, and you have no real interest in the underlying company other than how it might be affected by market news or economic changes.

In most cases, you don't know enough about the underlying company to determine if a drop in price is temporary or a reflection of a serious problem.

Your best course of action when investing in a stock (as opposed to a company) is to cut your losses at no more than 7 percent. When the stock drops that much, sell and move on to the next deal.

If you are investing in a company (as opposed to a stock), you have done your homework and know what's going on within the firm and its industry. You should know if a drop in the stock's price is temporary or a sign of trouble.

If you truly believe in the company, averaging down may make sense if you want to increase your holdings in the company. Accumulating more stock at a lower price makes sense if you plan to hold it for a long period.

This is not a strategy you should employ lightly. If there is a heavy volume of selling against the company, you may want to ask yourself if they know something you don't. The "they" in this case will almost certainly be mutual funds and institutional investors.

Swimming against the current can sometimes prove profitable, but it can also get you swept over the waterfall.[1]

AVERAGING UP

The results of averaging up can be similar to successful averaging down, but there is less risk involved. Averaging up works as a strategy to enhance the profits of an advancing stock price, and it can work with a stock price in a losing price position.

When a stock price suddenly takes a turn for the worse and the price declines significantly because of bad news, the investor holds the position, knowing the company and believing that the price decline is temporary. Eventually the stock price will reach a support level, and buyers will step in to stop the fall. The investor then buys more stock, averaging up as the price recovers.

Averaging up is buying specific amounts of stock at fairly regular intervals. It is a defensive strategy that protects the investor from falling prices. It is a part of a "buy on the dips" strategy. It is especially effective when a stock price is pushed down by an overall market decline, rather than specific problems with the company.

Let's take a look at the Toro Company, well-known for making heavy- and light-duty lawn equipment and snow throwers. The company has existed in Bloomington, Minnesota, since 1914 and has long held the reputation of making good, durable equipment. As Figure 24.1 shows, Toro's stock price readily follows the market. Toro's price dropped with the bear market. Once it hit bottom and started back up, there were multiple opportunities to average up.

There is other good news to recommend buying Toro. In November 2011, the company increased the amount of its dividend. In December 2011, it announced a record year of income. Also in December it announced another acquisition. So it has been an excellent stock with which to average up (see Table 24.1).

Essentially, when considering the average price per share, the last three purchases had built-in profits—nice to buy a stock with a built-in profit.

YES, YOU CAN BUY ALL AT ONCE

If you know the company and believe strongly, there is no reason not to buy all at once for the lowest possible price. It's just that periodic buying as the stock is rising is safer. Something new could happen to hammer down the price again. If you are buying periodically, you can take advantage of such situations. If you buy all at once, you can only be frustrated.

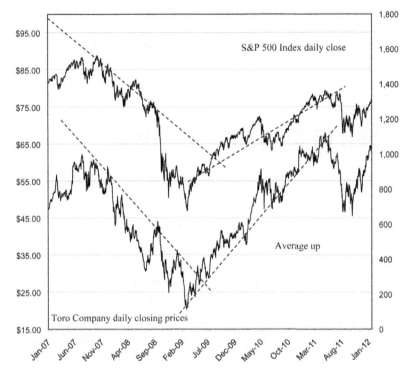

Data source: Yahoo! Finance Historical Prices

Figure 24.1   **Toro Co. and S&P 500 Index, 2008–January 2012**

Table 24.1   **Averaging Up with Toro Company Stock, 2009–2011***

Month	Amount	Price		Subtotal	Total Investment
June 2009	200 shares	$34	=	$6,800	$6,800
Dec. 2009	200 shares	$40	=	$8,000	$14,800
June 2010	200 shares	$50	=	$10,000	$24,800
Dec. 2010	200 shares	$60	=	$12,000	$36,800
June 2011	200 shares	$60	=	$12,000	$48,800
	1,000 shares	$48.80 average per share			

*Data Source: Yahoo! Finance Quote, TTC.

CHAPTER 25

"Sell in May and Go Away"

There are many beliefs about trading in the stock market. Some make a lot of good sense and others are quite unexpected. "Sell in May and go away," is somewhat of a surprise as a strategy.

Alexandra Twin has this to say about a certain widespread belief:

> Also known as the Halloween indicator, this is a variant of the stock market adage "Sell in May and go away," the belief that the period from November to April inclusive has significantly stronger growth on average than the other months. In such strategies, stocks are sold at the start of May and the proceeds held in cash (e.g., a money market fund); stocks are bought again in the autumn, typically around Halloween.[1]

Although it may be okay to sell in May and buy again in autumn, the results could be negative about 60 percent of the time. If you take five years and put the market on a stacked chart with each year on top of the others, rather than running them consecutively, it will look something like Figure 25.1. The figure stacks the years 2011, 2010, 2009, 2008, and 2007, one on top of the other. The years it might have been a good strategy were 2009 and 2010, when the

Data source: Yahoo! Finance Historical Prices

Figure 25.1   **S&P 500 Index, 2007–2011**

market dropped. Other years were not so good because the market rose during the May to October time period.

Whether it's good or not isn't the point. The point is are you a long-term investor or a short-term strategist? This is most definitely a short-term speculative strategy.

IT DEPENDS ON THE STOCK

A decision concerning when to buy should be based more on the stock's price history than anything. Buying in May and going away is still a speculative approach, and the drop from May to October might not happen. Also, you will have to figure out where to buy in again, and that can be difficult. Let's look at some individual stocks.

Data source: Yahoo! Finance Historical Prices

Figure 25.2   Results for Three Companies, Selling in May and Going Away

Figure 25.2 shows a three-year analysis of three different stocks: ExxonMobil (NYSE: XOX), 3M (NYSE: MMM), and United Technologies Company (NYSE: UTX). The figure shows what happened to the prices of the three stocks between May and October for 2009 to April 2012. If you owned these stocks and sold in May 2009 and 2010, you would done much better not to have sold them. However, in 2011, you would have done much better by selling in May and buying back for Halloween. This is a lot to go through for the potential of a few extra bucks that might or might not happen.

GET DEFENSIVE INSTEAD

A little finesse becomes important to the strategy in a president's third year in office.

> "Sell in May" takes on a different twist during the third year of a president's term in office," says Sam Stovall, chief investment strategist of Standard & Poor's. On average, the S&P 500 stock index rises 1.3 percent from May 1 through October 31, he reports. But in the third year of presidential cycles, returns during that same six-month period are 2.7 percent. Stock prices rise 70 percent of the time during the downer months of May, through October, when it's the third year of a president's term, he said.[2]

So where does that leave investors? Many have sizable gains, with the Dow Jones Industrial Average up after rising 18.82 percent in 2009, 11.02 percent in 2010, and 5.3% for 2011. But that isn't really a sell signal, and if you do sell, what are you supposed to do with your cash while you wait for the November rebuy?

Don't just sell, rotate.

Stovall believes that the best move for equity investors now isn't in stocks; it's in aggressive growth stocks and indefensive stocks, such as consumer staples and healthcare companies.

It's possible that rotating to "defensive stock" is a viable strategy, but the main point is that the phenomenon doesn't happen every year. Rotating positions can get expensive and end up losing money in the long term.

This chapter title is the kind of thing likely to appear in the *Stock Trader's Almanac*, which comes out every year. It is written by Yale and Jeff Hirsch. He also wrote a book called *Don't Sell Stocks on Monday*. Although his annually published Almanac statistics are interesting, investors should always keep two things in mind:

- Past performance does not predict future performance.
- The only certainty is change; if a consistent pattern appears and traders take advantage of it, the pattern will change.

BUY ON MONDAY AND SELL ON FRIDAY

For 37 years (1953 through 1989), the stock market had a tendency to drop on Mondays and rally on Fridays. The saying, "Buy on Monday, sell on Friday," became a well-known mantra for stock traders. Starting with 1990, the market pattern of correcting on Mondays ended. In fact, prices were typically no longer down on Mondays. Obviously, if a majority of investors start buying on Monday, the market will rally. When everybody became aware of the pattern, the pattern changed.

This can be a problem with many axioms about the stock market. When traders and the public become aware of the axiom, the patterns change. Technical trading patterns are somewhat the opposite. As more stock traders become aware and understand the technical patterns, the more accurate they become. Because people believe a drop will occur after the market hits a double top, traders make the sales to make it happen.

BE SKEPTICAL

The lesson to be learned is always to be skeptical of any formula regarding the stock market. The formula can change as investors trade on it with greater frequency, and even the good ones are wrong sometimes.

CHAPTER 26

Buy Stock Cheaper with Dollar Cost Averaging

Buying regular amounts of stock at set intervals is dollar cost averaging (DCA). If the price of the stock is rising, you will eventually be buying the stock with a built-in profit. The best time to use this strategy is when you are depending on income to buy the stock and do not have a lump sum of money to invest. Since you are investing a set amount of cash, you will be buying more shares when the price is down and fewer shares when the price is high.

DOLLAR COST AVERAGING FORMULA

DCA has a formula. Assuming that the same amount of money is invested each time, the return from dollar cost averaging on the total money invested is:

$$r = \frac{P_F}{\tilde{P}_P} - 1,$$

where P_F is the final price of the investment and $\tilde{P}_P$ is the harmonic mean of the purchase prices. If the time between purchases is small compared to the investment period, then $\tilde{P}_p$ can be estimated by the harmonic mean of all the prices within the purchase period.[1]

It works something like this: You decide that you will invest $8,000 in a stock. Each quarter you will invest $2,000 in The Gap (NYSE: GPS). Take a look at Figure 26.1. April 1, 2011, you would have paid $22.63 a share for a total of 88 shares. On July 1 you would have paid $18.28 a share for a total of 106 shares. On October 1, you would have paid $16.73 a share for a total of 119 shares. On December 29, you would have paid $18.55 for a total of 107 shares:

April 1, 2011	88
July 1, 2011	106
October 4, 2011	119
December 29, 2011	<u>107</u>
	420 shares total

The total cost is $7,924.84 (with the average cost per share of $18.87). If you had purchased all 420 shares on April 1, they would have cost $9,210.41, or $22.63 per share (these calculations do not include commissions).

LUMP SUM ALL AT ONCE

If you have a lump sum to invest, it might be best to buy all at once rather than mess around with dollar cost averaging. This is especially true when investing for the long term. Although as shown, dollar cost averaging does take advantage of price fluctuations. Forbes did some research. Here's what was found:

> Our recent research paper, *Does Dollar Cost Averaging Make Sense for Investors?* evaluates the performance of the following four distinct strategies over rolling 20-year periods between 1926 and 2010:

Data source: Yahoo! Finance Historical Prices

Figure 26.1   **The Gap, Dollar Cost Averaging, 2011–February 2012**

1. Lump Sum (LS) Investing (entire amount is invested at once)
2. "Basic" Dollar Cost Averaging (a set amount is invested every month, regardless of market performance)
3. Value Dollar Cost Averaging (more money is invested following a month with negative market returns; less following a month with positive returns)
4. Momentum Dollar Cost Averaging (more money is invested following a month of positive market returns; less following a month with negative returns)

For simplicity, we assumed zero transaction costs in the various DCA strategies. Perhaps contrary to what most investors would expect, our research revealed that the best performance consistently comes from Lump Sum Investing, with average annualized outperformance over DCA of nearly two percentage points over a period of 20 years. The second-best performance came from the Momentum Dollar Cost Averaging strategy, whereby the monthly amount invested is ratcheted up on the heels of good market performance. Over the period we examined, this strategy achieved superior returns when compared to the basic DCA approach more than 50% of the time.[2]

This brings up some interesting facts about a time-honored belief of DCA. Perhaps it's not the best approach, and lump sum could be the best way to go. Here is the conclusion:

> Conclusion: for Behavioral Investors,
> a New Twist on an Old Standby

> While LS investing is the clear winner when you look at the numbers, the reality is that investors are human beings with emotions for which hard facts and data sometimes are simply no match. That's where Momentum DCA can prove useful: while still an inferior alternative to LS investing, it offers the potential for higher returns than a basic DCA approach while providing the comfort of a measured, incremental approach to investors who might not quite be emotionally prepared to jump in with both feet. (To read the full research paper, look on the Internet for Gregg S. Fisher, *"Does Dollar Cost Averaging Make Sense for Investors?"*)[3]

VARIATIONS

Buying on the price dips, on a flexible one-month, two-month, or three-month basis could take even further advantage of price fluctuations. Buying more or less stock under preset conditions could also provide some advantages. Perhaps you could try buying based on the p/e ratio. This would be buying with increased value.

DON'T WORRY ABOUT THE MARKET

The message is that an investor can make good returns even though the market may be unstable. Every investor would like to "buy low and sell high," but that's not an easy thing to do. Markets fluctuate up and down. An investment strategy of dollar cost averaging takes advantage of this variability by consistently investing a fixed amount of money at predetermined intervals (monthly or quarterly). By doing this consistently, the fluctuations in the market value of the investment are smoothed out. The investor using this strategy purchases more shares of stock or a mutual fund when the prices are low and fewer when prices are higher.

NOTHING IS GUARANTEED

Of course, periodic investment plans such as dollar cost averaging do not ensure a profit or protect against loss in declining markets. But with investors using this strategy to continue making purchases through periods of low and declining prices, they gain from purchasing more shares at lower prices. The investors still must carefully select the specific investment, whether stocks, bonds, or mutual funds.

DON'T CONFUSE DCA WITH CONTINUOUS INVESTING

DCA is really not the same as continuous automatic investing like a mutual funds setup. Continuous automatic investing is set up for investors who contribute to investing as they earn. It's more like an automatic savings account without which the individual would probably save nothing.

DOLLAR COST AVERAGING HAS ITS CRITICS

As the above Forbes article shows, many people criticize of DCA as being a marketing tool to ease investors into the stock market. Keep in mind that the Forbes study might have different results with changing market conditions, even though the study was conducted over a 20-year period of time. The issue will probably continue to be debated. But the fact is that it usually works to provide the investor with a position in stocks at a slightly better price. This is especially true if you don't have a lump sum to invest but have money available only at certain times.

CHAPTER 27

The Perfect Hedge Is
Short Against the Box

Selling short "against the box" means to take a conservative position. It is a position with no loss potential and no gain potential. If an investor owns (long) 100 shares of IBM and sells (short) 100 shares of IBM, the investor's position is short against the box. The strategy is often called the "perfect hedge." If the price of IBM drops, there is no loss. Conversely if the price rises, there is no gain. For example:

- Long 100 IBM at $180 a share = $18,000
- Short 100 IBM at $200 a share = $20,000

If both positions are closed out, the profit is $2,000. If the stock price declines, the profit remains $2,000. If the stock price rises but the positions are closed out, the profit is still $2,000.

A short against the box position can be closed by selling the long position and buying back the short position, or by delivering the long shares to close the short. Physically delivering stock to close a short might require a letter of instruction to the broker. No orders are written on delivering, and generally no commission is charged.

The perfect hedge can be useful in a situation in which the investor currently owns the stock but does not have physical possession. This strategy can benefit the investor who is receiving stock from a corporate purchase plan but will not receive the certificate for a few days or weeks. With any short sale, margin requirements must be fulfilled.

NO LONGER A TAX ADVANTAGE

Things change in the stock market with tax laws. Changing the tax laws can also change what happens in the stock market. What was once a tax advantage might become neutral or even a disadvantage. That happened with short against the box.

> Before 1997, the sole rationale for shorting against the box was to delay a taxable event. According to tax laws that preceded 1997, owning both long and short positions in a stock meant that any papers gains from the long position would be removed temporarily due to the offsetting short position. All in all, the net effect of both positions is zero, meaning that no taxes need to be paid. Let's say that you have a big gain on some shares of ABC. You think that ABC has reached its peak and you want to sell. However, the tax on the capital gain may leave you under-withheld for the year and subject to penalties. Perhaps the next year you expect to make a lot less money, putting you in a lower bracket and causing you to want to take the gain at that time. However, the Taxpayer Relief Act of 1997 (TRA97) no longer allows short selling against the box as a valid tax deferral practice. Under TRA97, capital gains or losses incurred from short selling against the box are not deferred. The tax implication is that any related capital gains taxes will be owed in the current year.[1]

Figure 27.1 takes a look at the situation with Coach, Inc., a manufacturer of men's and women's accessories. It's probably most

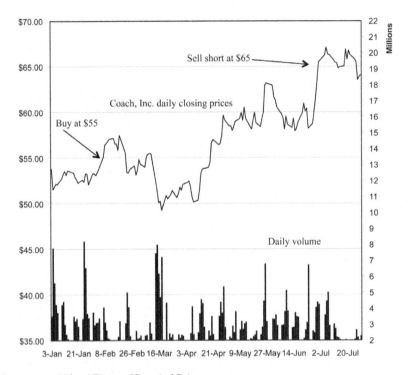

Data source: Yahoo! Finance Historical Prices

Figure 27.1   **Coach, Inc., January–July 2011**

well known for Coach purses. Say, for example, in early February 2011, you bought 1,000 shares at Coach for $55 a share for a total of $55,000. In mid-March, you watched the stock drop to $49.83 a share, but you decided to hang on. Toward the end of May, the price climbed up to $63.91 a share. It then promptly fell more than $10 a share. Then in early July, it climbed back up to $67.62 a share. That's great, but you have the nagging feeling that it will drop again. So you decide to try to take advantage of the situation and sell short at $65 a share. Since you bought the long position at $55 a share, you now have a built-in profit of $10 a share or $10,000 total.

As long as you hold both the long and the short positions you have that profit locked. Also if the price advances, you will not participate in further gains. If the price falls, you will not lose the amount that you have locked in.

Data source: Yahoo! Finance Historical Prices

Figure 27.2   Coach, Inc., 2011

Now look at Figure 27.2. This figure shows the full year of 2011 for Coach. As you can see, your concern was well deserved. The price dropped all the way to $48.63 in August. You could deliver the stock against the short sale, but at this point that would not make any sense. Just close out the short position by buying back.

We'll say you got lucky and bought back the short position at $50 a share, giving you a profit of $15 per share for a total of $15,000. Additionally, you still own 1,000 shares of Coach at $55 a share. The year ended with Coach just over $60.00 a share. Table 27.1 is an example of taking advantage of selling short Coach, Inc.

Table 27.1 Selling Short Coach, Inc., Data[2]

Date	Quantity	Buy Price	Sell Short Price	Close Short Price	Per Share Gain	Total Gain
Feb. 2011	1,000	$55.00				
July 2011	−1,000		$65.00			
Aug. 2011	1,000			$50	$15.00	$15,000 from short

Date	Long Quantity	Buy Price	Current Price		Potential Gain	Total Gain, Long and Short
Dec. 2011	1,000	$55.00	$65.00		$10,000 from long	$25,000

LONG IN THE ACCOUNT

Even though you may own the shares you wish to sell short, if you do not or are unable to deposit them in the brokerage account, normal margin account rules will apply. Also, if the long stock is not in the account, the stock must be borrowed. Obviously, if it is in the account, this is not a problem.

NOT IN A RETIREMENT ACCOUNT

Short sales of any kind cannot be made in retirement accounts because they must be made in a margin account. Margin accounts are not allowed in retirement accounts.

SHORT AGAINST THE BOX IS CONSERVATIVE

Short against the box is a conservative way to protect stock that you do not wish to sell or are unable to sell immediately. It might be stock from an inheritance or stock from a company stock purchase plan. Just make certain that you understand how a margin account works and that you have the resources to meet any calls.

CHAPTER 28

Diversification Is the Key to Portfolio Management

Here is an overly complicated example of diversification with an equally weighted portfolio.

The expected return on a portfolio is a weighted average of the expected returns on each individual asset:

$$E[R_P] = \sum_{i=1}^{n} x_i E[R_i]$$

where x_i is the proportion of the investor's total invested wealth in asset i.

The variance of the portfolio return is given by:

$$\underbrace{\text{Var}(R_P)}_{= \sigma_P^2} = E[R_P - E[R_P]]^2$$

Inserting in the expression for $E[R_P]$:

$$\sigma_P^2 = E\left[\sum_{i=1}^{n} x_i R_i - E\left[\sum_{i=1}^{n} x_i E[R_i]\right]\right]^2$$

Rearranging:

$$\sigma_P^2 = E\left[\sum_{i=1}^{n} x_i (R_i - E[R_i])\right]^2$$

$$\sigma_P^2 = E\left[\sum_{i=1}^{n}\sum_{j=1}^{n} x_i x_j (R_i - E[R_i])(R_j - E[R_j])\right]$$

$$\sigma_P^2 = E\left[\sum_{i=1}^{n} x_i^2 \underbrace{(R_i - E[R_i])^2}_{\equiv \sigma_i^2} + \sum_{i=1}^{n}\sum_{j=1, i \neq j}^{n} x_i x_j \underbrace{(R_i - E[R_i])(R_j - E[R_j])}_{\equiv \sigma_{ij}}\right]$$

$$\sigma_P^2 = \sum_{i=1}^{n} x_i^2 \sigma_i^2 + \sum_{i=1}^{n}\sum_{j=1, i \neq j}^{n} x_i x_j \sigma_{ij}$$

where σ_i^2 is the variance on asset i and σ_{ij} is the covariance between assets i and j.

In an equally weighted portfolio,

$$x_i = x_j = \frac{1}{n}, \forall i, j, ,$$

the portfolio variance then becomes:

$$\sigma_P^2 = n\frac{1}{n^2}\sigma_i^2 + n(n-1)\frac{1}{n}\frac{1}{n}\sigma_{ij}$$

And simplifying:

$$\sigma_P^2 = \frac{1}{n}\sigma_i^2 + \frac{n-1}{n}\sigma_{ij}$$

Now, taking the number of assets, n, to the limit gives:

$$\lim_{n \to \infty} \sigma_P^2 = \sigma_{ij}$$

Thus, in an equally weighted portfolio, the portfolio variance tends to the average of covariances between securities as the number of securities becomes arbitrarily large.[1]

My advice to this is forget about it. If you understand it, wonderful. If you can actually apply it to investing, excellent. But in the real world, it's totally unnecessary and probably a waste of time.

KEEP IT SIMPLE

Simply put, stock diversification is a strategy of investing in more than one company in a few different industries. Five to ten companies in at least three different industries will work for many investors. For example, you might invest in:

- Computers
- Healthcare
- Heavy industry

Choose several companies as targets in each area, and, through analysis, decide which ones have the best potential and set up your buying program. Obviously if you have larger assets, you can have additional industries and/or companies to invest in with your funds.

SOME DIVERSIFY INTO DIFFERENT ASSET TYPES

Even if you have substantial assets invested in real estate, precious metals, oil, and so on, keeping it simple will make you a happier and less confused person. In the 1980s, the big buzz word was "asset allocation." It was just another way to describe diversification and really did no better or worse. There are even formulas for balancing and rebalancing portfolios. Again, formulas are not a bad idea, but not necessarily a good one either. As always, it depends on what you as the investor are looking for in terms of financial achievement and risk tolerance. Also it depends how much money the investor has to invest.

DIVERSIFICATION DOESN'T ALWAYS HELP

When the economy or the stock market goes in the tank, no amount of diversification will be of much help. Diversification protects by being in an array of investments. If one or two suffer, you count on the others to bail you out. That's all it's really good for. When the whole market is down, diversification doesn't provide any protection.

BE CAREFUL WITH MUTUAL FUNDS

As mutual funds have proliferated in the investment market, many firms are diversifying by owning several different mutual funds. Yes, it's possible to have better diversification by owning more than one mutual fund, but find out what's actually in the fund. Request a list of assets or go on the Internet to one of the browser finance areas and under mutual funds enter the symbol of the fund you are interested in. Then go to the area labeled "Holdings." If necessary for comparisons, just print out the holdings list. Avoid funds that are investing in the same things. The only other rule is don't have too many. They will only complicate your life. Here's another consideration with mutual funds:

> Many mutual fund holders also suffer from being over-diversified. Some funds, especially the larger ones, have so many assets (i.e., cash to invest) that they have to hold literally hundreds of stocks and consequently, so do you. In some cases this makes it nearly impossible for the fund to outperform indexes—the whole reason you invested in the fund and are paying the fund manager a management fee.[2]

DIVERSIFICATION IS IMPORTANT

It is important to have diversification, no matter what kind of investments you have. Think of the poor investors who risked it all with Bernie Madoff or the other Ponzi schemes that became exposed. Many of those investors ended up with absolutely nothing.

EXCHANGE-TRADED FUND ALTERNATIVE

How about a mutual fund that trades like a stock? Some exchange-traded funds (ETFs) are highly speculative with a short-term focus, and others have a more conservative long-term approach. Here are some advantages:

- *Lower costs:* ETFs generally have lower costs than other investment products because most ETFs are not actively managed and because ETFs are insulated from the costs of having to buy and sell securities to accommodate shareholder purchases and redemptions. ETFs typically have lower marketing, distribution, and accounting expenses, and most ETFs do not have 12b-1 fees.
- *Buying and selling flexibility:* ETFs can be bought and sold at current market prices at any time during the trading day, unlike mutual funds and unit investment trusts, which can be traded only at the end of the trading day. As publicly traded securities, their shares can be purchased on margin and sold short, enabling the use of hedging strategies, and traded using stop orders and limit orders, which allow investors to specify the price points at which they are willing to trade.

In addition to the advantages just mentioned, following are several more advantages from Wikipedia: look in "Exchange-Traded Fund."

- Tax efficiency—ETFs generally generate relatively low capital gains, because they typically have low turnover of their portfolio securities. While this is an advantage they share with other index funds, their tax efficiency is further enhanced because they do not have to sell securities to meet investor redemptions.
- Market exposure and diversification—ETFs provide an economical way to rebalance portfolio allocations and to "equitize" cash by investing it quickly. An index ETF inherently provides diversification across an entire index. ETFs offer exposure to a diverse variety of markets,

including broad-based indices, broad-based international and country-specific indices, industry sector-specific indices, bond indices, and commodities.

- Transparency—ETFs, whether index funds or actively managed, have transparent portfolios and are priced at frequent intervals throughout the trading day.

Some of these advantages derive from the status of most ETFs as index funds.[3]

ETFs are an alternative, but they need to be delved into so that the investor can understand what the investment objective is and how speculative it is or can be.

SOME THOUGHTS ON DIVERSIFICATION

Yes diversification is important, but not as much as many people imagine. Ten to twenty stocks provide a lot of simple diversification. The diversification of most mutual funds is way overblown and overdone to the point of becoming a hindrance to performance.

Asset allocation is a wonderful concept, but it at least partly depends on the amount of money one has to invest. It tends to work better and more logically with very large sums.

Quality of securities should always be maintained. Forget the fish farms and monkey ranches and leave them for the high speculators. Whatever you invest in, be sure that you easily understand exactly where the profit is coming from and the details on risk.

Part 4

TRADING

In many ways, this entire book is about trading. It doesn't include "day trading," which can be a road to overtrading disaster for many investors. Instead it covers the short-, medium-, and long-term trading that might be practiced in your retirement account or in your regular brokerage account.

It used to be said that the only time to sell a stock is when you have found a new one to buy. With an extended bull market or even a new bull market, this has changed to something like, the only time to sell a stock is when you believe it cannot live up to your growth expectations. If your stocks are researched well before you buy them, most of the trading here will be buying rather than selling.

Why is it best to trade "at the market" or best available price (Chapter 30)? You might also ask why risk your entire trading strategy for a few extra cents per share? When the market moves, it moves. It doesn't sit there and wait for you to execute every order.

Why not buy a stock because it has a low price (Chapter 31)? Because there is a reason it has a low price, and the reason is very often the reason not to buy the stock at all. This trips up many beginning investors who believe that if they pay less money, they're not taking much risk. Frankly, the risk couldn't be much higher, but the stock price can and usually does go lower.

This part of the book also looks at the basic makeup of hedge funds. What they are and how they are designed. The Chapter 34 title, "Always Take Your Profits Too Soon," is a strategy that could easily be held by a hedge fund.

The biggest change in the stock market in the past decade is speed. If you look at the amount of daily volume today as compared to 10 years ago, you can easily see this. Large trades are being made in the blink of an eye. This speed is more likely to increase rather than decrease. Once the decision to invest is made, action should be swift, before the market moves on to a new situation.

The trading chapters can help you achieve greater results and profits.

CHAPTER 29

Never Short a Dull Market

A "dull" market is a sideways market, sometimes referred to as a trendless market. Movement is slow with an occasional advance followed by a modest correction. Volume tends to be below average. The following observations have often been attributed to Wall Street's Jay Gould: "Two old adages were frequently quoted in brokerage offices yesterday. One was that it would not do to sell the market when the sap was running up the trees, and the other was that it was dangerous to sell (short) a dull market."[1]

During dull or balanced markets, institutional investors are waiting for a good reason to get back into the market. The slightest good news or sometimes bad news that isn't as bad as expected can stimulate a strong rally. The rally can cause the price of the shorted stock to rise sharply, resulting in margin calls and eventually a loss. If there were no underlying strength, the market would be falling.

All lethargic markets have occasional rallies and corrections, although the price swings are generally not severe. If investors can identify where the heaviest volume occurs, they can determine whether the sentiment is bullish or bearish. If the volume on a correction (downswing) is consistently and significantly greater than the volume on a rally, the sentiment tends to be bearish.

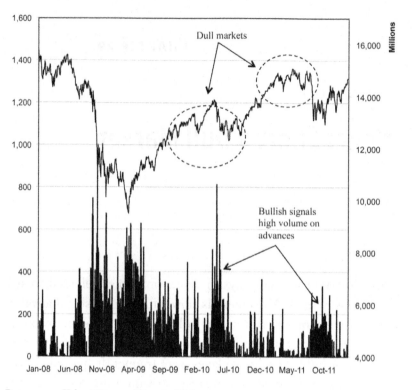

Data source: Yahoo! Finance Historical Prices

Figure 29.1   **S&P 500 Index, 2008–2011**

Figure 29.1 shows a dull market from September 2009 to September 2010. Making a short sale in this slow market probably wouldn't have been profitable. Most of the volume was low with occasional spikes on advances—a definite bullish signal. The same is true for December 2010 to July 2011. Although there is a good spot in August 2011, it was over in a flash, and the market started up again.

Although you might not want to sell short in a dull market, some professional investors will do just that in order to stir things up. A lot of short selling occurred during the second half of 2011. People were just trying to find some action in the stock market. Figure 29.2 shows the increase in volatility and volume. Volume tended to be heavier on the downward movements, and much of it was short

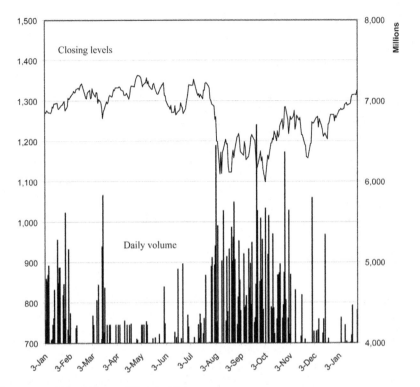

Data source: Yahoo! Finance Historical Prices

Figure 29.2   **S&P 500 Index, 2011–January 2012**

selling. There were many situations for short selling. As we came to the end of the year, the selling slowed and the market gained. The market went into 2012 on the rise, but with lower volume.

AN EXAMPLE

Most of us don't sell or sell short the whole market. We look for opportunities to sell short some stock. With the midyear drop in 2011 in the S&P 500 Index, Netflix followed suit. The company had announced higher fees and a cutback in services. This news was not well received by investors.

As Figure 29.3 shows, selling Netflix short between July and September of 2011 could have been an excellent strategy. The stock

Data source: Yahoo! Finance Historical Prices

Figure 29.3   **Netflix, Inc., 2011–January 2012**

dropped from $298 in July to $64 a share in November. One fortunate enough to execute that trade would have pocketed $230 per share in profits. Not bad for a short-term investment.

LOOK OUT FOR A SQUEEZE

Selling short is always a speculative strategy that requires patience and skill. Dull markets are notorious for sudden rallies that put the "squeeze" on short sellers. Traders refer to the rallies as being a "short squeeze" or "squeezing out the shorts." Short sellers caught in a squeeze run the risk of receiving a margin call for additional cash or marginable securities to be deposited in their accounts. If this does not happen they could be sold out by the brokerage firm at a loss:

> I always recall the old Wall Street adage: "Never sell a dull market short," says Eugene Peroni, portfolio manager at Advisors Asset Management. Peroni tells MarketWatch Radio's Larry Kofsky that "based on the relative volatility, it's actually fairly quiet and tame." So, he says, "this market might go higher before we get that much-anticipated pullback."[2]

"Never short a dull market" means to be careful with the underlying strength of stock prices in a stock market that has become lethargic and that has no clear trend. The underlying strength can turn to buying activity on the slightest positive news. The ensuing rally and resumption of the up trend creates a high-risk situation for the short investor.

CHAPTER 30

It's Best to Trade at the Market

Market orders have priority. It's important to remember that fact. A market order says that the investor is willing to buy or sell shares immediately at the "best available price." The order takes precedence over any other kind of order. It must be presented to the "trading crowd" by the specialist on the stock exchange at the earliest possible moment. In reality, a computer matches the vast majority of market orders. The result is a nearly immediate execution and report.

Here's what the Securities and Exchange Commission (SEC) says:

> A market order is an order to buy or sell a stock at the best available price. Generally, this type of order will be executed immediately. However, the price at which a market order will be executed is not guaranteed. It is important for investors to remember that the last-traded price is not necessarily the price at which a market order will be executed. In fast-moving markets, the price at which a market order will execute often deviates from the last-traded price or "real time" quote.[1]

IMPLICATIONS OF A MARKET ORDER

A market order says that the investor desires a fast execution of the trade whether it is a buy or a sell. The only time that delays can occur is when a broker is entering the order or if the stock exchange is swamped with orders and has to catch up.

A market order also implies that any price is acceptable. This fact is often forgotten until an investor pays more than expected for a stock purchase or receives less than anticipated on a sell. In a steady, evenly paced market, a buy order will be filled at or near the current offer on the stock quote and at or near the bid on a sell, but it is never guaranteed.

In a fast-market situation, an investor could pay a few or even several dollars more per share when the order is actually executed. This can be of real concern in a takeover situation in which, hypothetically, $20 or $60 or more per share might be paid with a market order. It is the main reason takeover offers are normally not announced during trading hours. However, rumors can suddenly appear and move the price of a takeover target significantly during the trading day. Announcements will usually appear after trading hours or during the weekend when the markets are closed. The uncertainty of price necessitates that buyers check the current trading price when placing an order to buy or sell stock.

A market order is quoted in terms of a "round lot." For most stocks this would be 100 shares. There can be exceptions. There can be a problem with thinly traded stocks because of current availability. If necessary, multiple round lots can be broken into smaller lots at different prices.

LIMIT ORDER CONTRADICTS INVESTOR INTENT

The main reason that it's best to trade "at the market" is simply that the market moves quickly. Order qualifiers such as price limits or "all or none" do not have the same priority as market orders and might not be executed. Directions can quickly and unexpectedly change, leaving the investor twisting in the wind with a limit order. When a decision has been reached, why should an investor take an action directly contradicting the strategy? "I want to buy some stock because I believe the price will rise, but I might be able to get it cheaper. So I place an order below the current price." Why do such a thing? Why buy a stock believing the price will go lower? On the other hand, why sell a stock believing that the price will rise? The action doesn't match the strategy.

The reason for placing a buy or sell of securities as a market order is to obtain an immediate execution at the best available price. If the investor nitpicks over a few cents per share, opportunity can be lost and the resulting cost of frustration and time lost is high. Such costs can easily be higher than any movement in the stock price while the market order is being placed. Do the analysis, make the decision, set the strategy, and stick with it when you're placing the order.

The only time to avoid using a market order is when a price is rising rapidly. If an investor is interested in a company whose stock price is rapidly moving up but the investor desires to have some control over the buying price, a limit order "or better" can be entered. The term "or better" is normally assumed, but in this situation its intent is to confirm that a limit order is being placed above the current trading price. This can be a valid strategy within an IRA where available funds are limited.

Let's say that XYZ Corp. is currently trading at $50 a share, up $5 for the day. An investor wants to buy the stock for his IRA and needs to have some control over the price. An order to buy 100 shares is placed with a limit of $51 or better for the day. Since the limit is about the current market price, it might be considered an error if the "or better" qualifier is not added. At this point either the order will be filled between $50 and $51 or it will not be executed.

Although this can be a good strategy on the buy side, it is different on the sell side. Although a similar order can be placed on the sell side, it might not be prudent. If the price is dropping rapidly and a decision has been made to sell, the stock should be sold as quickly as possible. There is a risk that placing a limit on the sell order will result in the order not being executed.

ERRORS HAPPEN

Placing a market order means to buy or sell stock at the "best available price." If an order is filled at a price substantially away from the quote given to the investor, the "time and sales" can be checked with the broker to see why the order was executed at a substantially different price from the one reported. Although errors are possible, they are usually the exception. Errors are not allowed to stand. The broker goes to the exchange or trading desk and has it corrected.

Another instance in which it might not be advisable to use a market order is with low-priced, usually thinly traded stock; for example, speculative stock that sells for less than $10 a share and trades only a few shares a day. In these situations a limit order is usually best, but, again, there is still the risk that it won't be executed.

FAIR AND ORDERLY MARKET

Exchanges and over-the-counter market makers strive to fill orders quickly and as close to the current price as possible. It's part of the integrity essential to maintaining a fair and orderly market. If a public market for securities does not operate with this integrity, it will cease to exist as a continuous public auction. Stock exchanges around the world, whether in emerging or developed markets, are striving to make their markets fair, orderly, and stable. Many have adopted rules to stop trading if a stock's price or the market fluctuates beyond a certain percentage in a trading session. Calling a halt to the trading won't stop declines, but it will provide everyone with an opportunity to learn about what's happening.

In most situations market orders work best because they can be executed rapidly at a reasonable fill price. Most of the time these advantages outweigh the benefits of placing a limit order, especially when it cannot be executed. If bad fills are being received, they should be checked for possible errors, and the strategy should be reexamined.

CHAPTER 31

Never Buy a Stock Because It Has a Low Price

Buying a stock simply because it has a low price is a risky strategy. It's especially risky if the investor doesn't find out why the price is low. Often investors are attracted to low-priced stocks that pay a dividend. The lower price pushes the dividend percent higher. The yield on the dividend might be 10, 15, or even 20 percent. Sometimes the companies are about to severely reduce or even eliminate that dividend. When they do so, the stock price plummets even further. The investor is then left with an extremely low-priced stock and no dividend.

HOW A STOCK CAN BE OVERSOLD

A stock is considered oversold when selling drives its price below its value. The then undervalued stock is expected to show some kind of rally in the next few trading sessions. Some analysts and investors don't believe an "oversold" situation can actually exist because the term implies that investors sold more shares than they intended to sell. Actually, the term "oversold" refers to the price at which a significant number of buyers come to the stock, believing it is worth more than the current market price indicates. It can be accompanied by higher trading volume.

At the other end, "overbought" is the price at which volume decreases and investors start selling because they believe the current market price is too high.

Technical analysts frequently use these two terms. Fundamental analysts might use "overvalued" or "undervalued." They would tend to look at the prices in relation to earnings and revenues.

As an example, let's look at Halcon Resources, Inc. (HK:NYSE), an independent oil and natural gas company engaged in the acquisition, development, exploitation, exploration, and production of oil and natural gas properties in Texas, Louisiana, and Oklahoma. On May 7, 2012 the current price was $9.56. Okay, it's got a low price, or does it? The current p/e ratio on that date was –188, and the current p/e ratio of S&P 500 stocks is about 20 average. In addition:

- Debt-to-equity ratio, 33.96 (anything more than 1.0 is a lot)
- Sales, $107.88 million
- 12-month sales growth, –4%
- 12-month earnings growth, 158%
- Institutional ownership, 2.15%

So there are some good factors (it does have sales) and some not so good. We have to wonder why there is virtually no institutional ownership. What do the institutional owners know?

The debt-to-equity ratio is a real deal killer. Halcon would need a lot more income to handle that debt. Let's look at the price chart shown in Figure 31.1.

The current price of $9.56 a share could tempt many an investor, but it obviously should not be the only reason for choosing the stock. Halcon could become a good stock in the future, but it would be a better strategy to follow it and see if it can climb out of debt and get some solid revenues and income.

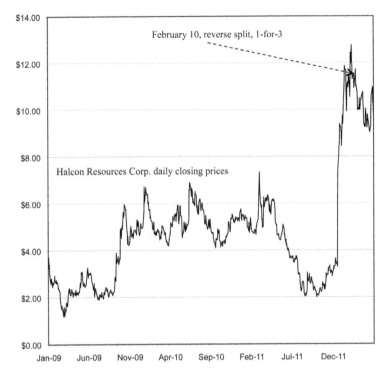

February 10, reverse split, 1-for-3

Halcon Resources Corp. daily closing prices

Data source: Yahoo! Finance Historical Prices

Figure 31.1 **Halcon Energy Resources, 2009–May 2012**

WHY DOES A STOCK HAVE A LOW PRICE?

Stocks have low prices because prices are determined by buyers and sellers in the stock market. If investors believe in the future of a company, they buy stock. If they have doubts about a company's future, they don't buy stock or they sell.

Company performance is always an important factor in stock market investing. Although it seems to be a statement of the obvious it should be understood and taken seriously. Here is another important view of performance:

> Most people would agree that the basic driver of stock price
> is company performance. If the company does well and its

profits increase year after year, the stock's price will generally go up over time. On the other hand, if the company
doesn't fare well and its profits remain stagnant or decrease,
the price of the stock will likely go down as well.

Because of this, stocks with a lower share price are typically riskier than stocks with higher-priced shares. Since the
likely reason the company's stock price is so low is that it
hasn't performed well, when you buy a low priced stock, you
are essentially betting that it is going to change its course
and start to perform well.[1]

The obvious point here is that price, although important,
should never be the only criterion for buying stock. It is a quick and
painful way to lose money in the stock market. We want investments
to make money. Any stock with a low price should be looked at carefully to determine why the price is low, and we need to figure out
what has to happen for the price to rise.

CHAPTER 32

Buy the Dips

Stock prices tend to move as a group, which causes the stock market to fluctuate. The market virtually never moves in a straight line. The stock market moves as anticipation changes, based on reactions to economic developments. Although starting in 1929 the market stayed down for four years, and starting in 1977 it stayed down five years, most market declines are more short term. Many last only four to six months. James Cramer, a renowned former hedge fund (Cramer and Company) manager on Wall Street, said, "For ten straight years, every time the stock market has taken a hit, you've made big money if you jumped in with both feet. A 'buy the dips' philosophy has outperformed any other strategy imaginable."[1]

Cramer goes on to say how the one exception to this rule was the market crash of 1987. But the biggest difference between then and the 2000s is the fact that interest rates were rising in 1987.

Notice that Cramer talks about the "stock market" taking a hit, not individual stocks. Dips caused by market declines are usually the most profitable; however, individual companies can have temporary setbacks that are resolved, and then the price recovers and climbs to new highs. When the dip is caused by market pressure, the reason why isn't so important. When the dip is just one individual specific stock, the reason why becomes extremely important. It's the time to find out why the stock price is down and what needs to happen for it to recover.

DIPS ON MARKET PRESSURE

A look at the price growth of Home Depot, Inc. (NYSE: HD) for 2011 and part of 2012, as shown in Figure 32.1, shows clearly that the major price dips were caused by market pressure. Sometimes Home Depot appears to be unaffected by a market dip, and other times it rises while the market falls. Clearly these are positive signs for the stock. Buying the stock at the lowest dip in August at $28.51 would have resulted in a $16.44 (58 percent) gain per share by the end of January 2012. Not bad for less than six months.

Data source: Yahoo! Finance Historical Prices

Figure 32.1   Home Depot, Inc., versus S&P 500 Index, 2011–January 2012

SELLING ON THE RALLIES

Buying on the dips can be used by the short-term speculator or the long-term investor. Some speculators follow a strategy of buying on the dips and selling on the rallies. Obviously, the ideal stock for this kind of trading is one that tends to fluctuate on a regular basis.

THERE IS A CONTRARIAN VIEW

There is always a contrarian view when investing is involved. If there wasn't, we'd all be billionaires:

> There is another issue: If the long-term return on stocks turns out to be positive, as most investors hope it will, then buying on the dips isn't likely to raise your return. As the market marches up sporadically over time, you may catch the occasional downdraft—but, on average, the successive dips will occur at higher prices than your starting point.
>
> What's more, many dips occur when markets are near record highs, points out Francis Kinniry Jr., an investment-strategy analyst at Vanguard Group. And a discount from an all-time high is hardly the same thing as a bargain.[2]

Whether this is a problem or not partly depends on whether you are intending to hold the stock long term or short term. Short term, you are still paying more for the stock than your original investment, and this will eat into your gains. Long term, you are still paying more but you have the advantage of time for the price to rise enough to justify the extra cost.

BUY STOP STRATEGY

Most of the dips shown in Home Depot's price were caused by market corrections. As we said, a speculator buying on these dips could have profited nearly 100 percent. The major difficulty with such a strategy is knowing when to make the move. A possible strategy, once the price drops, would be to place a buy stop order (on an exchange-traded stock) above the current price. That way the buy wouldn't be made until the stock moved upward. The stop could be lowered if the price continued to drop. A limit placed on the buy stop could give protection from an extreme upsurge.

The dips here could also be good for long-term investors. Price weakness, caused primarily by market weakness, can provide excellent opportunities to add stocks to a portfolio position.

IT'S A NO-BRAINER

To buy stock on price dips is a sound strategy, especially when those dips are caused by stock market corrections. Certainly, the stock market might keep correcting and enter a bear market, but this is not what usually happens. Most corrections stop quickly, and the market recovers. Individual stock prices that are influenced by the market create buying opportunities for both the speculator and the long-term investor. These opportunities do not usually last for a long period; therefore, the investor should have targets analyzed and selected in advance in order to be able to move swiftly.

CHAPTER 33

Order Modifications Can Cause Delays

Careful consideration should be given to any modification placed on an order because an order with qualifiers other than market order can take more time to be executed.

GOOD-TILL-CANCELED (GTC)

An order stays "open" until it is executed, canceled, or changed by the investor, or until it is canceled by the brokerage firm. Brokerage firms have different policies concerning how long they will carry an open order on their books. Many firms cancel at the end of 30 days or the end of the following month, whereupon the order must be reentered to remain open. Automatic cancellation helps the investor remember the open order by a cancellation notification and prevents duplication.

Open orders can be changed or canceled by the investor at any time; however, the investor should question the value of making several changes, usually referred to as *chasing*. It's usually better to make the trade than it is to chase a price. Changes are costly to brokerage firms, and those costs end up being passed on to investors. Also, too many changes can lead to confusion and costly errors.

DO NOT REDUCE

Buy and stop GTC orders are generally modified by the instruction DNR, which means "do not reduce." Most investors want an order filled even if it has become exdividend, which means that the investor is buying the stock without the current dividend. The stock's price is reduced by the amount of the dividend at the beginning of trading. Many firms require DNR designation on all GTC orders.

When an investor decides to change an open order, it is necessary to notify the broker of the existing, previously placed order. Otherwise, two orders could be executed, with the investor bearing responsibility for any liabilities. A new or change GTC order does not automatically cancel a previously entered order.

The advantage of the good-till-canceled order is its automatic feature. The order stays in effect, day after day, and it does not need to be reentered until it is changed or canceled. The investor's transaction will be executed when it is possible to do so, and it does not need constant attention. The disadvantage of using an open order is that doing so could cause delay. Situations may arise in which other limit orders have been placed at the same price. The investor's order execution is delayed by "stock ahead." Also, keep in mind that market orders always take precedence.

Market orders are automatically "day orders," but they may be entered GTC on thinly traded stocks. Some preferred stock and issues from small companies are not traded every day.

DAY ORDER

The day order is just what it says: it's an order placed for that day only. If the order cannot be executed by the end of the trading session, it is canceled. A notice of cancelation is sent to the broker: "firm nothing done." The broker notifies the investor. A day order can be changed or canceled by the investor at any time during the trading session.

Frequent traders or day traders are likely to use day orders. Their strategy is normally based on momentum that is building during the day, so they have no reason to keep an order open longer than the current trading session. The main disadvantage of using the day order is that the investor must wait for a status report at the end of the trading session. Obviously, the report can take a while to arrive after an exciting day in the stock market.

OB: OR BETTER

The phrase "or better" refers to the price that is most advantageous to the investor. "Or better" is always assumed with limit buy orders placed below or sell orders placed above the current trading price. Usually the OB designation is added to a buy limit placed at or above the current price and to sell orders at or below the current sell price. The OB designation clarifies the investor's intent to buy or sell. It is more like a code saying "this is not a mistake."

For example, let's say that the stock of ABX is trading at $21.25 and is up by $1.25 from the previous day's closing price of $20 a share. The investor wishes to buy ABX and take advantage of a continuing up trend; however, a market order could fill higher than the current ask price. This might present an extra problem in an IRA account that is limited to the funds available in the account. The investor is willing to pay as much as $21.50 but only if necessary.

The order is entered as a limit order OB: "Buy 500 shares of ABX at a limit of $21.50 OB, day order." If the order can be executed, the investor will buy the 500 shares for $21.50 or less. If the price is higher than the limit by the time the order is entered and stays higher, the order will be canceled at the end of the day.

AON: ALL OR NONE

The qualifier "all or none" can be used with multiple round lot or block orders. Block orders normally receive special handling through a brokerage firm's block order desk. The purpose of the modifier is to avoid a partial fill of the order.

If a person desires to buy 1,000 shares of BBB Corporation at $20.00 a share, with the stock currently at $19.75 to $20.00 a limit order might be entered at $20.00 for the day. It might be possible to buy only 500 or 600 shares at that price. The order can be filled for 500 shares at $20.00 a share, leaving the investor 500 shares short. If the AON modifier is added, there are only two possibilities at the end of the trading session: either the investor will have bought 1,000 shares of BBB at $20.00 a share or the order will have been canceled because it could not be filled.

IOC: IMMEDIATE OR CANCEL

The immediate-or-cancel order modifier is added to a limit that is at or close to an executable price. It specifies a maximum quantity, but it can be less. It says to buy (sell) 2,000 shares right now if you can. If you cannot do the 2,000, then buy (sell) 1,500 or 1,000 shares and cancel the remainder of the order.

FOK: FILL OR KILL

Although similar to the IOC, the fill-or-kill order says to make the transaction for the full amount of the order immediately or cancel the order. This differs from the AON, which allows some time to fill the order at the limit price.

NH: NOT HELD

Used primarily with large orders, the not held modification allows the floor broker to use time or price discretion for the effective execution of an order. NH indicates that the investor will accept what the floor broker can accomplish with an execution of the trade.

Note: During unusually fast markets, brokerage firms may accept only "market orders not held," meaning they are not held to a price based on the current price quotation. When the system becomes overloaded, orders ahead can change the price showing on the computer by the time an investor's order is cleared.

OLOS: ODD LOT ON SALE

Occasions can arise when an investor is selling a combination of a round low (normally 100 shares) and an odd lot (less than a round lot) of stock. An amount such as 125 shares of XYZ Company is a combination of the round lot of 100 shares and the odd lot of 25 shares.

If a limit order is placed to sell the stock, the investor might want to add the modification "odd lot on sale" to indicate that the round lot is available at the limit price, but the odd lot may be sold at the market price. This modifier simplifies the transaction and makes it easier to have the order executed. The odd lot portion of 25 shares could be charged an extra minimal fee, known as the "odd lot differential."

Placing a combination round lot/odd lot sell order with the odd-lot-on-sale modifier can make execution of the trade easier and faster. The only disadvantage is that the investor must accept a possible lower price for the odd lot.

MODIFIERS MAY BE NECESSARY

Modifiers such as price limits, AON, or IOK can have an impact on the speed at which an order is executed. Although there can be sound reasons for placing limits and other modifiers on buy and sell orders, in most cases the time saved by placing a market order is worth more than the time lost waiting for another 25 cents per share. Placing market orders will usually save the investor time and money.

CHAPTER 34

Always Take Your Profits Too Soon (Hedge Funds)

"Always take your profits too soon" is a phrase that probably originated with a hedge fund operator—one who wrapped up trades and unwrapped them just as fast. See the profit; take the profit. Another version says, "You will never lose money taking a profit too soon." So, what are these "hedge funds, " and why do we seldom hear about them or what they are doing?

HEDGE FUNDS: WHAT ARE THEY?

Although the Internet has a lot of information about hedge funds and how they operate, for many years it was very difficult to get any information. Part of this was the result of restrictions on how they could be advertised and partly was because people chose not to reveal information about them.

Hedge funds in one form or another have been around since the 1920s. They are pools of money assembled and invested by investment managers. Although there are many different types of hedge funds with different objectives, for the most part the investment managers do what they feel is best for the fund. They buy and sell securities, sell short, and trade options, futures, and other derivatives. This flexibility is the "hedge" against market reverses. As with all investment strategies, sometimes they work and sometimes they don't.

WHO ARE THE INVESTORS?

Hedge fund investors are made up of large pension funds, university endowments, foundations, and large net-worth individuals. They are open-end funds meaning that someone can join at any time. They tend to require large contributions of $500,000 or $1,000,000 to start an account. Hedge funds are not allowed to solicit investment from the general public (meaning they are not allowed to advertise):

> Hedge funds raise capital via private placement under Regulation D of the Securities Act of 1933, which means the shares are not registered. To comply with the private placement rules in Regulation D, hedge funds generally offer their securities solely to accredited investors. An accredited investor is an individual person with a minimum net worth of $1,000,000 or, alternatively, a minimum income of $200,000 in each of the last two years and a reasonable expectation of reaching the same income level in the current year. For banks and corporate entities, the minimum net worth is $5,000,000 in invested assets.[1]

HEDGE FUND FEES

Fees charged for hedge funds are management fees and performance fees. The management fee is usually between 1 and 4 percent annually, but it is calculated monthly. Performance fees are typically tied to a benchmark, such as the S&P 500 Index, and are charged on annual performance. Performance fees usually range from 10 to 50 percent annually. Supposedly this percentage gives the investment manager motivation to be successful. Losses are typically carried forward, although it can happen that a losing fund is closed out and a new one started.

STRATEGIES

There are four main strategies used by hedge funds:

1. Global macro strategy
2. Directional investment strategy
3. Event-driven strategy
4. Relative value (arbitrage) strategy

Managed futures or multistrategy funds may not always fit into these categories, but they are also popular strategies with funds.

Global Macro Strategy

In order to generate a risk-adjusted return, hedge funds take sizable positions in stock, bond, or currency markets in anticipation of global macroeconomic events to generate a risk-adjusted return.

Directional Investment Strategy

Directional investment strategies utilize market movements, trends, or inconsistencies when picking stocks across a variety of markets. Computer models can be used, or fund managers will identify and select investments. These types of strategies have a greater exposure to the fluctuations of the overall market than do market neutral strategies. Directional hedge fund strategies include US and international long/short equity hedge funds, where long equity positions are hedged with short sales of equities or equity index options.[2]

Event-Driven Strategy

Event-driven strategies concern situations in which the underlying investment opportunity and risk are associated with an event. An event-driven investment strategy finds investment opportunities in corporate transactional events such as consolidations, acquisitions, recapitalizations, bankruptcies, and liquidations. Managers employing such a strategy capitalize on valuation inconsistencies in the market before or after such events, and take a position based on the predicted movement of the security or securities in question. Large institutional investors such as hedge funds are more likely to pursue event-driven investing strategies than traditional equity investors because they have the expertise and resources to analyze corporate transactional events for investment opportunities.[3]

Relative Value (Arbitrage) Strategy

Relative value arbitrage strategies take advantage of relative discrepancies in price between securities. The price discrepancy can occur due to mispricing of securities compared to related securities, the underlying security or the market overall. Hedge fund managers can use various types of analysis to identify price discrepancies in securities, including mathematical, technical or fundamental techniques. Relative value is often used as a synonym for market neutral, as strategies in this category typically have very little or no directional market exposure to the market as a whole. Other relative value substrategies include:

1. Fixed income arbitrage: exploit pricing inefficiencies between related fixed income securities.

2. Equity market neutral: exploits differences in stock prices by being long and short in stocks within the same sector, industry, market capitalization, country, which also creates a hedge against broader market factors.
3. Convertible arbitrage: exploit pricing inefficiencies between convertible securities and the corresponding stocks.
4. Asset-backed securities (Fixed-Income asset-backed): fixed income arbitrage strategy using asset-backed securities.
5. Credit long /short: the same as long/short equity but in credit markets instead of equity markets.
6. Statistical arbitrage: identifying pricing inefficiencies between securities through mathematical modeling techniques.
7. Volatility arbitrage: exploit the change in implied volatility instead of the change in price.
8. Yield alternatives: non-fixed income arbitrage strategies based on the yield instead of the price.
9. Regulatory arbitrage: the practice of taking advantage of regulatory differences between two or more markets.
10. Risk arbitrage: exploiting market discrepancies between acquisition price and stock price.[4]

HOW WELL DO THEY DO?

Keep in mind the idea of a hedge fund is to hedge in order to lessen the impact of a declining investment value. In 2008, investments declined in value. How well did the hedge funds do?

Hedge funds posted disappointing returns in 2008, but the average hedge fund return of –18.65% (the HFRI Fund Weighted Composite Index return) was far better than the returns generated by most assets other than cash or cash equivalents. The S&P 500 total return was –37.00% in 2008, and that was one of the best performing equity indices in the world. Several equity markets lost more than half their value. Most foreign and domestic corporate debt indices also suffered in 2008, posting losses significantly worse than the average hedge fund. Mutual funds also performed much worse than hedge funds in 2008. According to Lipper, the average US domestic equity mutual fund decreased 37.6% in 2008. The average international equity mutual fund declined 45.8%. The average sector mutual fund dropped 39.7%. The average China mutual fund declined 52.7% and the average Latin America mutual fund plummeted 57.3%. Real estate, both residential and commercial, also suffered significant drops in 2008. In summary, hedge funds outperformed many similarly-risky investment options in 2008.[5]

It appears that during the crash of 2008, the hedge funds lost less money than other investments, thereby being a qualified success.

TO HEDGE OR NOT TO HEDGE

There are reasons why one might not wish to allocate a high proportion of assets to hedge funds:

1. Hedge funds are highly customized and not very transparent. Therefore it is hard to estimate the likely returns or risks.
2. Hedge funds' low relationships with other investments tend to go away during stressful market events, making them much less useful for any real diversification than they may appear.
3. Hedge fund returns are reduced considerably by the ultra high fee structures that are typically charged.

4. Hedge funds need much more regulation to protect the individual investor.
5. There are more Bernie Madoffs out there in the markets.

IF YOU HAVE THE MONEY, TAKE THE PLUNGE

If you have the qualifying assets and income and are tired of receiving less than adequate returns on part of your money, by all means jump in—after you get as much information as possible. If one fund won't give you the information you want, go to another. They are listed in various places on the Internet. Several have their own websites.

Part 5

GOOD IDEAS

It is easier to follow a few stocks well than it is to follow a
well full of stocks.

—S. A. NELSON[1]

S. A. Nelson was a close friend of Charles Dow, the founding father
of Dow Jones. Many investors are guilty of trying to follow too
many stocks—so many that they can't keep their facts straight. The
right number to follow is always an arbitrary decision, but if you follow the stocks you currently own and maybe as many as five others,
that should be plenty. If an investor owns stock of five companies
and follows five more, ten stocks are more than enough to follow on
a regular basis.

Several investment advisors are guilty of recommending too
many stocks in which to diversify or to follow. Possibly this is
intended to make the investor dependent on the advisor's expertise.
An investor wants to invest and make a certain return, but usually
doesn't want the effort to become a second job.

This part of the book also explores other good ideas in
investing—things that should be remembered like Chapter 36,
Greater Risk Means Greater Potential Reward. It just ain't necessarily so.

Keeping good records is an obvious advantage, and invest in what you know best is one of those simple rules that people often don't think about.

This part also goes into some definition of mutual fund investing in Chapter 38. It explores the advantages and a few disadvantages.

The part looks at some ideas that are still good and some that have lost their greatness.

CHAPTER 35

Follow a Few Stocks Well

Following stocks can be interesting and exciting, or it can be tedious and frustrating. For many investors it is the information that starts their day. They thrill to pouring over *The Wall Street Journal*, *Barron's*, *Investor's Business Daily*, and other financial journals. Others spend a great deal of time "surfing the net" to find out what happened in the stock market and then learn everyone's opinion about why it happened. Some of these fastidious readers seldom invest in the stock market; they just enjoy the changes, like watching a World Series game or perhaps the Super Bowl. They are the armchair investors who get enjoyment from seeing how the game plays out. For others, real investors, watching the market is not nearly as exciting as participating in its gains. Peter Lynch said it well when he said:

> It's absolute crap that people need to spend 60 hours a week analyzing companies. All you need are a few stocks to make money. If you find one stock a year, that's plenty. When I was running Magellan I had to find one a week but that was because I had billions of dollars. The average person needs only a few good stocks in a lifetime.[1]

LEARNING THE BASIC SKILLS

To become skilled in stock watching or tracking, one must have firsthand experience. An investor will learn more by owning a stock for two weeks than by watching a stock for two years. The reason is simple; ownership places money at risk. Risk of losing money greatly heightens one's attention. Losses that occur when the price drops are potentially real losses. More importantly, gains that occur when the price rises are potential profits; thus the company and its price progress become a magnet for the investor's attention.

During the first few days of ownership, investors are likely to learn more about the company than they will for the rest of the holding period. Hanging onto some of this enthusiasm can prove useful in making sound investment decisions.

THREE INFLUENCES ON STOCK PRICES

The price of a stock has essentially three main influences:

- Direction and strength of the overall stock market
- The current "play," or investing theme
- Earnings

Direction and Strength

At times, the direction and strength of the stock market are difficult to determine. However, reading opinions from the Internet, newspapers, magazines, and other available material can provide considerable information on strength and direction.

The Play

The "play," or theme, is usually found in the industry group or sector, such as technology, computers, the Internet, oil, healthcare, waste management, and so on. In some industries the play can be illusive, such as in fiber optics, drug rehabilitation, or lasers. The potential of lasers has excited people for more than 40 years, and yet few companies have accomplished much as "laser companies."

Play can be further complicated by a company's diversification into other industries, such as tobacco companies moving into food products.

Classifying stocks by theme, or play (merger, bad news, legal action, and others), helps to focus attention on what happens with the group. When the news headline says, "Stocks Were Up Today on Wall Street, Fueled by Strength in the Computer Technology Group," the computer investor's attention is drawn to the information. If OPEC members are fighting among themselves and producing too much oil, the prices of oil stocks drop. However, if oil-producing countries are in a cooperative mood, prices remain stable (or increase), oil company earnings increase, and the stock prices usually rise accordingly.

Earnings

The trick is to trade on the anticipation of earnings rather than on a specific earnings increase. Once the earnings increase (sometimes an earnings surprise) is announced, the price moves up immediately. Many investors buying at this point are actually buying the stock at inflated prices. When the reality of this becomes apparent, the price retreats. A small profit can quickly become a disappointing temporary loss:

Markets Slightly Up in Anticipation
of Positive Earnings Reports (AMZN, GM)

Major indices showed modest gains today as investors anticipated earnings calls from a few major corporations. In economic news, Federal Reserve numbers show that consumer credit in the US increased by more than $20 billion in the month of November, the largest increase in the past decade. In corporate news, Amazon (<u>AMZN</u>) struck a deal with Indiana's state government to start collecting state taxes there. It's the latest in a series of negotiations with state governments that the internet retailer has been involved in to face the long unaddressed issue of state sales taxes on online retailers in general. Meanwhile, General Motors (<u>GM</u>) is currently on pace to reclaim its title as biggest global auto seller, a position it has not held since Toyota (TM) dethroned it in 2008.[2]

A look at Figure 35.1 clearly shows buying in anticipation of earnings reports for both Amazon and General Motors. Amazon bumped up a bit and fell back, but once the report came out, it clearly

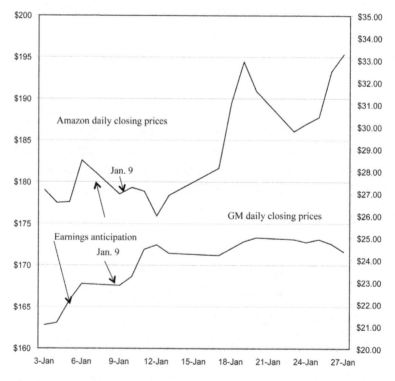

Data source: Yahoo! Finance Historical Prices

Figure 35.1   **Amazon versus General Motors, January 3–27, 2012**

was good news for the stock. GM's price rose and kept rising—a very good sign for the stock.

EARNINGS SURPRISES CAN BE NEGATIVE

Just as a positive earnings surprise can push a price higher, a negative earnings surprise can force a price lower. As stated, negative earnings surprises can even outweigh positive economic factors:

> Google's (GOOG) net revenue and earnings, though strong, fell short of analysts' expectations. The news was released on Thursday and was followed by a 8.38% drop in share price on Friday.
>
> Google's fourth-quarter profit, excluding the cost of stock options and the related tax benefits, was $9.50 a share, up from $8.75 a year ago. Analysts had expected $10.49 *a share*. Net revenue climbed to $8.13 billion from $6.37 billion a year ago. Analysts had expected net revenue of $8.4 billion.[3]

Google, Inc. (see Figure 35.2), a premier web browser, has done well as a stock since its beginning in August 2004. But even the best of companies eventually have earnings difficulties, and when Google had a problem, things happened. Notice the anticipation price drop in Figure 35.2. First a smaller drop from $668.88 to $622.46 and then a much larger drop from $639.37 to $569.49. That's a big drop ($99.39) in a short period of time. For the investor who believes in a stock like Google, Inc., this could be an excellent buying opportunity, although it might be good to see some recovery first.

A FEW GOOD STOCKS

It was in 1902 when S. A. Nelson made the statement cited in the introduction to Part 5: "It is easier to follow a few stocks well than it is to follow a well full of stocks." Nelson was an investor and as

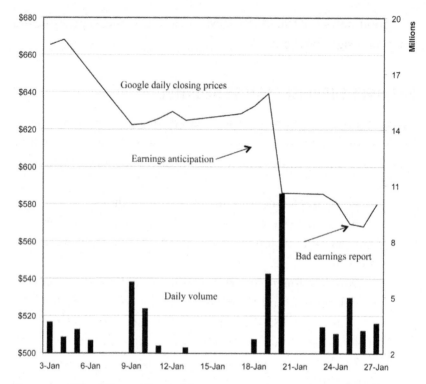

Data source: Yahoo! Finance Historical Prices

Figure 35.2 **Google, Inc., January 3–27, 2012**

noted a friend of Charles Dow. He was a publisher and an author of *The ABC of Stock Speculation*. For many years Nelson had watched investors knocking themselves out trying to analyze and track too many different stocks. When an investor analyzes too many stocks, it can lead to information overload.

Keeping up with daily changing events quickly becomes impossible and many investors are whipsawed on both sides of a price move. They buy at the top of a frenzied move and become disillusioned as the price turns and falls. Finally, they sell out at the bottom, only to see the price rise again.

The solution to information overload is to learn a great deal about a small number of stocks—the potential winners. Whether you follow three, five, or ten companies doesn't really matter. What matters is that you learn a lot about these companies. Understanding the information that will improve the price performance of these companies will enable an investor to select winners.

CHAPTER 36

Greater Risk Means Greater Potential Reward

s it true that greater risk means greater possible rewards? It is, but most people forget about the "risk" part of it and are totally shocked when their portfolio tanks. You might say the saying is sort of backwards. It should say, "Greater reward can come from greater risk."

Stocks have greater risk than bonds, but they also tend to make more money. Options and futures have greater risks than stocks, but if they are handled properly, they make considerably more money. There is a point of diminishing returns. It is here that greater risk doesn't necessarily mean that the potential reward will be higher. But the risk of losing goes much higher with these investments. There is no truly objective way to measure risk, no matter what the bank loan officers or life insurance people tell you. It's all mostly subjective—a best guess if you will. But let's look at some of the risks of owning common stock.

RISK WITH COMMON STOCK

There are three primary risks with common stock:

1. The price will trade in a narrow range and never move up.
2. The price will decline.
3. The price will go to zero.

What will likely prevent the above from happening?

1. The kind of business the stock is involved in
2. Steady increases in revenues
3. Steady increases in earnings
4. Manageable debt

To a large degree all these things are reflected in steady price growth. Although there can be times when prices run up on rumors and bandwagon emotions, it's normally not a lasting event and a reversal comes if earnings fail to fill in the picture. So what do we look for when we're trying to determine risk:

1. Steady price growth at least for the past year
2. Revenue growth and what is generating the money
3. Earnings growth and where the earnings are coming from (e.g., better revenues, layoffs, stock buybacks, etc.)

Analysis of these three things will give us a good picture of the growth strength of the company and help to estimate the risk involved. If you are dealing with investments that cannot be analyzed in this manner (i.e., derivatives, options, futures), assume that the risk is very high. But now we're looking at common stock only.

RISK METRICS

The NASDAQ website, http://www.nasdaq.com/services/riskMetrics .stm, has a risk indicator tool that measures the theoretical risk of any stock. It's called "Understanding RiskGrades" and appears to be very simple and very clever. It is free to use and shows the current risk level of the S&P 500 Index and the NASDAQ Index. It will show the risk level of any stock symbol you enter. The page has a detailed explanation of what is taken into consideration in calculating risk. The scale goes from 0 to 700 plus and graphs it in a simple straight line. Over 700 means extremely risky.

STOCKS FROM NASDAQ LIST

Table 36.1 shows some stocks from the NASDAQ Index and how they measure up.

All you have to do is make a list of stocks, usually low priced, and decide which one might bring you greater rewards. You should at least look at some of the basics to see what you are up against. Following are analyses of the two riskiest stocks shown in Table 36.1.[1]

1. Cybex International Inc. (NASDAQ: CYBI)
Current price (May 7, 2012)	$2.20
Current p/e	1.09
12-month revenues growth	+14%
12-month earnings growth	+158.80%
Debt-to-equity ratio	1.20
Type of business	Manufacturer of training and exercise equipment

2. Freeseas Inc. (NASDAQ: FREE)
Current price (May 7, 2012)	$1.03
Current p/e	−0.24
12-month revenue growth	+0.20%
12-month earnings growth	−418.10%
Debt-to-equity ratio	1.49
Type of business	Shipping company, based in Athens, Greece

Table 36.1   Risk Levels of Stocks Using Risk Metrics (May 7, 2012)[2]

Company Name	Risk Level
Bank of the Carolinas Corp. (NASDAQ: BCAR)	864
First United Corp. (NASDAQ: FUNC)	456
Cybex International Inc. (NASDAQ: CYBI)	967*
Freeseas Inc. (NASDAQ: FREE)	1,192*
Oak Ridge Financial Services Inc. (NASDAQ: BKOR)	713
Itron Inc. (NASDAQ: ITRI)	320
Apple Computer (NASDAQ: AAPL)	202
NASDAQ Index	157
S&P 500 Index	153

*The two highest-risk stocks.

Notice that in both of these companies the biggest problem is earnings. There's not enough money coming in to pay the bills and make a decent profit. To find out if these companies are viable turnarounds, one would have to find out how the income problem is being dealt with.

This is why the experts say, don't buy junk unless you can buy the whole company and turn it around. If that can be done, then greater risk would probably mean greater reward.

WHAT SOME PEOPLE SAY ABOUT RISK

Here are some quotations about risk from various sources.

"The goal is to win. It's not about making money. I have many much less risky ways of making money than this (buying Chelsea football club). I don't want to throw my money away, but it's really about having fun and that means success and trophies."

—ROMAN ABRAMOVICH,

RUSSIAN BUSINESSMAN

"Many people find vertical running frightening, and they would be right in thinking to create havoc in a company. Happily, I have always thrived on havoc and adrenaline."

—RICHARD BRANSON, ENGLISH BUSINESS MAGNATE, BEST KNOWN FOR HIS VIRGIN GROUP OF MORE THAN 400 COMPANIES

"I learned to embrace risk, as long as it was well thought out and, in a worst-case scenario, I'd still land on my feet."

—ELI BROAD, HE WAS CEO OF SUNAMERICA, NOW A SUBSIDIARY OF THE AMERICAN INTERNATIONAL GROUP, UNTIL 2000; AMERICAN BUSINESSMAN

"Risk comes from not knowing what you're doing."

—WARREN BUFFETT, AMERICAN BUSINESS MAGNATE, INVESTOR, AND PHILANTHROPIST. HE IS WIDELY CONSIDERED THE MOST SUCCESSFUL INVESTOR OF THE 20TH CENTURY.

"It's actually a relatively small number of people that really are those risk takers, and a relatively small number of people that end up really having an impact on the world."

—STEVE CASE, AMERICAN BUSINESSMAN, FOUNDER OF AOL

"Taking higher risks, such as borrowing to invest or investing in shares rather than interest-bearing securities, should, over time, magnify your returns."

—PAUL CLITHEROE, AUSTRALIAN TELEVISION PRESENTER, FINANCIAL ANALYST AND FINANCIAL ADVISOR

"To minimize risk and get the lifestyle you want by
utilizing a car means purchasing and maintaining a
safe car, using the seat belts and driving safely. To get
the lifestyle benefits (more money) from investing in
growth assets, such as shares and property, time is the
equivalent of a safety belt."

—PAUL CLITHEROE

"The greatest risk is the risk of riskless living."

—STEPHEN COVEY, AMERICAN EDUCATOR,
AUTHOR, BUSINESSMAN AND MOTIVATIONAL SPEAKER

"All economic activity is by definition "high risk." And
defending yesterday—that is, not innovating—is far
more risky than making tomorrow."

—PETER DRUCKER, INFLUENTIAL WRITER,
MANAGEMENT CONSULTANT,
AND SELF-DESCRIBED "SOCIAL ECOLOGIST"

"The value of having everybody get the complete picture
and trusting each person with it far outweighs the risk
involved."

—BILL GATES, AMERICAN BUSINESS MAGNATE,
COMPUTER PROGRAMMER, AND PHILANTHROPIST

"That it is perfectly proper to buy stocks for speculation.
There is no crime in that. When you buy stocks for
speculation it is perfectly proper to take speculative
factors into account, which are different from investment
factors."

—BEN GRAHAM, BRITISH-BORN AMERICAN
ECONOMIST AND PROFESSIONAL INVESTOR

"When somebody asserts that a stock has an earning power of so much, I am sure that the person who hears him doesn't know what he means, and there is a good chance that the man who uses it doesn't know what it means."

—BEN GRAHAM

"Most of the time common stocks are subject to irrational and excessive price fluctuations in both directions as the consequence of the ingrained tendency of most people to speculate or gamble . . . to give way to hope, fear and greed."

—BEN GRAHAM

"The stock market resembles a huge laundry in which institutions take in large blocks of each other's washing–nowadays to the tune of 30 million shares a day—without true rhyme or reason. But technologically it is remarkably well-organized."

—BEN GRAHAM

"One of the major biases in risky decision making is optimism. Optimism is a source of high-risk thinking."

—DANIEL KAHNEMAN, ISRAELI AMERICAN
PSYCHOLOGIST AND WINNER OF THE 2002 NOBEL
MEMORIAL PRIZE IN ECONOMIC SCIENCES

"Instead, to be financially free, we need to learn how to make mistakes and manage risk."

—ROBERT KIYOSAKI, AMERICAN INVESTOR,
BUSINESSMAN, SELF-HELP AUTHOR, MOTIVATIONAL
SPEAKER, FINANCIAL LITERACY ACTIVIST, AND
OCCASIONAL FINANCIAL COMMENTATOR

"Speculation is a hard and trying business, and a
speculator must be on the job all the time or he'll soon
have no job to be on."
                              —JESSE LIVERMORE, EARLY 20TH CENTURY
                                                STOCK SPECULATOR

"Investing without research is like playing stud poker
without looking at the cards."
                              —PETER LYNCH, WALL STREET STOCK INVESTOR,
                                   CURRENTLY A RESEARCH CONSULTANT
                                        AT FIDELITY INVESTMENTS

"This is not like pure science where you go 'A-ha!' and
you've got the answer. By the time you've got 'A-ha!,'
Chrysler's already quadrupled or Boeing's quadrupled.
You have to take a little bit of risk."
                                                —PETER LYNCH

"An important key to investing is to remember that
stocks are not lottery tickets."
                                                —PETER LYNCH

"Take risks. Ask big questions. Don't be afraid to make
mistakes; if you don't make mistakes, you're not reaching
far enough."
                              —DAVID PACKARD, COFOUNDER OF HEWLETT-
                         PACKARD (1939), SERVING AS PRESIDENT (1947–1964),
                         CEO (1964–1968), AND CHAIRMAN OF THE BOARD

"Don't spend your whole life working for what you don't want, instead of for what you do want. Sometimes it takes risk, it gets scary, but if you're going to do it, work toward something that matters to you."

—DR. PHIL, BEST KNOWN AS DR. PHIL, IS AN
AMERICAN TELEVISION PERSONALITY, AUTHOR,
PSYCHOLOGIST, AND THE HOST OF THE TELEVISION
SHOW *DR. PHIL*, WHICH DEBUTED IN 2002.

"To make money, you will have to take risks, even if it's just your time on the line. The key to risk-taking is knowledge."

—STUART WILDE, BEST KNOWN FOR HIS WORKS
ON METAPHYSICS, SELF-EMPOWERMENT,
AND SPIRITUALITY[3]

CHAPTER 37

Buy a Good Banking Stock
with a Nice Dividend

Some of Charles Dow's advice included that investors should buy a good banking stock. In fact he added that this would be better than trying to double one's money in a week. Banking stocks used to be the stalwarts of the financial world. They used to advertise how many billions of dollars they held in their very safe bank. Rather like McDonald's with their, "More than 10 billion sold." So, what happened?

IT ALL CHANGED

As complicated as finance and banking can be, it's difficult to pinpoint who or what caused the situation that allowed the banks to fail with their subprime mortgages. Jimmy Carter with the Community Reinvestment Act is credited with starting it, and every president since has had some hand in the banking downfall. That's the trouble when you lighten up with regulations. You lighten up by ten, and that becomes ten thousand. There's a reason why the regulations were there in the first place.

Years ago banks were not allowed to conduct business in states other than their own. The reason given was that they could get too powerful with all that money. That was done away with, and guess what happened? Not only did they become more powerful, but they went drunk crazy with all that money. As usual it's the little guy who has to pay for it all.

The best of motives were behind the action—to relax restrictions so that less wealthy people could afford to own property. Who can argue with that? The trouble is that this change touches lending institutions where they live and breathe.

MONEY CAN'T SIT AROUND

When you deposit money in a bank, it can't just sit there and do nothing. It can earn money only if it's on the move, being lent out at some kind of interest rate. This is why George Bailey in the old movie *It's a Wonderful Life* couldn't give the people their money from the Bailey Building and Loan. The money was loaned out and earning interest. It works the same today.

BANKS REALIZED SOMETHING

Banks realized that they could charge more interest money for "subprime mortgages," and the race was on. More interest being charged meant more profits, and this meant higher salaries and bonuses for everyone. If the federal government wanted the money lent out, this meant that it would help any financial institution that had a problem. Right? Well, strangely enough, yes and no. The federal government would pick and choose which bank to help.

For example, in 2008, the federal government bailed out Bear Stearns, Fannie Mae, and Freddie Mac. It bailed out the Goldman Sachs Group, Inc. (with help from Berkshire Hathaway) and American International Group. Additionally it bailed out Citigroup, Inc., and gave a "bridge loan" to General Motors Corp. and Chrysler LLC. In 2009, it was Bank of America's turn since it was taking over a failed Merrill Lynch. These are just a few of the bailouts.

The totals are staggering, a $700 billion bailout program. (See the full list of several hundreds of bailouts at *The New York Times Business.*[1])

The banks involved were not small institutions. They were the biggest and the best. What they did was nearly disastrous, but they just figured the government would bail them out and pay their all-important bonuses.

Citigroup was a nice bank stock with a good dividend until 2008. The stock price and its dividend grew at a steady pace (see Figure 37.1).

Citigroup had some trouble from 2000 to August 2002, but turned around and started a nice up trend in price to 2008. The price went from $26.00 to $56.00 in that time frame. That's moderately

Data source: Yahoo! Finance Historical Prices

Figure 37.1   **Citigroup, Inc., 2000–January 2008**

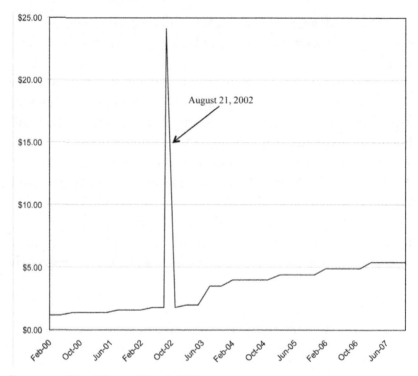

Data source: Yahoo! Finance Historical Prices

Figure 37.2   **Citigroup, Inc., Dividends, 2000–November 2007**

reasonable growth for a conservative bank stock with a good dividend. The volume surge at the end of the figure is most definitely an approaching storm. Let's take a look at that dividend for the same time period (see Figure 37.2).

The dividend in 2000 was a modest $1.20 a share. Not great, but not terrible either. All of a sudden August 21, 2002 comes along, and a whopping $24.15 is paid out, making all the individual shareholders ecstatic. Special dividends are paid by many companies occasionally. Dividends continue to increase, and by 2007 they are up to $5.40. Not too bad for a nice bank stock with a good dividend. Remember, during this time money is flowing out of the bank to people and businesses that won't be able to afford to pay it back. After all "greater risk means greater potential reward." So, in 2008,

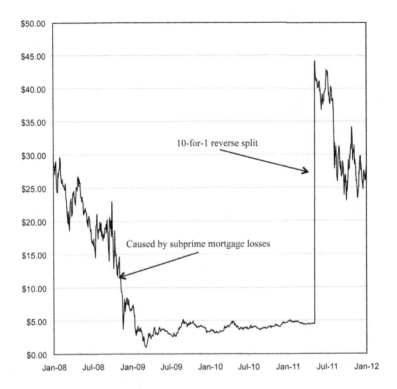

Data source: Yahoo! Finance Historical Prices

Figure 37.3 **Citigroup, Inc., 2008–January 2012**

the mud hit the fan. Take a look at what happens to that "nice bank stock, with a good dividend" (see Figure 37.3).

It makes you want to say ouch. A stock that was worth more than $500 a share just a few years ago declines to $30 a share and then all the way down to $1.22 a share. Was this a good time to buy? Some people thought so. Was it high risk? Extremely. And as if that weren't enough, the bank decided to do a 10-for-1 reverse split. Notice that the price goes from $4 a share to $44 a share and then drops to $24 a share. Ain't economics wonderful? But what about that good dividend? Take a look at Figure 37.4 and see where the dividend went.

In 2008, the dividend had already fallen to $3.20 a share. But then in October 2008, it started to fall some more. Save money;

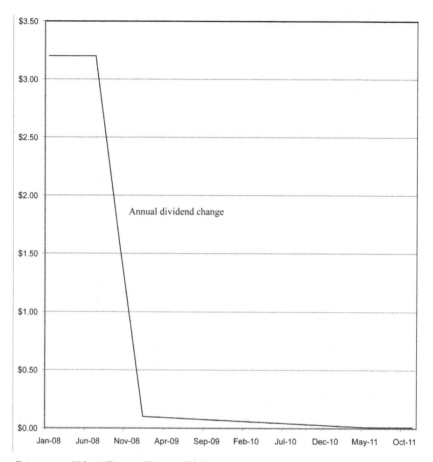

Annual dividend change

Data source: Yahoo! Finance Historical Prices

Figure 37.4   **Citigroup, Inc., Dividends, 2008–2011**

don't pay dividends. By the time it slowed in 2011, it was all the way down to a penny a share. A lousy stinking penny. Not even enough for a bubble gum machine anymore.

THE GOVERNMENT CAN'T BAIL OUT EVERYONE

Although most people would agree that the government should help out where it can, it cannot possibly hope to bail out everyone. This was possibly the largest chunk of money in the world lent out to people who couldn't afford to pay it back. This problem was compounded when the chain reaction of unemployment, lower real estate values, wars, and other conflicts came along at the same time.

NO SUCH THING AS A FOOLPROOF STOCK

Although Charles Dow was trying to come up with a basically safe stock that any investor could feel comfortable with, it just can't be done. All common stocks have risk, and you can't escape it. The same is true of all investments. That is why you should learn as much as you can about the market and investing. Then proceed with a certain amount of skepticism and caution.

CHAPTER 38

Invest in Mutual Funds, and Don't Worry About It

Mutual funds have been around for many years. The first mutual funds in the United States started in the 1890s. According to the Investment Company Institute, at the end of 2010, there were 7,581 mutual funds in the United States with combined assets of $11.8 trillion. By comparison the total dollar value of the December 2011 New York Stock Exchange was $14.242 trillion.[1]

WHAT IS A MUTUAL FUND?

Essentially, a mutual fund is a pool of money invested into several different securities, thus providing the primary advantage of diversification. Mutual funds also have some ease of investment by often allowing low contribution amounts and reasonable liquidity for buying and selling.

What Are the Main Advantages?

The primary advantages of mutual funds include:

- Greater safety with automatic diversification
- Liquidity, usually the same as with stock and other securities
- Professional management of buying, selling, or holding securities
- Participation in investments that may be available only to larger investors
- Service and convenience, such as getting regular interval payouts
- Government oversight similar to stock
- Ease of comparison of one fund's performance to another, similar to stock

What Are the Main Disadvantages?

The main disadvantages of mutual funds include:

- Fees
- Less control over timing of gains
- Less predictable income than dividends or individual stock sells
- Less opportunity to customize
- Some funds are proprietary to one provider
- Some are closed to new members
- Some funds are gigantic
- Hidden fees (soft dollars)
- Bad performance compared to the market
- Not protected from market crashes
- Buy price is based on day's closing prices
- Sell price is based on day's closing prices
- Cannot do a short sale
- Cannot use margin

A LOOK AT DIVERSIFICATION

"Don't put all your eggs in one basket." Because if you drop the basket, all is lost. The same holds true with stock or other securities. It's better to spread your money around in different securities so that if one or two perform badly, the others will be good. That's all well and good, but overdiversification can lower the fund's total return on investment. Let's look at some diversification. Following is a fund summary for T. Rowe Price (T. Rowe Price Equity Income, PRFDX):

> The investment seeks to provide substantial dividend income as well as long-term growth of capital. The fund will normally invest at least 80% of net assets (including any borrowings for investment purposes) in common stocks, with 65% in the common stocks of well established companies paying above-average dividends. It invests most assets in U.S. common stocks and may also invest in foreign stocks in keeping with the fund's objectives.[2]

The description gives a good idea of what kind of investing the fund does. Additional detailed information is available from the T. Rowe Price website at http://individual.troweprice.com/public /Retail/hUtility/Search-Results?vgnextrefresh=1.

Table 38.1 shows how performance has been for T. Rowe Price.

The table shows us a few things, perhaps the most important of which is that when the market gets hammered (as it did in 2002 and 2008), so does a mutual fund. Diversification does not protect the investor from bear markets. Second, there are times when the S&P 500 Index outperforms the mutual fund—five to be exact, as shown in Table 38.1. But also the fund outperformed the index for five years. In 2002, the fund had less of a loss at –13.04 percent compared to the index at –22.10 percent. In 2004, the fund gained 15.05 percent, with the market at 10.88 percent. Again in 2006, the fund was up 19.14 percent, with the market up only 15.79 percent.

Table 38.1   Calendar Year Total Returns: T. Rowe Price Equity Income
(PRFDX) versus S&P 500 Index

Year	Equity Income Annual Return	S&P 500 Index
2002	−13.04%	−22.10%
2003	25.78%	28.69%*
2004	15.05%	10.88%
2005	4.26%	4.91%*
2006	19.14%	15.79%
2007	3.30%	5.49%*
2008	−35.75%	−37.00%
2009	25.62%	26.46%*
2010	15.15%	15.06%
2011	−0.72%	2.05%*
10-year annualized returns	**10.59%[3]**	**2.67%[4]**

*S&P 500 outperformed the mutual fund in 5 out of 10 years.

The fund had less of a loss in 2008 than the S&P 500, with a slightly better gain in 2010. And 2011 was a disappointment for both, with the S&P 500 doing slightly better.

The 10-year annualized performance is significantly better with the mutual fund than with the S&P 500 Index. It should be, because the index has more stocks to pull down on the annual return. This is one of the problems in investing in stock index funds. Too many stocks are involved.

WHAT'S IN THE FUND?

In the old days, the only way to find out what was actually in a mutual fund was to order the information from the company. A mailed request would generally bring a prompt response. Things might have changed since the asset list was printed, but at least you were able to get some feel for what the fund contained.

Now things are different because of the Internet. Just go to your web browser financial page and enter the fund's letter symbol (for this fund it is PRFDX). When information on the fund appears, just click on "Holdings," and it will list many of the top current investments. The pages will normally list only the top 10 or top 25 holdings with general descriptions of the remainder. A complete listing of the holdings can be obtained at the company's website, but it might not be totally current. Table 38.2 shows the top 25 holdings for T. Rowe Price.

If you're thinking that checking mutual fund portfolios for stock investing targets would be a good idea, you are absolutely correct. Just remember that the information isn't usually brand new, so you have to dig a little deeper. You can see the type of stocks the fund is invested in which can help you decide if it's the best place for your money.

HOW DOES IT COMPARE?

Figure 38.1 shows price tracking on the T. Rowe Price fund and the S&P 500 Index. The fund tracks with the index quite well, although we saw in earlier performance that the numbers can vary during market volatility. The figure also illustrates that if you buy shares in the fund, buying on the dips is an excellent strategy.

WHAT ABOUT FEES?

If you are buying into the T. Rowe Price fund, the minimum initial investment is $2,500. If it's for an IRA, the minimum initial investment is $1,000. Minimum additional contributions are $100 each time.

It is a "no-load" fund, with no sales charge to buy into or get out of the fund. The annual management fee as of January 31, 2011 was at 0.70 percent, according to T. Rowe Price. The company further

Table 38.2   T. Rowe Price Equity Income (PRFDX) Top 25 Holdings
(22.9 Percent of Total Assets)[5]

Ticker	Company Name	% Net Assets	% YTD 2011 Return
N/A	Reserve Invt-SBI	3.89	n/a
CVX	Chevron Corp.	2.90	−3.39
GE	General Electric Co.	2.60	4.80
XOM	Exxon Mobil Corp.	2.39	−0.93
JPM	JPMorgan Chase & Co.	2.26	13.83
RDS.A	Royal Dutch Shell PLC ADR	1.98	−1.18
AXP	American Express Co.	1.86	7.70
T	AT&T Inc.	1.84	−0.66
WFC	Wells Fargo & Co.	1.71	8.89
USB	U.S. Bancorp	1.54	5.58
TWX	Time Warner Inc.	1.44	4.29
HD	Home Depot, Inc.	1.41	5.78
JNJ	Johnson & Johnson	1.41	0.17
MMM	3M Co.	1.39	6.88
MSFT	Microsoft Corporation	1.31	15.14
ETR	Entergy Corp.	1.24	−5.01
PFE	Pfizer Corp.	1.24	−0.51
KMB	Kimberly-Clark Corporation	1.21	−2.05
IP	International Paper Co.	1.21	6.01
DIS	Walt Disney Company	1.20	4.88
MUR	Murphy Oil Corporation	1.19	6.44
EXC	Exelon Corp.	1.17	−8.37
MRK	Merck & Co. Inc.	1.16	−8.37
APC	Anadarko Petroleum Corp.	1.13	5.48
MMC	Marsh & McLennan Companies, Inc.	1.12	2.21

Data source: Yahoo! Finance Historical Prices

Figure 38.1   T. Rowe Price Equity Income Fund versus S&P 500 Index

states that the fee is expressed as an annualized percentage of the total assets and is what shareholders pay for mutual fund operating expenses and management fees. The size of the fund is $37.5 billion. The expense ratio is disclosed in the prospectus.

SOFT DOLLARS (HIDDEN FEES)

Mutual funds and other institutional investors can have "soft dollars" hidden in their transaction fees. This directly affects the gain for the investor and is probably impossible to detect and measure:

> In soft dollar arrangements, the brokerage commissions are
> higher than they would be for an "execution only" trading

relationship, and over time investment performance may suffer by that higher commission cost. Because institutional funds can trade a significant number of shares every day, the soft dollars add-up quickly. The amount of soft dollars institutional funds use is quite high (estimated in 2007 to be in excess of 11 billion dollars). (Note that soft dollar amounts do not have to be disclosed to anyone, not even the agencies responsible for oversight, so only estimates are available.) Because hard dollars eventually end up being reported as part of the management fee the fund charges its investors, soft dollar transactions are also a way for funds to lower their apparent fees (even though investors pay for the expense). But, over time, investment performance will deteriorate if the soft dollars are not used to purchase research that enhances performance. And the performance of individual investment accounts will deteriorate if the benefits of the services are not allocated back to the accounts that paid the extra commissions for the services.[6]

At this time soft dollars are just a part of the cost of doing business with a mutual fund. If you are buying your own stock, this is obviously not a problem.

COMMISSIONS PAID

There are a number of different ways of charging investors to buy into a mutual fund. Typical share classes for funds sold through brokers or other intermediaries are:

1. Class A shares usually charge a front-end sales load together with a small 12b-1 fee.
2. Class B shares don't have a front-end sales load. Instead they have a high contingent deferred sales charge, or CDSC, that declines gradually over several years, combined with a high 12b-1 fee. Class B shares usually

convert automatically to Class A shares after they have been held for a certain period.

3. Class C shares have a high 12b-1 fee and a modest contingent deferred sales charge that is discontinued after one or two years. Class C shares usually do not convert to another class. They are often called "level load" shares.

4. Class I shares are subject to very high minimum investment requirements and are, therefore, known as "institutional" shares.

5. Class R shares are for use in retirement plans such as 401(k) plans. They do not charge loads, but they do charge a small 12b-1 fee.

6. No-load funds often have two classes of shares:
   a. Class I shares do not charge a 12b-1 fee.
   b. Class N shares charge a 12b-1 fee of no more than 0.25 percent of fund assets.

   Neither class of shares charges a front-end or back-end load.[7]

(Note: 12b-1 refers to a withdrawal charge that declines over time. Classes A and B refer to voting rights and Class C refers to a constant sales load structure.)

BUY AND SELL PRICES

With mutual funds, you buy and sell shares based on the closing price of the day. This tradition goes back to before the age of good computers. It was virtually impossible to come up with an accurate price during the day, when all the prices are constantly changing. The tradition continues. Obviously this means that you can't day trade mutual funds.

Note that exchange-traded mutual funds (ETFs) are bought and sold on the stock exchange just like regular common stock.

Therefore, they follow the same rules as common stock and are not bound by the restrictions of mutual funds.

TYPES OF MUTUAL FUNDS

There are many different types of mutual funds, and within the categories many have different objectives. Learn about the type of fund you are considering and its objective. Following are some of the types of mutual funds.

Open-End Funds

By regulation and practice, open-end mutual funds must be willing to buy back their shares from their investors at the end of every business day at the net asset value (NAV) computed that day. Net asset value is the total money the fund is worth, divided by the number of shares outstanding. Most open-end funds also sell shares to the public every trading day; these shares are also priced at the NAV. A professional investment manager manages the portfolio by buying and selling securities as appropriate. The total investment in the fund will vary based on share purchases, share redemptions, and fluctuation in market. Any number of shares in the fund can be sold to investors.

Closed-End Funds

Closed-end funds issue shares to the public once, when they are created through an initial public offering (similar to shares of a company's stock). Their shares are then listed for trading on a stock exchange. Investors who no longer wish to invest in the fund sell their shares to another investor in the market; the price they receive may be significantly different from net asset value. It may be at a "premium" to net asset value (meaning that it is higher than net asset value) or, more commonly, at a "discount" to net asset value (meaning that it is lower than net asset value). Like common stock the price of the fund's shares are determined by the market activity. A professional investment manager oversees the portfolio, buying and selling securities.

UNIT INVESTMENT TRUSTS

Unit investment trusts (UITs) issue shares to the public only once, when they are created. Investors can redeem shares directly with the fund (as with an open-end fund), or they may also be able to sell their shares in the market. Unit investment trusts do not have a professional investment manager. Their portfolio of securities is established at the creation of the UIT and does not change. Some allow substitution of securities if one closes out (such as a company being bought out or going under). UITs usually have a close-out date set at the time of the fund's creation.

Exchange-Traded Funds

The exchange-traded fund (ETF) is often structured as an open-end investment company, although ETFs may also be structured as unit investment trusts, partnerships, investment trusts, grantor trusts, or bonds (as an exchange-traded note). ETFs combine characteristics of both closed-end funds and open-end funds. Like closed-end funds, ETFs are traded throughout the day on a stock exchange at a price determined by the market. However, as with open-end funds, investors normally receive a price that is close to net asset value. To keep the market price close to net asset value, ETFs issue and redeem large blocks of their shares with institutional investors.

INVESTMENTS AND CLASSIFICATION

Mutual funds follow a basic structure based on what the fund will do and will not for its investments. Their objectives are managed by a portfolio manager who is supported by a team of market analysts. There are many different kinds of funds.

Mutual funds may invest in many kinds of securities. The types of securities that a particular fund may invest in are set forth in the fund's prospectus, which describes the fund's investment objective, investment approach and permitted investments. The investment objective describes the type of income that the fund seeks. For example, a "capital appreciation" fund generally looks to earn most of its returns from increases in the prices of the securities it holds, rather than from dividend or interest income. The investment approach describes the criteria that the fund manager uses to select investments for the fund.

A mutual fund's investment portfolio is continually monitored by the fund's portfolio manager or managers, who are employed by the fund's manager or sponsor.

Mutual funds are classified by their principal investments. The four largest categories of funds are money market funds, bond or fixed income funds, stock or equity funds and hybrid funds. Within these categories, funds may be sub-classified by investment objective, investment approach or specific focus. The SEC requires that mutual fund names not be inconsistent with a fund's investments. For example, the "ABC New Jersey Tax-Exempt Bond Fund" would generally have to invest, under normal circumstances, at least 80 percent of its assets in bonds that are exempt from federal income tax, from the alternative minimum tax and from taxes in the state of New Jersey.[8]

Bond, stock, and hybrid funds may be classified as either index (passively managed) funds or actively managed funds.

Money Market Funds

Perhaps the most familiar mutual fund is the simple money market fund. It is usually attached to a brokerage account and used to earn interest on amounts of cash that might be temporarily parked in the account waiting to be used for a stock or other securities purchase.

The following is a more detailed description of what they are and how they work.

> Money market funds invest in money market instruments, which are fixed income securities with a very short time to maturity and high credit quality. Investors often use money market funds as a substitute for bank savings accounts, though money market funds are not government insured, unlike bank savings accounts.
>
> Money market funds strive to maintain a $1.00 per share net asset value, meaning that investors earn interest income from the fund but do not experience capital gains or losses. If a fund fails to maintain that $1.00 per share because its securities have declined in value, it is said to "break the buck." Only two money market funds have ever broken the buck: Community Banker's U.S. Government Money Market Fund in 1994 and the Reserve Primary Fund in 2008.[9]

Bond Funds

Bond funds invest in fixed income securities. Bond funds can be subclassified according to the specific types of bonds owned (such as high yield or junk bonds, investment-grade corporate bonds, government bonds, or municipal bonds) or by the maturity of the bonds held (short term, intermediate, or long term). Bond funds may invest in primarily U.S. securities (domestic or U.S. funds), in both U.S. and foreign securities (global or world funds), or primarily foreign securities (international funds).

One of the problems with open-end bond funds is that they effectively never mature. They may contain bonds that reach maturity, but those bonds are immediately replaced by others. This means that they will fluctuate both in value and yield. An actual bond or a closed-end fund keeps the same yield until maturity and will mature at face value. Also, many bond funds are allowed to trade derivatives to enhance their yield. This can make them be a higher risk.

Stock Funds

Stock funds (sometimes called equity funds) invest in common stocks. Stock funds may invest in U.S. securities (domestic or U.S. funds), in both U.S. and foreign securities (global or world funds), or foreign securities (international funds). They may focus on a particular industry or sector.

Stock funds may be subdivided along two dimensions:

1. Market capitalization
2. Investment style (i.e., growth vs. blend/core vs. value)

The two styles are displayed in a grid known as a "style box."

Market capitalization tells the size of the companies a fund invests in, based on the value of the companies' stock times the number of shares. Market capitalizations are typically divided into the following categories:

- Micro cap
- Small cap
- Mid cap
- Large cap

While the specific definitions of each category vary with market conditions, micro cap stocks usually have market capitalizations below $300 million, small cap stocks have market capitalizations below $2 billion, medium cap between $2 and $10 billion, and large cap stocks generally have market capitalizations of at least $10 billion. Funds are also classified in these categories based on the market caps of the stocks that it holds.

Stock funds are also subclassified according to their investment style: growth, value, or blend (or core). Growth funds seek to invest in stocks of fast-growing companies. Value funds seek to invest in stocks that appear cheaply priced. Blend funds are not biased toward either growth or value.

Hybrid Funds

Hybrid funds invest in both bonds and stocks or in convertible securities. Balanced funds, asset allocation funds, target date or target risk funds, and lifecycle or lifestyle funds are all types of hybrid funds.

Hybrid funds can be set up as funds of funds, meaning that they invest by buying shares in other mutual funds that invest in securities. Most funds of funds invest in affiliated funds (funds managed by the same fund sponsor), although some invest in unaffiliated funds (managed by other fund sponsors) or in a combination of the two.

Funds investing in funds can have some difficulties trying to avoid duplication. This obviously limits their selections. But they hire teams of experts to deal with these problems.

Index Funds (Passively Managed) and Actively Managed Funds

An index fund or passively managed fund attempts to match the performance of a market index, such as the S&P 500 Index, while an actively managed fund seeks to outperform a relevant index, through improved security selection.

As an index the S&P 500 represents a good portion of the stock market, but not all the stocks are winners. Therefore, some managers take the index as a benchmark and improve on it, hoping to beat the index performance.

A LOT TO KNOW

This is a lot to know. Most investors who are essentially forced into a group of mutual funds with their retirement plan at work usually have little idea what their money is in or what other choices are available. That's not good. Take the time to find out. Companies generally have meetings to explain what's available or at least have a phone number or e-mail address where you can get information.

You have worked very hard for that money, and your future may depend on the results of your investment, so take the time to find out what it is and what might be better for your specific situation.

CHAPTER 39

Invest in What You Know Best

Know thyself.

—SOCRATES

Diversification in an investment portfolio is always advisable; however, investing in an industry or a company where you have been employed can be profitable as well. If you work in the auto industry, for instance, it is logical for you to do some investing in automobile stocks. Someone who has worked for Ford Motor Company for several years will undoubtedly have special insight into how the company works. With that background, an investor could also have a unique understanding of the vendors used by Ford. Working directly with a supplier provides knowledge of a company's ability to supply products and services that could be worth more than spending numerous hours analyzing that vendor's balance sheet.

A pharmacist should have insight into the potential growth of pharmaceutical companies, and an electrical engineer could do well investing in high-tech companies. Investing in companies related to the investor's background is logical, but it is not done often. Doctors invest in aerospace stocks, aerospace engineers invest in drug companies, and drug company employees invest in high-tech computer companies.

SIGNIFICANCE VERSUS PUBLIC RELATIONS

We're all more or less vulnerable to public relations, and since most investors are unfamiliar with what's real and what is window dressing, it is difficult to discern what information is significant. However, the same people often have tremendous firsthand knowledge about the workings of their own industry. They might have 10 or 20 years of experience—experience that can be used as a basis for analysis. Their work experience gives them advantages not available to the stock analyst. Most good analysts would love the opportunity to work for 30 days in the companies they follow and do the work incognito. The knowledge gained would be priceless. However, analysts do not have the time for such an activity, much less the opportunity.

When investors already have the work experience, it only makes sense to make good use of the knowledge. If the stocks they select do well, consider the profits a work-related bonus for using job-related information.

KEEP AN EYE ON COMPETITION

Competitive companies might even be better stock targets. People sometimes know more about the competition than they do about their own companies. A person working for IBM might actually know more about Compaq, just as the Compaq employee might well know that IMB's most recent development will generate strong sales.

Investing in the stock of a competitor can be an excellent strategy. It offers these advantages:

- No emotional involvement
- Early observation of developments

- Easily followed financial growth
- Insight into problems

Investing in the stock of companies with which one has practical working knowledge will not guarantee success, but it can make the analysis more meaningful and improve the chances of success. In addition, an investor can keep an eye on the competition's successes and failures, which will also be a valuable resource for the investor's regular employment.

SHOULD YOU OWN STOCK IN YOUR OWN COMPANY?

Deciding whether to own stock in the company you work for depends on what shape your company is in at the current time. Obviously, if your company is in good shape and growing at a steady pace, you'll want to own some stock. If it's not doing so well and you are looking for a new job, maybe sell off the stock. In either case, your company should never be your only investment. Terrible surprises can be looming over the horizon, surprises that can reduce your stock investment to zero.

Look at the poor employees at Enron back in 2000 and 2001, more than 20,000 employees. Shareholders lost nearly $11 billion when Enron's stock price, which hit a high of $90 per share in mid-2000, fell to less than $1 by the end of November 2001. They were terribly blindsided. So, yes, own some of your own employer's stock, but diversify too. Own some stock in other companies.

The authors of the recent study, "Do Individual Investors Have Asymmetric Information Based on Work Experience?," put the theory to the test:

> The goal of the study was to see if individual investors preferred "professionally close" stocks (meaning stocks of companies in fields related to their profession) and if they could outperform a benchmark essentially by buying what they

know. The study also looked at the performance of investors buying stock of the companies they work for, as well as other companies near where they live. The following is a summary of their findings:

- Individuals failed to diversify their human capital, over-weighting stocks in their industry of employment.
- Individuals didn't earn abnormal returns when trading professionally close stocks. On a one-year level, a port-folio of stocks related to investors' areas of expertise had a negative alpha of about 5 percent (meaning investors performed worse than the benchmark). Also, the stocks they sold outperformed the stocks they bought by about 4 percent annually.
- Individuals traded excessively in professionally close stocks, showing that investors felt more confident trading stocks of companies they knew.
- Advanced degrees didn't provide any benefit. Those with a Ph.D. didn't generate abnormal returns.
- Local proximity provided no advantage.

The authors concluded: "Our findings are consistent with both familiarity and overconfidence being the behavioral driver behind our results."[1]

The study does not invalidate the concept of buying stock in the company you work for, but it does raise some important considerations about investing in what you know or think you know.

LOOK FIRST AT WHAT YOU KNOW

The learning curve regarding investing is steep, and mistakes can be costly. Investing in companies an investor knows and under-stands significantly reduces the amount of information that must be learned. This can lead to quick understanding and fast decisions when it comes time to buy or sell the stock.

As the study above suggests, there is a caution that comes along with this and this is to be careful not to be too emotionally involved with stock of companies you know. You still have to do basic analysis to measure performance and trends. It's possible to believe too strongly in their capabilities. Keep your normal market skepticism that you would have with a company you know nothing about. Base your decisions on analysis of the facts and not on emotions. In the words of Peter Lynch, former fund manager of Fidelity Magellan: "Your investor's edge is not something you get from Wall Street experts. It's something you already have. You can outperform the experts if you use your edge by investing in companies or industries you already understand."[2]

IF YOU DON'T KNOW IT, LEARN IT

Take the time to understand what the investment is and what the money is invested in. Know how it works for you. Normally it doesn't take much time, and it becomes quite interesting as you delve into the information.

ESPECIALLY KNOW YOUR RETIREMENT PROGRAM

Ask most people what's in their retirement program, and either they don't know or they'll say some mutual fund. They have no idea what's in the fund or what its objectives are. They stay in the same fund their company put them in at the beginning. Most likely the fund or funds are far too conservative, aren't making much money, and never will.

When most companies start employees out on a retirement program, they choose the most conservative investment. The trouble is that the employees never get around to changing to a program that will better fit their needs. The funds chosen are nicely conservative, but too much so. If you have such funds, at least take the short time to find out what their investment objectives are and what is in them. It's important.

Part 6

CAUTION

The first chapter in this part, Give Stop Orders Wiggle Room, simply means to place a stop order far enough away for the current trading price so that it doesn't tempt the specialist into execution of the order. Although sell stops are used, the preference is that they never be executed. On the other side, when buying, you want buy stops filled only when the stock price is having a strong upward movement.

No matter what the indicators are currently saying, it's inevitable that something can happen to completely override and overrun them. A perfect example was the terrorist attack on the New York World Trade Center. A market that was beginning to indicate recovery from an economic recession suddenly turned south again. More recently, the credit rating downgrade on U.S. Treasury debt overrode the indicators, even when we knew it was likely to happen.

The investor should always be wary of "penny stocks." There is a reason that the price is that low. Unless you want to buy a controlling interest and manage the company (not recommended), stay away from this kind of investment, no matter how tempting.

Simple advice, like be wary of stock tips (from anyone) or be careful with a margin account, is basic common sense. Many people are completely caught by surprise with their first margin call, and that should not be the case. Margin calls happen only when the margined stock price is moving, information that is constantly available.

Is the "triple (quadruple as of 2008) witching hour" of options and futures expirations still a threat to stock market stability, or has that also changed? The effects of it for 2011 and the future are examined.

CHAPTER 40

Give Stop Orders
Wiggle Room

A "stop order" is an order to buy or sell stock when it reaches or passes a predetermined price. Buy stop orders are placed above the current trading price, and sell stop orders are placed below the current price. Once activated, the stop order becomes a market order that says that the broker will make the trade at the best available price.

If you believe that the price of a stock is going to drop an unacceptable amount, sell the stock. Don't even consider a stop order. Why give the money away when you don't have to? This is the most important rule of all sell stop orders. They should be used carefully and cautiously during times of uncertainty.

WHEN USING STOPS

Wiggle room is important when you are placing stop orders, whether buying or selling stock. Essentially, it allows the stock price to move in "normal" market swings without activating the stop. Allowing for wiggle room means placing the stop order close enough to the current price to prevent a loss on a sell or activate a buy on an upward move, but far enough from the current price so that it will be triggered only by a larger-than-normal move. Orders are activated as market orders (unless limits are added) when the price is traded on or past the stop price.

When buying, the investor wants the buy stop to be activated only if the stock price is making a strong move upward. On the other side, no one really wants the sell stop order to be filled unless the price is declining at a disturbing rate. Consequently, the buy stop is usually placed closer to the current trading range than is the sell stop. It is good to give the sell stop enough room for the price to fall during a small market correction without activating the stop.

SELL STOP

Some people say to place a sell stop $2 away from the current price; others say take losses at 10 percent. The problem with these solutions is the probability that the orders will be executed. The $2 sell stop is so close to the current price that the exchange specialist can easily be tempted to tick the price down and execute the order. The specialist is allowed to do just that. And locking all stops into a 10 percent loss is also not a good idea. Some stock prices will swing 10 percent every week; others every day. Instead, what does make sense is to look at a price chart, such as the one shown in Figure 40.1, to see the price trading range for Kraft Foods, Inc. (NYSE: KFT).

A possible level for a stop sell order on Kraft Foods, Inc. (Figure 40.1), would be about $32 a share. This is below the strong support level of $34 and $35 a share. If the stock price falls through that support, it's headed for the next support at $31 a share. Falling through that level could result in significant losses since the current price is at $38.47 a share. At this point, it would not be a good idea to raise the sell stop above the $32 level. Even that is relatively close to the current price and could be unexpectedly executed.

The point here is that looking at a graph of the stock prices gives you a realistic idea of where to put a stop loss order and give it enough wiggle room. Stop loss orders should be used for unexpected emergency price declines only. They should not be used as a way to

Strong support

Sell stop at about $32 a share, January 2012

Data source: Yahoo! Finance Historical Prices

Figure 40.1 **Kraft Foods, Inc., 2011–January 2012**

sell stock. If the price is moving down gradually, either sell the stock at the market price or remove the sell stop order if you believe the downward movement to be a temporary situation.

TRAILING STOP

As discussed in Chapter 10, the trailing stop order might be the route to go. It has an advantage with a stock that has a rising price and will help to protect profits without having to continually be reentered. It is similar to the stop loss order, but you use it to protect a profit as opposed to protecting against a loss. If you have a profit in a stock, you can use the trailing stop order to follow it up. You enter the trailing stop order as a percentage of the market price. If the market price declines by that percentage, the trailing stop becomes a market order, and your broker sells the stock. If the stock continues to rise, the trailing stop follows it up since it is a percentage of the market price. This protects your additional gains. A trailing stop order also needs a certain amount of wiggle room.

AN ALTERNATIVE OPTION

Instead of a stop loss order, an investor can buy a "protective put" which leaves the control in the hands of the investor instead of giving it to the market:

> Many investors employ stop loss techniques to reduce their loss or to capture an unrealized gain. Stop loss prices can be set at or below recent lows, or based on the volatility of the stock or at a set percent that the investor does not wish to lose.
>
> Protective put options offer investors another way to reduce the risk of a loss in their stock. Buying an out-of-the-money put where the strike price is just below the stock price, gives the investor the lowest price they can sell their stock. If the stock falls below the strike price, you can still sell your shares at the strike price. On the other hand, you can sell the put option since it will have risen in price as the price of the underlying shares fall. Many professional investors use protective put options.[1]

The disadvantages are that the investor has to pay for the puts, and they will eventually expire and have to be replaced. But even so, it could be worth the extra hassle just to have the protection and the control.

BUY STOP

A buy stop is an aggressive buying approach that says you want to buy the stock only when the price is making a significant advance.

Unlike the sell stop, this is an order you want to see executed but only if the price is moving.

Placing the buy stop order also requires some study of the current trading range. The distance to establish between the buy stop price and the current trading price of the stock is a matter of personal decision, but it should be at least partially based on trading range analysis. A price chart can be of great assistance in selecting a good buy stop price. Just remember that the ideal situation is to catch the stock as the price moves and continues upward.

Look at the price of Apple Computer during the first half of 2011 (Figure 40.2). The price traded in a narrow range between $330 and $360 a share. Then in June it dropped to $315.32. Most

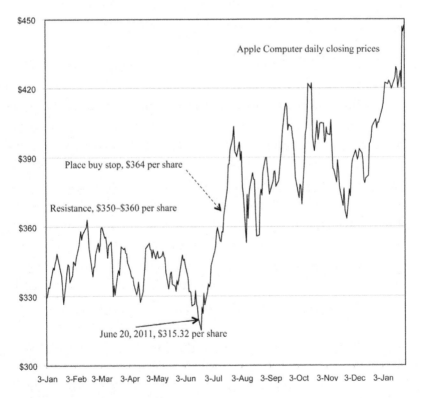

Data source: Yahoo! Finance Historical Prices

Figure 40.2   Apple Computer, Inc., 2011–January 2012

people didn't believe it would stay there, so placing a buy stop just above the $360 resistance made sense. If it broke through that resistance, in all likelihood the price would keep climbing. That is just what it did—it broke through resistance and went up all the way to $446.66, a very nice advance for the second half of 2011 into 2012.

LIKE MEDICINE, USE ONLY WHEN NECESSARY

An important point to remember about the use of buy or sell stop orders is: if you believe a price will go up or will weaken and fall, forget using a stop and place a market order to buy or sell. It doesn't make sense to give the money away. Stops should be used only if there is considerable uncertainty or you'll be out of town for the next month (in which case you shouldn't have an order in).

GOOD TILL CANCELED

Stop orders should be entered good till canceled (GTC), see Chapter 33 for a full explanation of GTC. Find out how long the GTC order will remain open since the term has different meanings to various brokerage firms. Some orders stay in until the end of the month; others are canceled in a month. Stop orders can also be changed. They can be raised on the sell side if the price keeps rising or lowered on the buy side. A recent price chart should be consulted before an order is changed.

The sell stop can provide protection for profits, and it can also limit loss in a severe decline. But remember that it should be far enough away from the current price to avoid having it triggered by a minor move. It needs wiggle room.

The buy stop can be placed closer to the current price because it is an order the investor wants triggered. Limit prices can also be placed on stops, but the limits might prevent the order from being filled. However, with a buy stop, a limit order can prevent the order from being filled on a sudden price move resulting from a takeover announcement.

CHAPTER 41

Indicators Can Meet Overriding Factors

No matter what the current indicators are saying, they
can be overridden by other, unexpected factors.

—S. A. NELSON

At the end of July 2011, things were looking good. We appeared to be climbing out of the bear market of 2008, moving on to the next bull market (see Figure 41.1). Volume was a little light but not a big concern. The government and President Obama threw some money at some problems, and things were looking better.

Basically, the stock market indicators weren't looking great, but they were looking better. Then came the announcement from Standard & Poor's that it was lowering the AAA rating on the debt of the United States to AA+. Many people would say that it was long overdue and more than fair:

Wall Street had its worst day since the 2008 financial crisis, as fearful investors reacted to the United States losing its coveted AAA credit rating. All three major U.S. stock indexes sank between 5% and 7%, pushing the Dow below 11,000 for the first time since last November. U.S. stocks

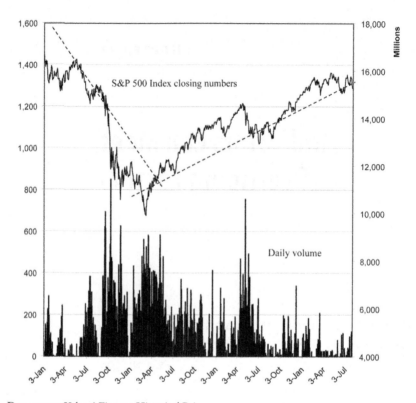

Data source: Yahoo! Finance Historical Prices

Figure 41.1   **S&P 500 Index, 2008–July 2011**

have fallen 15% during the past two weeks. Though observers said S&P's downgrade shouldn't matter all that much, the market wasn't buying it.

"Investors are having one reaction to the downgrade: sell first and ask questions later," said Paul Zemsky, head of asset allocation with ING Investment Management.

Even if investors dismissed the downgrade, they'd still have to contend with the European debt crisis and rising fears of a new U.S. recession. Those are the factors that led to a drop of more than 6% last week, the worst since the financial crisis of 2008. The Dow Jones industrial average (INDU) sank 635 points, or 5.6%, to 10,810. The S&P 500

(SPX) lost 80 points, or 6.7%, to 1,120. And the Nasdaq Composite (COMP) dropped 175 points, or 6.9%, to 2,358. Few companies were spared. All members of the Dow 30 and all members of the S&P 500 traded lower.[1]

Talk about your indicators being overridden. Nothing does it quite like an S&P downgrade. Standard & Poor's is one of the premium raters of debt instruments in the world. It publishes research and analysis of stocks and bonds and is owned by McGraw-Hill. It is one of the big three rating agencies, along with Moody's Investor Service and Fitch's Ratings.

LONG-TERM CREDIT RATINGS

Standard & Poor's rates borrowers on a scale from AAA to D. Intermediate ratings are offered at each level between AA and CCC (e.g., BBB+, BBB, and BBB–). For some borrowers, the company may also offer guidance (termed a "credit watch") as to whether it is likely to be upgraded (positive), downgraded (negative), or uncertain (neutral).

Here is a look at the details of Standard and Poor's debt ratings and how they are determined.

Investment Grade

AAA: An obligor rated AAA has extremely strong capacity to meet its financial commitments. AAA is the highest issuer credit rating assigned by Standard & Poor's.

AA: An obligor rated AA has very strong capacity to meet its financial commitments. It differs from the highest-rated obligors only to a small degree. Includes:

AA+:   Equivalent to Moody's Aa1 (high quality, with very low credit risk, but susceptibility to long-term risks appears somewhat greater)

AA: Equivalent to Aa2

AA–:   Equivalent to Aa3

A: An obligor rated A has strong capacity to meet its financial commitments but is somewhat more susceptible to the adverse effects of changes in circumstances and economic conditions than obligors in higher-rated categories.

A+:   Equivalent to A1

A: Equivalent to A2

BBB: An obligor rated BBB has adequate capacity to meet its financial commitments. However, adverse economic conditions or changing circumstances are more likely to lead to a weakened capacity of the obligor to meet its financial commitments.

Non-Investment Grade (Also Known as Junk Bonds)

BB: An obligor rated BB is less vulnerable in the near term than other lower-rated obligors. However, it faces major ongoing uncertainties and exposure to adverse business, financial, or economic conditions, which could lead to the obligor's inadequate capacity to meet its financial commitments.

B: An obligor rated B is more vulnerable than the obligors rated BB, but the obligor currently has the capacity to meet its financial commitments. Adverse business, financial, or economic conditions will likely impair the obligor's capacity or willingness to meet its financial commitments.

CCC: An obligor rated CCC is currently vulnerable, and is dependent upon favorable business, financial, and economic conditions to meet its financial commitments.

CC: An obligor rated CC is currently highly vulnerable.

C: Highly vulnerable, perhaps in bankruptcy or in arrears but still continuing to pay out on obligations

CI: Past due on interest

R: An obligor rated R is under regulatory supervision owing to its financial condition. During the pendency of the regulatory supervision, the regulators may have the power to favor one class of obligations over others or pay some obligations and not others.

SD: Has selectively defaulted on some obligations

D: Has defaulted on obligations and S&P believes that it will generally default on most or all obligations

NR: Not rated[2]

There are also short-term issue credit ratings not shown here.

So a look at the meaning of a Standard & Poor's downgrade shows what caused the stock market to panic. Up until this point the U.S. credit rating had always been AAA, which meant that it was the highest grade debt available. U.S. government debt is always backed by the "full faith and credit of the United States Government," all of which means that it's backed by the government's ability to raise taxes if necessary to pay off the debt.

Effectively the downgrade is saying there is doubt that the U.S. government can raise enough taxes to service or pay off the huge amount of debt.

Take a look at Figure 41.2 to see the effect the downgrade had on the S&P 500.

It was ouch, ouch, ouch all the way down. The indicators weren't just overwhelmed; they were hit by a tsunami. The biggest surprise is that there wasn't more damage done. One moderating factor was probably the preliminary news warning that such a downgrade could be coming soon. This from *The Wall Street Journal*, August 6, 2011:

> The downgrade from S&P has been brewing for months. S&P's sovereign debt team, led by company veteran David T. Beers, had grown increasingly skeptical that Washington policy makers would make significant progress in reducing the deficit, given the tortured talks over raising the debt ceiling. In recent warnings, the company said Washington should strive to reduce the deficit by $4 trillion over 10 years, suggesting anything less would be insufficient.[3]

So the stock market had partly discounted the fact that the rating would probably be downgraded. This is just one example of the kind of bad news that has the power to override positive stock market indicators. In 2011 and the first half of 2012, foreign debt problems and employment problems around the world have also had their

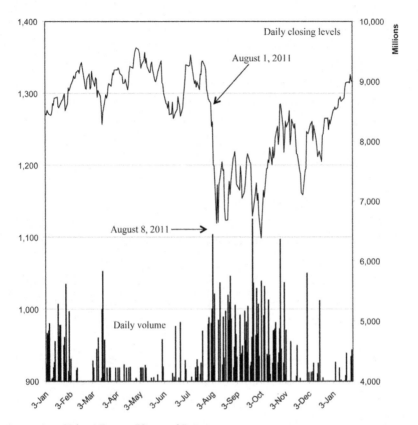

Data source: Yahoo! Finance Historical Prices

Figure 41.2   **S&P 500 Index, 2011–January 2012**

daily effect on the market. A lot of it was bad news one or two days and good news the next, all of which influenced the stock market.

Here is a list of some other possible overrides:

- Funding for a large project (such as a corporate takeover) can fail to materialize at the last minute, sending the entire market into a spin.
- A U. S. Treasury bond auction might not go as well as expected, thereby causing interest rates to rise.
- Unemployment data showing that it is a growing problem.

- An earthquake, flood, fire, hurricane, or other natural calamity can unexpectedly send the market down.
- War or a related event can break out and have negative global economic situations.
- Oil from the Middle East can become threatened.
- A national scandal can appear in the news.
- The U. S. dollar can weaken and fall too low, or strengthen and rise too high.
- Interest rates might be raised with the intention of slowing the economy.
- Economic distress in places other than the United States (such as the Asian crises in 1998) can have a negative impact on our stock market.
- An economic indicator such as the producer price index (PPI), housing starts, or even inflation might be worse than expected.

Any of these events, as well as others, can appear suddenly and cause the stock market to change direction. It can happen even when all indicators are showing a strong and stable market.

CURRENT EVENTS AND THE MARKET

It has been said that "information makes the market." More accurately, it is the reaction to the information that makes the market. The reaction is partly anticipation. The stock market will often rise on good news and fall on bad news. When the bad news is expected, the market often ignores information because it has already been discounted. The market made its adjustment before the news appeared.

The kind of current events having an effect on the stock market are something like these:

- *Internal developments:* Hyper-speed computerized sell-offs
- *World events:* Debt and problems in other countries

- *Inflation and interest rates:* Going up or stagnating
- *Exchange rates:* Always on the move, sometimes negative
- *Hype:* Always a problem of some kind or another

Understanding the economic implications of the news can help the investor know what to expect in the stock market. It's important to know what scares investors and what gets them excited with anticipation. The knowledge can help the investor comprehend the sudden market corrections or rallies.

Indicators, whether technical or fundamental, are important but they can be overridden by other events or situations.

CHAPTER 42

Beware the Penny Stock

Penny stocks are defined as stocks with a price per share of less than $5 (or less than $1 in some cases). Many of them trade on the OTC/BB (Over the Counter, Bulletin Board) stock exchanges, where they are sometimes known as pink sheet stocks, and they might have symbol extensions like .PK or .OB.

Penny stocks have certain characteristics:

1. The price per share is low, usually $5 or less, but can be higher.
2. The price will often go lower than anyone can imagine.
3. The low price makes these stocks targets for manipulation.
4. The stocks tend to trade "thinly," sometimes going for weeks without a buy or sell.
5. At times it's nearly impossible to find buyers for investors wanting to sell.
6. Reverse splits of 10-for-1 happen occasionally to boost the price.
7. The risk is exceptionally high.

VOLATILITY

A typical "blue-chip" stock with a price of $20 will typically fluctuate by only 1 to 2 percent per day, while a penny stock could easily go up or down 10 or 20 percent or more. In fact, it is not uncommon to lose 80 percent of your investment within a week!

SCAMS

"Alert! XYZ is at $0.024 and is expected to hit $0.35 at the end of the week!" You have probably received several e-mails like this. Penny stocks are subject to frequent spam e-mail attacks.

In the classic "pump and dump" scheme, a person or company will buy some stock and then e-mail thousands of people telling them that stock is going to go up a large amount. Many readers of this e-mail will buy that stock, causing the price to go up dramatically because of the law of supply and demand.

Investors erroneously think they are buying regular stock, like 3M or Coke, only at low prices, but they are not. Many of these stocks barely exist and don't have much of a real business behind them. They are in a class by themselves.

Once the stock price has gone up, the scammer will sell his or her shares for a sizable profit. The stock price will then usually drop back down significantly because the stock was overvalued. This results in many unsuspecting investors losing lots of money. This is a common problem and the Securities and Exchange Commission actively tries to detect these scams and charge the criminals who run them.

LURE OF MYTHS

Some investors believe (erroneously) that big, successful companies started out as penny stocks. Myths about once being able to buy

IBM at 50 cents a share and 3M at 19 cents a share crop up in occasional conversation. They talk about Mr. Hewlett and Mr. Packard building computers in their garage and using shares in the company as wages. Such beliefs are seldom based entirely on fact; rather, most are partial truths at best. The truth is that very few companies started out tiny and made it big, at least as far as penny stock is concerned.

The amount of risk in the low-price situation increases dramatically as the price of the stock drops even lower. It can be true that reward potential increases as risk increases, but this is often not the case with penny stocks. If a company whose stock is selling for about 50 cents has two or three employees left (who are looking for work), and are unable to manufacture product or even ship product, that company will most likely go out of business, and the stock price will drop to zero.

I CAN AFFORD TO LOSE A THOUSAND

Despite the risk, some investors are attracted to stocks like these. The usual statement you hear is, "I thought I'd invest a thousand dollars on a flier. If I lose it, okay, but I might get lucky." In the vast majority of cases they don't get lucky, and the $1,000 is gone. Typically, the odds are better in horse racing or on a trip to Las Vegas, where they can at least get some entertainment for their money.

PENNY STOCK AND THE SECURITIES AND EXCHANGE COMMISSION

The SEC has comments concerning penny stocks. These include:

> The term "penny stock" generally refers to low-priced (below $5), speculative securities of very small companies. While penny stocks generally are quoted over-the-counter, such as on the *OTC Bulletin Board* or in the *Pink Sheets*, they may also trade on securities exchanges, including foreign

securities exchanges. In addition, penny stocks include the securities of certain private companies with no active trading market.

Before a broker-dealer can sell a penny stock, SEC rules require the firm to first approve the customer for the transaction and receive from the customer a written agreement to the transaction. The firm must furnish the customer a document describing the risks of investing in penny stocks. The firm must tell the customer the current market quotation, if any, for the penny stock and the compensation the firm and its broker will receive for the trade. Finally, the firm must send monthly account statements showing the market value of each penny stock held in the customer's account.

Penny stocks may trade infrequently, which means that it may be difficult to sell penny stock shares once you own them. Because it may be difficult to find quotations for certain penny stocks, they may be impossible to accurately price. Investors in penny stocks should be prepared for the possibility that they may lose their whole investment.

For more information, read the penny stock rules section of our *Broker-Dealer Registration Guide.* You may also want to review the penny stock rules (Securities Exchange Act Rules 3a51-1 and 15g-1 through 15g-100).

Before you consider investing in the stock of any small company, be sure to read our brochure, *Microcap Stock: A Guide for Investors.*[1]

THINGS TO WATCH OUT FOR

Watch out for high-pressure sales techniques. Investing in a legitimate emerging company is long term. A good little company is usually not going to skyrocket in a couple of weeks. Sure Google did, but it came out at $100 a share, so it was not a penny stock. Building a sound company takes years; you have a few days or weeks to decide whether the investment is right for you.

Do not invest in any security without being told exactly how your money will be spent. Be sure you know which properties the company plans to buy with the offering proceeds and how much money is to be spent on management and promoters.

Be very wary if your trade confirmation is marked "unsolicited" if your broker did in fact solicit the trade. While it may be a simple mistake, unscrupulous penny stock brokers often mark the confirmation as unsolicited to avoid the registration laws and the "fair, just, and equitable" standard. Watch for misstatements about your net worth, income, and account objectives as well. Investing in penny stocks is speculative business and involves a high degree of risk. Often brokers will enhance the new account card to make it seem that you are suitable for a penny stock investment when you are not.

Be alert to placement in your account of securities you did not agree to purchase. In some instances a broker may try to pressure you into purchasing the stock, claiming that since you have the stock, you must pay for it. In other cases the broker is temporarily "parking" the securities in your account, perhaps to meet the minimum distribution of an Initial Public Offering (IPO), or for any number of reasons. In some cases an unauthorized trade is simply a mistake, but in any case, complain immediately, both orally and in writing to your broker, your broker's manager, and the Securities Division.

BUY DIRECT—SELL TO WHOM?

Sometimes penny stock can be purchased directly from the company, but the company might not be willing to buy the shares back when the investor is ready to sell. Unless the investor wants to own a controlling interest and manage the company, the super-low-priced penny stocks are usually best avoided.

TAKE A FLYER

If you feel an overwhelming urge to "take a flyer" on a penny stock, one way to lower the risk is to buy only those shares on which you can obtain reliable research information about the company. Use the same fundamental analysis approach as you would use to buy blue-chip stocks for a long-term investment. This will at least give you some idea about the company's prospects.

CHAPTER 43

Be Wary of Stock Ideas from a Neighbor

Charles Dow, in 1900, commented on the tendency of individuals to invest in a widely speculative stock, taking more risk than they would with their own businesses. Often the speculative investments are based on hearing about it from a friend.

Even today stockbrokers hear investors admit that they are interested in a speculative issue of stock because "a neighbor told them." Such stock recommendations can come with the best intentions, but they should be viewed with caution.

STOCK TIPS

The tip you get might be a good one. However, it might have been a good tip some time ago. The best stock ideas usually don't wait around for the investors to make their move. By the time the friend or neighbor has spread the word, it's too late to take any useful action. Learning more about the tip is a better strategy. Even though timing is often of the essence, answering a few questions such as the following can help prevent a costly mistake:

- Where did the idea originate?
- Could it be just a rumor?
- Did a broker recommend the stock?
- Did the idea appear in a financial journal?

Sometimes a tip can be traced quickly to a reliable source; other times the source is illusive. The frustrating fact is that the greater the reliability of the source, the less time there is to take action. If the tip was discussed in *The Wall Street Journal, Investor's Business Daily, The New York Times*, or other such notable publications, the action has probably already occurred.

There are times when the action gets going as a rumor is being discussed, but this is the exception. If the source of the idea is a coworker or indeed a neighbor, some friendly conversation might shed valuable light on the rumor. Was the source a vision, a dream, wishful thinking, or anything else? Spending time to ask can save you money.

It is also important to find out the nature of the tip. For example:

- How speculative is it?
- Is it short-term, a buyout rumor, and by whom?
- Is it more long term; a merger, new contracts, or new revenue growth?
- Is the stock price less than $10 a share?
- Is the stock marginable, so you can borrow money to buy more?

Also, if the stock cannot be bought on margin, then the number of investors, especially institutions that might be interested, is limited.

Buyout rumors have a way of suddenly appearing and disappearing. Sometimes they are based on sound information; other times they are pure fabrication. The truth sounds as good as the falsehood. The stock price can rise just the same. There are also rumors that turn into announcements, only to run into a stone wall.

RUMORS

The year 2008 was not a good one for the stock market. It was made even worse by numerous false rumors, supposedly started by some unscrupulous hedge fund managers to drive stock prices down. Finally, the SEC got angry and started prosecuting some of the rumor mongers. The following is from *The New York Times*:

> The Securities and Exchange Commission announced on Sunday that it and other regulators would begin examining rumor-spreading intended to manipulate securities prices.
>
> The timing of the announcement, made before the markets opened in Asia, was meant to warn broker-dealers, hedge funds and investment advisers to quell any spreading of rumors before trading started Monday.
>
> "Traders know there is false information in the market. They need to think twice if they are going to pass it on," said Lori Richards, director of the S.E.C.'s Office of Compliance Inspections and Examinations.
>
> "It's important that firms be aware of their supervisory and compliance obligations to prevent violations of the securities law," Ms. Richards said.
>
> The examinations are expected to begin Monday and will focus on what policies firms have in place to prevent the passing of false information. The intent is to stop malicious rumors without hampering the natural exchange of information in the marketplace.
>
> These examinations will focus on compliance and supervisory policies. In addition, continuing investigations will look at potential wrongdoing. In addition to the S.E.C., the Financial Industry Regulatory Authority and New

York Stock Exchange Regulation will be conducting the examinations.[1]

Since it announced its intention to investigate those spreading rumors, the SEC has stepped up to the plate and has been investigating and prosecuting people who have been spreading the rumors. However, the rumors still appear occasionally.

Facebook, planning an initial public offering for early 2012, had a false rumor appear. The following is from *The Wall Street Journal*:

> Facebook took action to quelch a rumor that it had made public the phone numbers of all users of the social network.
>
> Many users of the service Wednesday began circulating posts warning their friends that the phone numbers of their contacts are now visible to everyone on Facebook. The warning went something like this: "ALL THE PHONE NUMBERS of your contacts are now on Facebook! . . . Please repost this on your status, so friends can remove their numbers and thus prevent abuse if they do not want them published."
>
> The company responded by posting an update to the Facebook fan page stating that the feature, called Contacts, is neither new nor does it disclose information more broadly than before.
>
> "Rumors claiming that your phone contacts are visible to everyone on Facebook are false," the company wrote. "Our Contacts list, formerly called Phonebook, has existed for a long time. The phone numbers listed there were either added by your friends themselves and made visible to you, or you have previously synced your phone contacts with Facebook. Just like on your phone, only you can see these numbers."
>
> Facebook has taken to its own page to dispel myths about itself less than a dozen times, Chin said. She said the

company uses the approach when it sees a rumor is trend-
ing in Facebook traffic or if the company starts receiving an
influx of emails.

The most frequent rumors circling on the social network are that Facebook is going to start charging users and
that it's going to shut down its services, she said. The company tried to stop the rumor that it will start charging users
money by putting a line into its log in page that says Facebook does not and never will charge users for its service. It
still sees the rumor pop up, though.[2]

Obviously, these rumors are a big frustration for Facebook or
any company. Why do the rumors appear? Who knows? Maybe
they're started by somebody with a low self-image trying to make
trouble for someone else, or someone trying to manipulate the stock
of a specific company.

The Bear Stearns Companies firmly believes its demise as an
international bank was caused by negative rumors in 2008. Granted,
it had problems resulting from the mortgage financial meltdown,
but the rumor mills did much damage also.

DECISION MAKING

Here are some questions to ask when you're trying to reach a decision about a stock tip:

- How does the purchase or sell fit into an investment
  strategy?
- How much risk currently exists with other investments?
- What proportion of the portfolio is in the risk category?

When assessing a stock tip, consider how the stock fits into
the broader investment strategy and goals. If some funds have been
established as speculative money, by all means make use of them.

However, limiting and controlling risk whenever possible is always prudent.

RISK AND REWARD

Investing in the stock market always has an element of risk. Some risk is low and often is lessened over time. Other risk is high and is strictly short term. Greater risk does not always bring greater rewards. Before investing in high-risk, speculative situations, it is worthwhile to ask a few extra questions and do some research on the initial source of your information. This will not eliminate risk, but it can allow you to at least enter an investment being aware of the risk, an awareness that may prompt you to go in another direction.

Whether it's a stock tip from a neighbor or a friend or a hot tip from an Internet blog or chat room, tips are always fraught with high risk and often little in the way of rewards. They should be approached with reserved skepticism.

CHAPTER 44

Heavily Margined, Heavily Watched

To "margin" is to borrow money using stocks or other securities as collateral. The borrowed funds can be used for any purpose (the cash can be withdrawn), although the money is most commonly used to buy more stock or other marginable securities. A margin can be a useful tool to leverage investments for greater profits. In essence, an investor puts up one-half the value of the stock purchased on margin.

KNOW THE MARGIN RULES

Here is some information on the group that regulates stocks purchased on margin and other investment firms in the United States.

The Financial Industry Regulatory Authority (FINRA) is the largest independent regulator for all securities firms doing business in the United States. FINRA's mission is to protect America's investors by making sure the securities industry operates fairly and honestly. All told, FINRA oversees nearly 4,450 brokerage firms, about 161,065 branch offices and approximately 629,755 registered securities representatives.[1]

Following are some of the key rules you should know.

Use of Margin Accounts

An investor purchasing securities may pay for the securities in full or may borrow part of the purchase price from a securities firm. If the investor chooses to borrow funds from a firm, it is necessary for the investor to open a "margin account" with the firm.

The portion of the total purchase price that the investor deposits is called margin and is the investor's initial equity in the account. The loan from the firm is secured by the securities that are purchased by the investor.

Margin Requirements

The terms on which firms can extend credit for securities transactions are governed by federal regulation and by the rules of FINRA and the securities exchanges. This area focuses on the requirements for marginable equity securities, which include most stocks. Some securities cannot be purchased on margin, which means that they must be purchased in a cash account and that the investor must deposit 100 percent of the purchase price.

In general, under Federal Reserve Board Regulation T, firms can lend an investor up to 50 percent of the total purchase price of a stock for new, or initial, purchases. Assuming that the investor does not already have cash or other equity in the account to cover the share of the purchase price, the investor will receive a "margin call" from the firm. As a result of the margin call, the investor will be required to deposit the other 50 percent of the purchase price.

The rules of FINRA and the stock exchanges supplement the requirements of Regulation T by placing "maintenance" margin requirements on investor accounts. Under the rules of FINRA and the exchanges, the investor's equity in the account must not fall below 25 percent of the current market value of the securities in the account. Otherwise, the investor may be required to deposit more funds or securities in order to maintain the equity (ownership) at the 25 percent level. The failure to do so may cause the firm to force the sale of—or liquidate—the securities in the investor's account in order to bring the account's equity back up to the required level.

Here's an example of a margin transaction. If an investor buys $100,000 of securities on Day 1, Regulation T would require the investor to deposit a margin of 50 percent or $50,000 in payment for the securities. As a result, the investor's equity (ownership) in the margin account is $50,000, and the investor has received a margin loan of $50,000 from the firm that issued the securities.

Let's say that on Day 2 the market value of the securities falls to $60,000. Under this scenario, the investor's margin loan from the firm would remain at $50,000, and the investor's account equity would fall to $10,000 ($60,000 market value less $50,000 loan amount). However, the minimum maintenance margin requirement for the account is 25 percent, meaning that the investor's equity must not fall below $15,000 ($60,000 market value multiplied by 25 percent). Since the required equity is $15,000, the investor would receive a maintenance margin call for $5,000 ($15,000 less the existing equity of $10,000). Because of the way the margin rules operate, if the firm liquidated securities in the account to meet the maintenance margin call, it would need to liquidate $20,000 of securities.

INVESTMENT FIRM PRACTICES

Investment firms have the right to set their own margin requirements—often called "house" requirements—as long as they are higher than the margin requirements under Regulation T or the rules of FINRA and the stock exchanges. Firms are allowed to raise their maintenance margin requirements for specific, volatile stocks to ensure that there are sufficient funds in their investors' accounts to cover large price swings. These changes in firm policy often take effect immediately and may result in a maintenance margin call. An investor's failure to satisfy that call may cause the firm to liquidate a portion of the investor's account.[2]

UNDERSTAND MARGIN CALLS: YOU CAN LOSE MONEY FAST, WITH NO NOTICE

If your account falls below the issuing firm's maintenance requirement, the firm will make a margin call to ask you to deposit more cash or marginable securities into the account. If you are unable to meet the margin call, the firm will sell your securities to increase the equity in your account up to or above the firm's maintenance requirement.

Always remember that your broker may not be required to make a margin call or otherwise tell you that your account has fallen below the maintenance requirement level. In this case, your broker may be able to sell your securities at any time without consulting you first. Under most margin agreements, even if the firm offers to give you time to increase the equity in your account, it can sell your securities without waiting for you to meet the margin call.

ASK QUESTIONS

If you deal with margin accounts, be sure to ask yourself the following questions:

- Do you know that margin accounts involve a great deal more risk than cash accounts in which you fully pay for the securities you purchase?
- Are you aware that you may lose more than the amount of money you initially invested when buying on margin? Can you afford this?

- Did you take the time to read the margin account agreement?
- Did you ask your broker questions about how a margin account works and whether it's appropriate for you to trade on margin?
- Did your broker explain the terms and conditions of the margin agreement?
- Are you aware of the costs you will be charged on money you borrow from the issuing firm and how these costs affect your overall return?
- Are you aware that your brokerage firm can sell your securities without notice to you when you don't have sufficient equity in your margin account?

For more information about margin trading, visit the website of FINRA at http://www.finra.org/.

INTEREST CHARGES

Brokerage firms make money on margin accounts from the interest they charge on the loans and also from commissions on the larger transaction sizes that buying on margin allows. However, lending money carries risks for the brokerage firms similar to the risks that banks face when lending: the borrower may not want to or may not be able to pay back the money borrowed. The interest rate charged can vary from brokerage firm to brokerage firm and can change without notice to the investor.

UNMET CALLS

If the required margin is not maintained, the brokerage firm has every right to sell securities in the account to cover the amount or prevent further loss, without notifying the investor beforehand.

This is a common occurrence when the stock market takes a big nosedive. Investors who are out of town, sometimes on vacation, return to find their stock portfolios decimated. Many will still owe money to the brokerage firms.

Protect the margin position with careful and deliberate attention. Brokers are often amazed at the number of investors who make stock purchases just before they leave on vacation.

In fact, it is usually not the best time to buy any stock and can be exactly the wrong time to increase a margin position. A lot can happen to the stock market in a week or two. Most people leaving for vacation have enough to do without keeping an eye on the market.

MARGIN STRATEGIES

Margins can be used with minimal risk and maximum impact, but doing so requires care and attention. Margin positions can be well maintained by your implementing a few simple strategies:

- *Daily observation*: Keep an eye on the developing market situation by computer, cell phone, or communication with a broker.
- *Extra precautions:* Take extra precautions when leaving town on a vacation or a business trip. Consider making special arrangements with the broker to have someone bring money or fully paid securities to cover any possible maintenance calls. Keep in touch. Although cell phones make a big difference with communication today, it can still be a good idea to reduce or totally pay off a margin debt if your trip will be for an extended period of time.
- *Place protective orders:* This could be a good situation for stop loss orders carefully placed.
- *Be extra cautious with a short position:* A short position has potentially unlimited risk since there is no limit to how

high the price of a stock can rise. Carefully placed buy stop orders can help control this risk.

USE MARGIN FOR LEVERAGE

Margin can be a useful tool for leverage when buying securities. It should be used carefully and deliberately. Like all investment strategies, an investor must have a basic understanding of the workings of margin before using leverage. It is possible to learn more about using margin by asking a broker for information, finding books on the subject, or searching the Internet.

NEVER, EVER, EVER

Do not ever under any circumstance use borrowed margin funds to buy a car or house. Use the funds for investment securities only.

CHAPTER 45

Beware the Triple (Quadruple) Witching Hour

Tis now the very witching time of night,
When churchyards yawn and hell itself breathes out.
Contagion to this world.

—WILLIAM SHAKESPEARE, *HAMLET*

The triple witching hour is the last hour of the stock market trading session on the third Friday of every March, June, September, and December, 3:00–4:00 p.m., eastern time.

On those days, four kinds of securities expire:

- Stock market index futures
- Stock market index options
- Stock options
- Single-stock futures

For many years it was just the "Triple Witching Hour," then in November, 2008, the Single-stock futures were added to make it "Quadruple." The simultaneous expirations generally increase the trading volume of options, futures, and the underlying stocks, and occasionally increases volatility of prices of related securities. Single-stock futures also expire, so that the final hour on those days is sometimes referred to as the "quadruple witching hour." In the past these days could wreak havoc on what some referred to as "freaky Friday." Now, trading circuit breakers limit huge swings in the stock market. These limits prevent the short sellers and computerized traders from driving the market down dramatically. Even so the potential for a hyperactive stock market is still with us.

CIRCUIT BREAKERS

The following is an explanation of how circuit breakers function to moderate the negative actions taking place in the stock or commodities markets.

> This is when a major stock or commodities exchange stops trading temporarily because an index, or even an individual stock, has fallen a certain percentage during a trading day. The purpose is to prevent a market or stock price free-fall by trying to rebalance buy and sell orders.
>
> For example, if the Dow Jones Industrial Average falls by 10 percent, the New York Stock Exchange (NYSE) might halt market trading for one hour. There are other circuit breakers for 20 percent and 30 percent declines.
>
> In addition to market-wide circuit breakers, the Securities and Exchange Commission approved market rules on a trial basis in 2010, allowing circuit-breaker pauses for certain individual securities whose prices move 10 percent or more in a five-minute period.
>
> These circuit-breaker pauses apply to stocks in the S&P 500 Index, the Russell 1000 Index, and several hundred exchange traded products. They halt trading in the applicable security in all U.S. markets for five minutes.
>
> When were market circuit breakers first conceived? The markets instituted circuit breakers in the wake of 1987's

"Black Monday." On Oct. 19, 1987, the market plunged 508.32 points, 22.6 percent, or $500 billion lost in one day. This was the largest one-day percentage drop in history until that time.

Circuit breakers were first used in October 1989, following a major stock market drop.

Until 1997, the markets used a point drop rule—that is, looking at how many points the markets declined, rather than the percentage of the move, to trigger circuit breakers to stop trading.

This point-drop rule caused trading to halt on October 27, 1997, even though the decline was only about 7 percent. The rule was subsequently changed to respond to percentage drops rather than point drops. The rules have since been changed back to point drops as well as percentage declines.

When do market circuit breakers kick in?

The rules for using circuit breakers have changed over the years, and are usually calculated on a quarterly basis.

On June 30, 2011, the NYSE issued these guidelines for using circuit breakers:

Level 1 Halt

A 1,200-point drop in the Dow industrial average before 2 p.m. ET will halt trading for one hour; for 30 minutes if between 2 p.m. and 2:30 p.m. ET; and have no effect if happens at 2:30 p.m. or later, unless there is a level 2 halt.

Level 2 Halt

A 2,400-point drop in the Dow industrials before 1 p.m. will halt trading for two hours; for one hour if occurs between 1 p.m. and 2 p.m.; and for the remainder of the day if at 2 p.m. or later.

Level 3 Halt

A 3,650-point drop will halt trading for the remainder of the day regardless of when the decline occurs.

The percentage levels were first implemented in April 1998, and the point levels are adjusted on the first trading day of each quarter. In 2011, those dates are January 3, April 1, July 1, and October 3.

What Is Rule 48?

Unlike a circuit breaker that stops stock trading, the Securities and Exchange Commission's Rule 48 makes it easier and faster to open the stock markets—when there are fears that the market could open with a lot of volatility that would disrupt trading.

Where circuit breakers and Rule 48 may be related is the rule could be used the day after a circuit breaker has been enforced.

Rule 48 speeds up the opening by suspending the requirement that stock prices be announced at the market open. Those prices have to be approved by stock market floor managers before trading actually begins. Without that approval, stock trading can begin sooner.

To invoke Rule 48, an exchange would have to determine that certain conditions exist that would cause market disruptions. Those conditions include:

- Volatility during the previous day's trading session
- Trading in foreign markets before the open
- Substantial activity in the futures market before the open
- The volume of pre-opening indications of interest
- Government announcements

Rule 48 was approved by the SEC in December 2007.

It's been invoked twice: on Tuesday, January 22, 2008, and on Thursday, May 20, 2010. In 2008, the stock markets were subject to great volatility over fears of a global recession and in 2010, the European debt crisis caused panic buying and selling.[1]

The only criticism has been that the circuit breakers haven't been put in place soon enough. There are times when the market moves well beyond the set parameters before the breakers are implemented. But they are serious, they are used, and they are effective for stabilizing a tail-spinning stock market.

BAD NEWS CAN ALSO HAVE AN IMPACT

If significant economic news comes out at the same time that the expirations occur, the volatility can be magnified. But this can confuse the issue, and it's difficult to tell if it was news that made the market volatile or if the triple witching was more to blame.

If we look at 2011 (see Figure 45.1), it's clear to see that the triple or quadruple witching hour was pretty much ignored by the stock market. Apparently the circuit breakers are having an impact and have changed the situation.

The market of 2011 had its own freaky problems to deal with without reacting to the witching hours. This is sometimes the case with problems in the market. A fairly simple adjustment occurs, and it all settles down until the next crisis comes along.

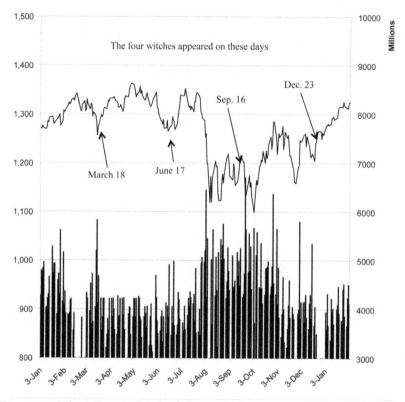

Data source: Yahoo! Finance Historical Prices

Figure 45.1   S&P 500 Index, 2011–January 2012

Part 7

SURPRISES

S tock market surprises come in all shapes and sizes, some pleasant and some not. Where analysts were expecting 23 cents a share in improved earnings and get 32 cents a share is a very pleasant surprise.

Fraud is an all too common experience related to investing. The Bernie Madoff scandal was devastating to many investors, whether directly or indirectly. The good news is that the scandal resulted in a closer examination of many other illegal scams and put them out of business.

A stock split, which we deal with in this part, is a neutral surprise. Although many people consider them positive events, the facts can be quite different. Some are positive for a short time and then neutral or even negative.

What about the end-of-year "Santa Claus rally" effect? Is it real? Can an investor take advantage of it? How and when does it work exactly?

Most other surprises in the stock market are bad surprises. All of a sudden the hot stock is down 10 bucks and heading lower. It might be because of fraud or because the company is facing a major lawsuit.

Safety in numbers can be found with well-run investment clubs. From such clubs the investor can learn a great deal about the stock market. Serving on analysis committees and making presentations to the rest of the group can be quite instructive and worth checking out.

Surprises also can bring personal and financial growth.

CHAPTER 46

Avoid Heavy Positions in Thinly Traded Stocks

The terms "heavy position" and "thinly traded" can mean different things to different investors. A *heavy position* for one might be 5,000 to 10,000 shares; for another it could mean a few hundred shares. *Thinly traded* might describe a stock that doesn't trade on some days, or it could describe a stock that trades low volume, such as fewer than 5,000 shares a day. Many stock traders consider anything less than 10,000 shares a day as thin. The terms are not absolute.

UNUSUALLY LOW-PRICED

Thinly traded stocks also tend to have relatively low prices, often below $3 a share. A problem can arise in this way: although it is relatively easy to buy 10,000 shares of thinly traded stock, it could be difficult to sell the position. Selling might necessitate breaking the block into smaller segments of 5,000 or 3,000 shares, or even 1,000 shares. The share "hitting the bid" (pushing the price lower by selling) can be damaging to any profits. The investor can also be charged additional commissions if the buys or sells cannot be executed on the same day.

Figure 46.1 shows what many thinly traded stocks look like on a graph. A quick glance shows that the stock didn't trade every day in January 2012. With this stock the volume is all over the board from zero to 16,000 shares in a day. The future of this stock does not look great. This is why it is unnamed. No point in kicking it when it's down.

Many thinly traded stocks cannot be graphed like the one shown in Figure 46.1 because the information isn't readily available. In fact the availability of any information on many of the companies that issue the stock is a serious problem. It just isn't there. In the old days we would say, "They just don't have room for all

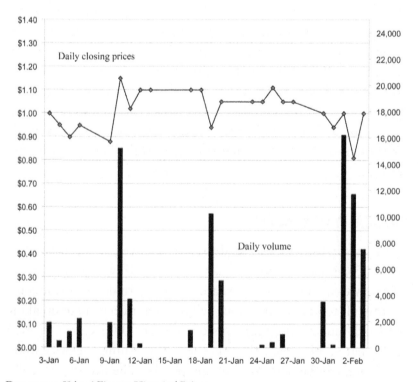

Data source: Yahoo! Finance Historical Prices

Figure 46.1   Thinly Traded Stock, January 3–February 2, 2012

that information in the phone booth they use for an office." But the phone booths have all but disappeared.

This is from the SEC, dated January 26, 2012:

> The Securities and Exchange Commission today charged a Fort Lauderdale-based firm and its founder with conducting a fraudulent boiler room scheme in which they hyped stock in two thinly-traded penny stock companies while behind the scenes they sold the same stock themselves for illegal profits.[1]

BE CAREFUL ON THE PHONE

Brokers get business by making "cold calls," which means they call from a phone book, a reverse directory, or another listing and sell investments to people they have never met. This activity is not illegal in the United States, although it is illegal in other countries. Most cold callers are reputable brokers just trying to make a living, and they are trying to meet investors' objectives. However, the chop-shop stockbrokers couldn't care less about objectives other than their own. They are trained for the quick, hard sell. Their philosophy is to, "Let the buyer beware."

Chop-shop stockbrokers are difficult to control. The new promoters gain control over cheap stock or dominate the markets for thinly traded stocks and then push them on the public, using crews of brokers reporting to them.

Neither the National Association of Securities Dealers (NASD) and the Securities and Exchange Commission's highly visible campaign against small-stock abuses nor the recent spate of criminal prosecutions have made a significant impact on chop houses. Although regulators have shut down a handful of cold-calling powerhouses, the vast majority of questionable firms remain untouched.

So be careful on the phone. The best thing to do is hang up, especially if the broker puts you on hold after mentioning a large number gain or interest percent. It's an old gimmick to let people think about that high number for a few seconds and then come back on the line to sell them something. Just hang up while you're on hold.

Take a look at another thinly traded stock. American Care-Source Holdings, Inc. (NASDAQ: ANCI). American CareSource Holdings operates as an ancillary services company that offers access to a national network of ancillary healthcare service providers in the United States. Find more information at its website: http://www.anci-care.com/. Take a look at the price graph in Figure 46.2.

While this might become an excellent stock in the future, at this point it is more than speculative. To become interesting to investors, it needs a huge increase in sales and earnings. There is some institutional ownership, just over 15 percent, but not really enough to bring attention to the company. Mutual fund ownership

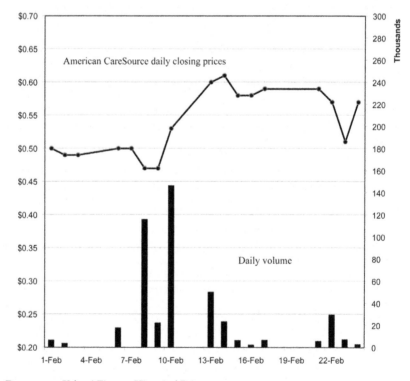

Data source: Yahoo! Finance Historical Prices

Figure 46.2   American CareSource Holdings, Inc., February 2012

is almost nonexistent at .05 percent. The company appears to be mostly owned by insiders at 32.30 percent.

You can see from Figure 46.2 that a big volume day is 146,000 shares. At 53 cents a share that's not much movement. With this stock a huge price movement is from 53 cents all the way up to 60 cents. You can say that if you bought enough shares, it would be worthwhile. The trouble is that buying all those shares would push the price out of sight, and then it would have to go up a lot farther for you to double your money—although this might make the current shareholders happy.

PRICES CAN BE MANIPULATED (ILLEGALLY)

Almost every month we see examples of crooked investment brokers or firms stealing money from people. Here is an example.

> The United States Securities and Exchange Commission (Commission) today announced a civil action against First Resource Group LLC and its principal David H. Stern alleging that they fraudulently touted stock in two thinly-traded microcap companies, sold each company's stock at the same time they were touting it, and manipulated the markets in both penny stocks in violation of the antifraud provisions of the federal securities laws. According to the SEC's complaint, at various times from December 2008, to May 2010, First Resource and Stern, and telemarketers they employed, fraudulently solicited brokers to purchase stock in TrinityCare Senior Living, Inc. and Cytta Corporation. The complaint alleges that while First Resource and Stern were recommending the purchase of the securities of the two microcap companies, Stern sold First Resource's shares of TrinityCare and Cytta unbeknownst to the investors who were purchasing the stocks, a practice known as scalping. Further, the complaint alleges that while Stern was selling the stocks, he was also purchasing small amounts of the

stocks in order to create the false appearance of legitimate trading activity to induce the investors to purchase shares in both companies. The SEC also alleges that Stern and First Resource acted as unregistered broker-dealers.[2]

USE CAUTION TAKING SPECULATIVE POSITIONS

Although thinly traded stocks might be worth a light speculative position of a few hundred shares held for a long-term investment, they should probably not make up a significant position for short-term trading. Short-term trading would easily lead to investors being "whipsawed"—that is, losing money in both directions, losing on both the buy and the sell. Also, learn about the company (make a visit if possible), and don't buy the stock on the word of some cold-calling "cowboy." Brokers are required to know their clients' investment objectives. Thinly traded stocks will not fit well into any growth or income portfolio.

RELATED TO PENNY STOCKS

Penny stocks are often thinly traded and easily lend themselves to fraud and unreasonable markups that are almost impossible to detect. The stock markets depend on investors at all levels being essentially honest and straightforward. The problem is that a dishonest firm or broker can come along and wreak havoc just by ignoring some of the rules. It takes a while for them to be caught, and in the meantime they can do millions of dollars' worth of damage. Thinly traded and penny stocks are prudently best avoided.

CHAPTER 47

Fraud Is Unpredictable

Anything can happen in the stock market. It is possible to research and select a stock or other investment that is about to double or triple in price, and it is possible to buy a stock that is about to fold the tent and head toward the cellar. The most difficult bad news to anticipate is fraud. Investors buy stock based on the assumption that the company is being straightforward with its financial information. Because of this assumed honesty, it is nearly impossible to see fraud coming. The devastating impact of fraud hits the professional investor as well as the individual.

I'd very much like to be able to say, "Take a look at the chart of Bernie Madoff's fund and see what happened." But I can't say that because there wasn't anything to look at—no information. It was all just: put your faith in Bernie and hope for the best.

The first suspicions to be made official were back in 1999. Analyst Harry Markopolos actually complained to the SEC saying that what Madoff claimed to be doing was not possible. Bernard Lawrence Madoff was finally arrested on December 11, 2008, and charged with securities fraud. Why did it take the SEC so long to investigate?

For some reason people are especially attracted to those who lie to them the most. The reason is simple. The ones telling the lies have the best story. Since they are making up the facts, their story sounds terrific. When other people trust them, why shouldn't we. There is also the belief that if they are lying they would have been caught.

The damage Madoff caused was not only the $17 to $20 billion he stole, but the total destruction of trust in America's financial system and its regulators. Bernie started in the securities business as a penny stock seller. Isn't that fitting? He worked his way up to the largest Ponzi scam ever perpetrated. It alone threatened the entire financial system of the United States. Not exactly a noble achievement. But the point is that it was not easily predictable by the individual investor. Supposedly there are stories that many large firms refused to do business with him because they thought he was crooked. Well duh? You gotta wonder why they didn't say something. Apparently Bernie was so big that everybody was afraid to say anything.

Reportedly when investors did ask how he was operating, they were told it was "a secret." Well, folks, if you ever hear that, it's time to leave the building. Just hope that you can get your money back.

SOMETIMES IT'S NOT FRAUD

Individual stock prices can drop suddenly with no apparent reason. News announcements might be slow to come forward. The drop might have just been a fluke. A large investor decides to do some portfolio rearranging; another large investor sees a significant sell and adds to the mix.

Occasionally investors will bring lawsuits against companies because the price has dropped. Although this is not a favorable event, it is not the same as fraud.

SELL SOON

It can be prudent to quickly sell at the first sign of fraudulent activity. Most institutional investors will quickly sell all or part of their positions, which causes the price to plummet. This is why it is important to find out as soon as possible why a stock has had a sudden, severe drop in price. The investor must discover the reason for the bad news and take action.

FRAUD IS STILL HAPPENING EVERYWHERE

Here are some headlines from 2012 about frauds:

- "Tokyo Stock Market Rocked by Madoff-Style Fraud and Chinese Backdoor Listing," by Stephen Harner, *Forbes International*, February 27, 2012.
- "Munich Prosecutors Conduct Raids in Insider-Trading Case," by Karin Matussek, Bloomberg, March 1, 2012.
- "Director Deals—Scottish American Investment Company Plc (SCAM)," StockMarketWire.com., March 7, 2012.

It is unfortunate that investing fraud will likely always be with us. As long as there is money to be made, scammers will try to get your funds. This is why it is so important to check out the information on any investment.

USE CARE WITH INTERNET TRANSACTIONS

In recent years the Securities and Exchange Commission has become concerned about fraudulent securities available via the Internet. Apparently, some unscrupulous individuals are surfing right into people's life savings. Following are some of the approaches they use.

The Pyramid Scheme

It's called a pyramid, because it involves a growing amount of people and their money. The first people entering the pyramid often get big returns, but investors entering later usually lose everything. The high returns come from new investors and go to the earlier investors. Eventually it all collapses. One online promoter claimed that you could "turn five dollars into $60,000 in just three weeks."[1]

According to the SEC, this was just an electronic version of the classic pyramid scheme. It's well suited to online activities, where a lawbreaker can send messages to 1,000 people with the click of a mouse button.

The Risk-Free or Low-Risk Scheme

Here are some other approaches used by Internet scam artists:

1. "Exciting, low-risk investment opportunities" to participate in exotic-sounding investments, including wireless cable projects, prime bank securities, and eel farms, have been offered online.
2. One promoter attempted to get people to invest in a fictitious coconut plantation in Costa Rica, claiming that the investment was similar to a bank CD, with a better investment rate.

At times these cons will misrepresent the risk by comparing their opportunity to something an investor considers safe, such as a bank certificate of deposit. The obvious intent is to make the investor comfortable. If it's "just like a CD," there's nothing to worry about. In the United States, to be "just like a CD," an investment would have to be backed by the FDIC up to the first $100,000. Anything less than that isn't like a CD. Some schemes don't even have an investment product to sell. Like Bernie's plan, they just have people send in money.

The Pump-and-Dump Scam

It is common to see Internet messages posted online urging readers to buy a stock quickly because it is poised for rapid growth. Often the writer claims to have "inside" information about an impending development or will claim to use an "infallible" combination of economic and stock market data to pick stocks.

According to the SEC, the promoter might be an insider who works for the company and will gain by selling shares after the stock price is pumped up by gullible buyers.

The Internet advice might also be a suggestion to sell a stock. It might be a short seller who stands to gain if the price goes down. The ploy is often used with little-known, thinly traded stock. The individual investor is left holding the bag after a whirlwind of activity.

INVESTIGATE BEFORE INVESTING

Print out a copy of any online solicitation. Make certain to copy the Internet address (URL), and note the date and time that you saw the offer. Save the printout in case you need it later. Check with your state securities regulator or the SEC to see if it has received any complaints about the company, its managers, or the promoter. Don't assume that people are who they claim to be. The investments that sound the best could be figments of someone's crooked imagination.

Check with your trusted financial advisor, your broker, or your attorney about any investment you learn about online. You can also ask the promoter where the firm is incorporated. Contact that state's secretary of state and ask if the company is indeed incorporated there, with a current annual report on file.

Don't assume that the access providers or online services have approved or even screened the investment. They don't do that sort of thing. Anyone can set up a website or advertise on the Internet without anything being checked for legitimacy or untruthfulness.

Before you invest, always obtain written financial information such as a prospectus, annual report, offering circular, and financial statements. Compare the written information with what you've read online, and watch out if you're told that the information is not available.

If a company is not registered or has not filed a Form D with the SEC, call the SEC's Office of Investor Education and Assistance at (202) 942-7040 or contact your state securities regulator. You can also visit the SEC's website at www.sec.gov or contact it by e-mail. Regular mail can be sent to:

> Securities and Exchange Commission
> Office of Investor Education & Assistance
> 450 Fifth Street, NW Mail Stop 11-2
> Washington, D.C. 20549

FRAUD IS DIFFICULT TO SPOT

The advice heard so many times is true, "If it sounds too good to be true, it probably is." Easy to think, but sometimes difficult to follow. In the past this advice might have kept many people away from companies like Microsoft, Apple Computer, or Google when they first started. They were not fraudulent investments in any way, and that is what the scam artist is counting on to gain investors' confidence.

A personal visit to a company can be helpful, but again it doesn't ensure the integrity of the information. Companies tend to be good at putting on a dog-and-pony show for investors and brokers. Even the worst of companies can usually put together a good show for an interested audience. Often, the best information about a company comes from outside sources that are more objective.

Usually the best defense is to avoid companies where there is any doubt involved. If evidence of fraud appears, sell out quickly and take the loss.

CHAPTER 48

There's Always a Santa Claus Rally

Santa Claus is coming to town, and to the stock market. To the old-time purist, any rally between Thanksgiving and Christmas Day is a Santa Claus rally. Actually, virtually any rally in the months of November or December was credited to the Santa. Nowadays the so-called Santa Claus rally is combined with what used to be called the "year-end rally" and falls on the last five days of the year and the first two trading days of the next year.

It's the buying season, a time when some retailers make their yearly profit. Consumers go shopping with a frenzy and not only for gifts to place under a tree. Many excited shoppers also buy themselves presents. The Friday after Thanksgiving remains the busiest day of the year for most retailers. Consumers have been saving money and curbing their impulses just for this day. It's only natural that the buying frenzy would extend to the stock market.

10 YEARS OF RALLIES

Although some years the rallies are barely there, most years have a decent year-end rally. Figure 48.1 shows that years 2004 to 2007

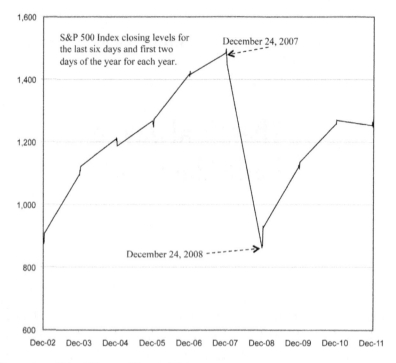

Data source: Yahoo! Finance Historical Prices

Figure 48.1   Santa Claus Rallies, 2002–2011

rallied quite nicely to the end of the year. Santa ran out of steam at the end of 2007 and in 2008. The second half of the year was still reeling from the effects of the banking crooks and the investment crooks, although there was a small rally at the very end of the year. Years 2009 through 2011 showed Santa rallies with some recovery from the debacle and may move toward a new bull market.

NOT ALL POSITIVE

Jeff Hirsch, author of *The Stock Trader's Almanac*, published by Wiley, has some bad news about what happens when the Santa Claus rally fails to appear.

"If Santa Claus should fail to call, bears may come to Broad and Wall [Street]," says Hirsch. In 1999 and 2000, as well as in 2007–2008, the warnings of no Santa Claus rallies were harbingers of doom that investors would have been well served to pay attention to. Hirsch himself notes the limitations of basing an investing strategy on seven trading days. It's data mining, and as Hirsch puts it, "If you torture numbers long enough, you can get them to say anything." What these numbers are telling us is we best pay at least some attention to the trading at the end of next month.[1]

Can a Santa Claus rally be a harbinger of a down market for the following year? Maybe. It may or may not happen, but it's worth noticing the end-of-the-year figures of the stock market.

Is there always a Santa rally? The only *always* in the stock market is price fluctuation. Because the stock market trades in anticipation of higher or lower prices, it frequently surprises investors with rallies or corrections. Although it is possible to have a bearish trend in the last two months of the year, there will likely be some kind of rally. Some of these rallies will be significant; others quite modest:

> A recent Forbes article notes that the Santa Claus rally has resulted in an average December market gain of 2.0 percent since 1990. Roughly 81 percent of the time, stocks have risen in December since 1990.
>
> The explanation most often used is that investors are buying stocks in anticipation of the January effect, where stocks typically rise as well. Another explanation I've read asserts that stocks increase in January as a result of investors buying back the stocks they sold in December to harvest the tax losses.[2]

There is a repetitive tendency of the stock market to rally between the months of November and December. If it's before the last week of the year, it's referred to as, "Santa Claus came early." If a rally occurs in January, it's called "the January effect." An investor can take advantage of such rallies by patiently waiting for them to appear and then deciding to take a profit.

THE JANUARY EFFECT (SANTA COMES LATE)

There are three concepts underlying the January effect:

1. January is a predictor of how stocks will perform for the rest of the year.
2. Small and hammered-down stock will outperform larger stocks in January.
3. The first five days of the new year are enough to predict the rest of the year's performance.

Does it work? Like any indicator, the answer is yes and no:

While the historical numbers can vary from one researcher to the next, they all generally point in the same direction: Small caps usually *do* outperform large caps during the first month of the year.

For example, Bank of America Merrill Lynch strategist Steven G. DeSanctis has found that the Russell 2000 Small Cap Index has outperformed large caps more than 70% of the time since 1926. He also notes that January usually is the best month for small caps; they've averaged a gain of 4% in that month.

University of Kansas professors Mark Haug and Mark Hirschey broadly confirmed the idea, discovering that between 1927 and 2004, small-cap stocks outperformed large caps by an average of 2.5 percent in the first month of the calendar year.[3]

It appears that the math does support the assumptions. Although this doesn't mean that it will happen next year or the year after. It's a difficult trading strategy to take full advantage of, but it is a phenomenon that should be observed by investors. In 2011 and 2012, all indexes were up in January both large and small caps. The first five days were up as well, although one could probably accuse traders of making the first five days up just to put a positive spin on the year. This would not be considered illegal price manipulation because it would be to the investors' benefit.

TAKE ALL ANOMALIES WITH A GRAIN OF SALT

All stock market anomalies should be doubted more than relied upon either because the conditions that created them have changed or because they were overridden by other factors. However, you should be aware of them, because occasionally a situation will come along you can take advantage of and come out a winner.

CHAPTER 49

A Stock Price Splits
When It Gets Too High

L ike so many things involving the stock market, price splits are kind of a combination of yes and no. On the no side is Warren Buffett with Berkshire Hathaway. The BRK.A share is $121,404 (one share is a round lot), and the BRK.B is $80.00 a share (for the poor folks to buy). How about Apple? Apple is at $582.22 a share. Shouldn't it split soon? One would think so. And of course we can't forget Google at $603.16 a share. All this suggests that a high price is not always a factor in deciding on a two-for-one, three-for-one, or three-for-two, or some other forward split. Many people state that the split is neces-sary to make the stock affordable to more investors. Yeah, right. More likely it's for the free publicity that a split will bring to the company. Companies are like rock stars or movie stars. When their life gets dull, they have to do something dramatic to get some good free press. Many resort to stock splits or share buyback programs.

TYPES OF SPLITS

It's the *forward split* that is considered a neutral-to-positive event. On the other hand, a *backward* or *reverse split* is considered a very negative event. The reverse split lowers the number of shares and increases the current price. If you have 1,000 shares of stock at $1.00 per share, a 10-for-1 reverse split would leave you with 100 shares at $10.00 a share. The problem is that the price usually doesn't stay at the new higher level for long but drops back toward the bottom.

WHO HAS THE MOST SHARES?

Microsoft has 8.39 billion shares outstanding at this moment in time. By contrast Berkshire Hathaway A has 1.65 million shares outstanding. If we calculate the market capitalization, which is number of shares multiplied by price, it looks like this:

- Microsoft, $253.40 billion
- Berkshire Hathaway A, $198.22 billion

So Microsoft is about 28 percent larger than Berkshire Hathaway A. That's big.

BAD NEWS, GOOD NEWS

There are times when the announcement of a stock split seems to be for the purpose of softening the blow of bad news. Company ABC might make a great fanfare to announce a three-for-one split and then a couple of days later announce earnings weakness. This is not unlike what can happen with stock buyback announcements. Whether the strategy works is difficult to say, but it does happen.

MESSY SPLITS

A forward split that is two-for-one, three-for-one, or sometimes five-for-one is often just a clean split with nothing additional in the pot. But occasionally a stock will split five-for-four or four-for-three with additional cash or preferred stock thrown in the kitty. Sometimes preferred stock and warrants are added. These messy splits can be big headaches for professional investors who often avoid them completely.

Here is some interesting information about the growth and splits of Coca Cola, better known around the world as "Coke."

> Sometimes, not splitting would mean that few people could afford even a single share. If, in its 80-odd-year history as a public company, Coca-Cola (NYSE: KO) had never once split its stock, one share would be priced at well more than $200,000 today.
>
> Not too many people could afford even a single share. In fact, Coke has split so many times in its history that if you had bought just one share when it went public in 1919, you'd have more than 4,600 shares today.[1]

This seems to support the argument that splits help to keep the price down at a level where individual investors can afford the stocks, rather than having them soar to astronomic levels for only institutional investors.

ARE SPLITS GOING AWAY?

In the good old days, news of a stock split often fired up the stock market. Almost everything jumped up a few points. Then it was takeover and merger fever driving the market. Now it seems to be more stock buybacks squeezing a few extra dollars into those share prices. A look at Table 49.1 suggests that stock splits have gone away.

It's difficult to find much recent news about new stock splits. There are a few out there, but not many. In 2010, analysts were already discussing the demise of stock splits.

"WHERE HAVE ALL THE STOCK SPLITS GONE? LONG TIME PASSING"

Are they going away? If so, what's replacing them and why? Take a look at some interesting facts about stock splits.

Table 49.1 **Selected Stock Splits[2]**

Company	Size	Years
Oracle Corporation (NASDAQ: ORCL)	2-1	1989
	2-1	1993
	3-2	1995
	3-2	1996
	3-2	1997
	3-2	1999
	2-1	2000 (March)
	2-1	**2000 (October) Last**
Microsoft Corporation (NASDAQ: MSFT)	2-1	1987
	2-1	1990
	3-2	1991
	3-2	1992
	2-1	1994
	2-1	1996
	2-1	1998
	2-1	1999
	2-1	2003 Last
Intel Corporation (NASDAQ: INTC)	3-2	1987
	2-1	1993
	2-1	1995
	2-1	1997
	2-1	1999 Last
EMC Corporation (NYSE: EMC)	3-2	1987
	2-1	1993
	2-1	1995
	2-1	1997
	2-1	1999 Last

(continued)

Table 49.1   Selected Stock Splits *(continued)*

Company	Size	Years
General Electric (NYSE: GE)	2-1	1971
	2-1	1983
	2-1	1987
	2-1	1994
	2-1	1997
	3-1	2000 Last
IBM (NYSE: IBM)	5-4	1964
	3-2	1966
	2-1	1968
	5-4	1973
	4-1	1979
	2-1	1997
	2-1	1999 Last

Ten years ago there were 83 stock splits, last year there was just one, and tomorrow will be the first one this year (a small note below on reverses and stock dividends). Traditionally splits were used to keep stocks in a price range. The concern was that if prices were too high, investors, especially individuals, would not buy them. So, as a stock price went up, to say 150% or 200% of its acceptable level, speculation would start on a split, causing the stock price to raise more. After another 10%–20% gain, enough to cushion the stock in case it got caught in a down draft after the split, the issue would split. Decades ago (I'm old), there were services which charged a fee to alert you via a beeper (I hope you remember what a beeper is) when a split was announced so you could buy the stock (no one cared what the issue was), make a short-term profit, and move on—ah, life was good, and easy (not really).

That was then. Now splits are out of fashion. Besides stocks not being high in price (unless you compare it to the March 2009 lows), splits are expensive, and the cost of maintaining odd-lots is equally as high. Secondly, companies are not as scared about high prices. The $37.40 average price 30 years ago when the S&P 500 was at 135.76 compares to the $42.11 average of today with the Index at 1067. The logic for splits is gone, there is no need for them and in the current cost conscious environment there is no room for them. So, why do I think that stock splits will return? The logic of psychology. I think, which is short hand for saying I have absolutely no evidence or facts to back up my opinion, that investors like splits: more shares; a belief that it proves the stock has done well; and a belief that management thinks the stock will continue to do well. All illogical, non-professional, and on par with not selling a stock that is up 90% just because you want to say it doubled—but that's what investor psychology is about. No big pressing investment insight here, a few charts below (and attached in the file), and a note of an unusual event in the current market trend, maybe.[3]

BULLISH WITH ATTITUDE

A stock split announcement tends to convey a bullish attitude and a feeling that the company is doing something for the benefit of the investors. This benefit doesn't bear close examination but conveys a kind of corporate warm, fuzzy feeling. Also with respect to psychology, a split makes investors feel like they are getting something for nothing, even though they aren't. It's always best to be skeptical.

Stock splits do make shares more affordable for the individual investor, but this doesn't really do anything for the company. In fact it makes more work—more information for the company to send out and get back. It's a stretch to say that extra work is advertising for the company, but it certainly doesn't hurt.

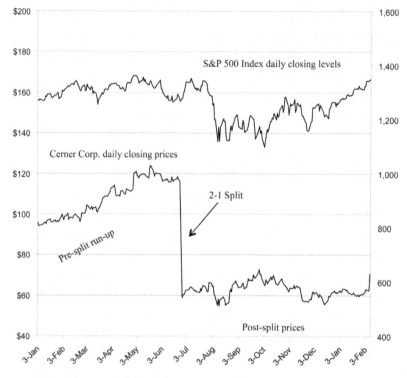

Data source: Yahoo! Finance Historical Prices

Figure 49.1   **Cerner Corp. 2-1 Split, 2011**

Figure 49.1 shows the effect of a 2-1 split on Cerner Corp. back in June 2011. The stock was enjoying a nice advance prior to the split, but it went rather flat after the split. Part of this can be attributed to the market pullback, but it does show that the split didn't do much to help the stock price growth. The S&P 500 Index is included in Figure 49.1 just for comparison.

EVERYTHING IS SPLIT

It's important to remember that all the data relating to a stock are split by the amount of the split. With a 2-1 stock split, the number of shares is doubled and:

- The price per share is cut in half
- The dividend per share is cut in half
- The earnings per share are cut in half
- The revenues per share are cut in half
- The debt per share is cut in half
- Everything else per share is cut in half

SPLITS COULD COME BACK

Splits will return in a big way if companies decide they are necessary. It's impossible to say when this might happen, but maybe when the economy settles down, assuming such a thing is possible. The investors this will help the most are the ones who want to hold stock shares in their IRAs and other retirement accounts.

CHAPTER 50

Join the Club

We could start a club. We could get a bunch of people together, pool our money, and get rich together. Plus we'd learn something about the stock market.

That's often the way it starts; someone suggests a club and talks up the idea to friends, neighbors, and other acquaintances. They meet monthly to discuss the market and stocks, as well as to make some investment decisions. Some clubs do well; some become famous or infamous, like the "Beardstown Ladies," who wrote a book claiming to earn more than 23.4 percent on their "sensible" investing. However, their errors were eventually exposed when an article appeared in the *San Francisco Chronicle* and another in *Chicago* magazine.

In 1998, an article in *Chicago* magazine asserted that the group's stated returns had included the new investments made by its members, and that when computed in conventional fashion, their annual rate of return for 1984–1993 was actually 9.1 percent, considerably less than the 14.9 percent return on the S&P 500 during the same period. Outside auditor Price Waterhouse, hired by the club, confirmed the subpar 9.1 percent annual rate for 1984–1993. The auditor also discovered the Beardstown Ladies' annualized return was 15.3 percent when all of 1983–1997 was included; this was better than the average stock fund at the time, but still worse than the S&P 500 return of 17.2 percent for the same period.[1]

Many at the time said the error was not an intentional act of deception, still it did cause more loss of faith in the stock market.

The Internet has become a large resource for investment clubs, supplying research and other information to subscribers. Although investment clubs aren't for everyone, they can be a useful source of information and education for the individual investor.

NATIONAL ASSOCIATION OF INVESTORS CORPORATION

Investment clubs generally aren't phony pyramids or other schemes created for an investor to "get rich quick." The National Association of Investors Corporation (NAIC; also known as "Betterinvesting"), for one, is a not-for-profit organization devoted to assisting individual investors form and operate investment clubs. Currently there are more than 13,000 clubs with about 120,000 individual members.

The NAIC stresses four principles for successful, long-term investing:

1. Invest regularly, regardless of market conditions.
2. Reinvest all earnings.
3. Invest in growth companies (and growth mutual funds).
4. Diversify to reduce risk.

Investors need help when starting an investment club and the NAIC is one of the organizations available to provide that help. Their vast resources can provide invaluable assistance to clubs that are just starting out.

The heart of the NAIC approach to investing is the third principle—investing in growth companies. The primary tool to evaluate common stocks is a two-page form with a semi-log graph on the front called the Stock Selection Guide (SSG). The SSG dates to the founding of the organization and was created by George A. Nicholson.[2]

Following is contact information for the NAIC:

Member Services
E-mail: service@betterinvesting.org
Toll free: (877) 275-6242
Tel: (248) 583-6242
Fax: (248) 583-4880
Monday–Friday 8:00 a.m– 6:00 p.m. (ET)
Closed Saturday and Sunday

BetterInvesting Magazine
Editor e-mail: bi@betterinvesting.org
Toll free: (877) 275-6242, ext. 3047
Tel: (248) 583-6242, ext. 3047
Fax: (248) 583-4880

Home Office
711 West 13 Mile Road
Madison Heights, MI 48071

Mailing Address
BetterInvesting
P.O. Box 220
Royal Oak, MI 48068

Office Hours
Monday–Friday 8:30 a.m.–5:00 p.m. (ET)
Closed Saturday and Sunday

Website:
www.betterinvesting.org

HOW DOES A CLUB FUNCTION?

Most clubs have simple rules that can be changed as necessary. Usually, clubs are groups of 10 to 20 people or more, often organized as a legal partnership (for tax purposes). They meet on a regular basis, such as monthly. Club officers are elected, and members are asked to actively participate through the following activities:

1. Attending the monthly meeting
2. Making a monthly contribution, often a $20 minimum, with no maximum
3. Researching and following the progress of a specific company's stock or a group of stocks that the club owns or has targeted for investment.

Based on its strategy, the club invests money in the stock market and normally has one or two members authorized to place trades with a stockbroker. Each member has shares of the investment portfolio, depending on the amount of money the member has contributed.

With a low monthly minimum, virtually anyone can afford to belong to a club. The main requirements are a willingness to work, learn, and get along with the other members. Obviously, a mutually agreed-upon system of resolving differences is necessary.

In Business Together

Since the club is a legal partnership, all the members are effectively in business with each other, with all the advantages and problems that this can engender. Trust is essential. The organization sets broad goals of education so that members can learn about investing in the stock market, capital gains, and making a profit.

Club members need to understand that gains can be minimal or even nonexistent for the first couple of years. Often clubs place restrictions on early withdrawals. Eventually, club members start their own individual portfolios, supported by the knowledge and skills they learned by being an investment club member.

Federal Taxes

Here is a brief summary of some of the Internal Revenue Service's tax requirements for investment clubs.

- *Identifying number.* Each club must have an "employer identification number" (EIN) to use when filing its return. The club's EIN also may have to be given to the payer of dividends or other income from investments recorded in the club's name. If your club does not have an EIN, obtain Form SS-4, "Application for Employer Identification Number" from the IRS. Mail the completed form to the Internal Revenue Center where you file the club's tax return.
- *Tax treatment of the club.* Generally, an investment club is treated as a partnership for federal tax purposes, unless it chooses otherwise. In some situations, it can be taxed as a corporation or a trust.

INVESTMENT CLUBS AND THE SEC

Investment clubs usually do not have to register themselves or register the offer and sale of their membership interests with the SEC. But since each investment club is unique, each group should explore, examine, and decide if it needs to register in compliance with securities laws.

Two laws can relate to investment clubs:

1. Under the Securities Act of 1933, membership interests in an investment club may be securities. If this is the case, the offer and sale of membership interests could be subject to federal regulations.

2. Under the Investment Company Act of 1940, an investment club may be an investment company and regulated accordingly.

For further information, contact the Securities and Exchange Commission at http://www.sec.gov/, and do a search for "Investment Clubs."

STATE REGULATIONS

State securities laws can differ from federal securities laws. To learn more about the laws in your state, contact your state securities regulator. You can also visit the North American Securities Administrators Association (NASAA) website at: http://www.nasaa.org.

TRUST RESULTS, BUT AUDIT THEM

Obviously trust is important. But it's also necessary to create safeguards to protect both the investors and those in charge of the money. As much as possible, remove the opportunity for mistrust; decrease the temptation, and make it difficult for someone to walk off with the money. Also, establish a system to ensure that investment policies and decisions are being followed.

SUCCESS IS IN THE SETUP

The most difficult thing for a group of people to do is make a decision. Because the initial setup is so important to the successful operation of a club, remove or moderate the decision-making process by relying on experience. Contacting an organization like the NAIC for their suggestions accomplishes much of the difficult organizational work and simplifies the decision-making process.

Notes

Part 1

Chapter 1

1. Peter Lynch and John Rothschild, *One Up on Wall Street*, second edition, New York: Simon & Schuster, 2000.
2. Market Intelligence Center Staff, "Good Stock, Bad Stock: Amazon (AMZN) vs. Netflix (NFLX)?" Amazon.com, October 26, 2011.
3. Charles Riley, "Diet Coke Fizzes Past Pepsi," *CNN Money*, March 18, 2011.
4. Peter Lynch and John Rothschild, *One Up on Wall Street*, New York: Simon & Schuster, 2000.

Chapter 2

1. "Stocks Prices Double in 3 Years, but It's Becoming a Lonely Party," Associated Press, March 8, 2012.
2. Doug McIntyre, "8 Stocks That Could Double in Value in 2012," *Daily Finance*, December 23, 2011.

Chapter 3

1. PR Newswire, United Business Media, press release, December 21, 2011.
2. Ibid.
3. Jon Ogg, "2011 Stock Buybacks on Fire, Over $34 Billion (PFE, UNP, GME, ERTS, GD, TUP, MHS, VZ, UNM, MO, AZN, SYMC, YUM, DGX, COH, TIF, INTC) 24/7 Wall St. Wire," February 4, 2011, http://247wallst.com/2011/02/04/2011-stock-buybacks-on-fire-over-34

-billion-pfe-unp-gme-erts-gd-tup-mhs-vz-unm-mo-azn-symc-yum-dgx
-coh-tif-intc/#ixzz1hZhTrfLK.

4. Nelson D. Schwartz, "Business Day," *New York Times*, November 21, 2011.

5. RTT Staff Writer, "FMC Corp. Authorizes $250 Mln of Stock Buybacks, Boosts Quarterly Dividend," RTTNews.com, February 17, 2012.

6. Gillian Rich, "Time Warner Cable Beats, Plans $4 Billion Buyback," *Investor's Business Daily*, January, 26, 2012.

7. YCharts Staff, "Nordstrom Authorizes $800 Million Stock Buyback and Increased Dividend," YCharts, http://ycharts.com/analysis/story/nordstrom _authorizes_800_million_stock_buyback_and_increased_dividend.

8. StreetInsider.com Staff Writer, "Alaska Air (ALK) Approves 2-for-1 Split, New $50M Buyback," February 16, 2012, available at StreetInsider.com.

9. Alex Sherman, "Comcast Authorizes $6.5 Billion Buyback," Bloomberg Businessweek.com, February 15, 2012, available online.

Chapter 4

1. Staff Writer, "The AAII Sentiment Survey," 2011+, American Association of Individual Investors, published ongoing.

2. Irene Aldridge, "How Profitable Is High-Frequency Trading?" *Huffington Post*, July 26, 2010, http://www.huffingtonpost.com/irene-aldridge/how -profitable-are-high-f_b_659466.html.

3. Graham Bowley, "High-Frequency Trading," *New York Times*, October 10, 2011.

4. Ibid.

Chapter 5

1. Hilary Kramer, "Seven Bellwethers to Watch Closely," The Trading Deck, MarketWatch, *Wall Street Journal*, December 23, 2011.

2. David Zielenziger, "IBM's Earnings Beat Estimates: Could They Be Tech Bellwether?" *International Business Times*, October 17, 2011.

Part 2

Chapter 6

1. Peter Lynch and John Rothschild, *One Up on Wall Street*, second edition, NewYork: Simon & Schuster, 2000.

2. Jim Cramer, "There's Always a Bull Market," *The Street*, June 23, 2006, http://www.thestreet.com/story/10292267/1/theres-always-a-bull-market.html.

3. Peter Lynch and John Rothschild, *One Up on Wall Street*, second edition, New York: Simon & Schuster, 2000.

Chapter 7

1. Hans E. Wagner, Trading Online Markets LLC, April 16, 2009, http://www.tradingonlinemarkets.com/Articles/Technical_Analysis/MACD_Indicator.htm.
2. Daryl Guppy, "Head and Shoulder Pattern," Guppytraders.com, 2010, http://www.guppytraders.com/gup344.shtml.
3. Currently published by Orient Paperbacks, India; its ninth, revised edition appeared on July 25, 2009.

Chapter 8

1. Fortune Editors, "Bill George's Corporate Dream Team," *CNN Money*, August 24, 2011.
2. "Tracking the Nations Bank Failures," http://graphicsweb.wsj.com/documents/Failed-US-Banks.html, January 2008 to August 2011.

Chapter 9

1. Hibah Yousuf, "Insider Selling on the Rise—Bear Signal?" *CNN Money*, November 7, 2011, http://money.cnn.com/2011/11/06/markets/insider/selling/index.htm.
2. Sarah N. Lynch and Aruna Viswanatha, "Chicago Consultant Charged with Insider Trading on Carlyle," Reuters, March 15, 2012.
3. H. Nejat Seyhun, *Investment Intelligence from Insider Trading*, Cambridge, MA: MIT Press, 2000.
4. Steve Kroft correspondent, "Congress: Trading Stock on Inside Information?" November 13, 2011. Copyright 2012, CBS Interactive Inc., reprinted with permission of CBS News Archives.
5. The report "Insiders" received quite a reaction the week after it aired. Democratic Congresswoman Nancy Pelosi's office called the report a "right-wing smear." And Republican Speaker John Boehner's office called his inclusion in the story "idiotic." But now at least 93 members of Congress have signed on as cosponsors of the Stock Act, and for the first time the bill has been introduced in the Senate.
6. Justin Rohrlich, "Insider Trading Laws Do Not Apply to Members of Congress, No, Seriously," Minyanville Business News blog, October 13, 2011, http://www.minyanville.com/businessmarkets/articles/raj-rajaratnam-galleon-insider-trading-rajaratnam/10/13/2011/id/37373.

7. Committee on Ethics, Statutes and Rules Governing Disclosure of Financial Interests, Ethics in Government Act of 1978, http://ethics.house .gov/financial-dislosure/statutes-and-rules-governing-disclosure-financial -interests.

Chapter 10

1. Joshua Kennon, "Intro to Stock Trading," 2012, *About.com Guide.*

Chapter 11

1. Gerald Loeb, *The Battle for Investment Survival,* New York: Wiley, 1996.
2. Peter Lynch and John Rothschild, *One Up on Wall Street,* second edition, New York: Simon & Schuster, 2000.
3. Data from MSN.com, quotes, MAT, and more on Mattel, 2012.

Chapter 12

1. StockCharts.com—ChartSchool, a subscription chart service with some complimentary information, http://stockcharts.com/help/doku .php?id=chart_school:chart_analysis:support_and_resistance.
2. Ibid.
3. Ibid.

Chapter 13

1. Matthew Schifrin, "Martin Zweig: Turbo Charged Value Stocks," *Forbes Magazine,* February 23, 2009, http://www.forbes.com/2009/02/23/zweig -growth-value-personal-finance_marty_zweig.html.
2. Robert Holmes, "What If There's a Bear Market in 2012?" TheStreet. com, December 29, 2011.
3. Ibid.

Part 3

Chapter 14

1. Yahoo! Finance, Quote, DOM, Profile, 2012.
2. Yahoo! Finance, Quote, HE, Profile, 2012.
3. Yahoo! Finance, Quote, SO, Profile, 2012.
4. Yahoo! Finance, Quote, WDC, KLAC, SBUX, JBL, HURC, 2012.
5. Yahoo! Finance, Quote, BMY, DE, GE, 2012.

Chapter 15

1. Michael Ervolini, "Why We Can't Sell Our Losers," Forbes.com, Intelligent Investing Panel, November 9, 2002.
2. Data from Yahoo! Finance, Quotes, EK.
3. Joe, "Sell Your Losers Before 2011 Ends," retirebyforty, November 30, 2011.

Chapter 18

1. "Division of Market Regulation: Responses to Frequently Asked Questions Concerning Regulation SHO," Securities and Exchange Commission, http://sec.gov/divisions/marketreg/mrfaqregsho1204.htm.
2. Data from NASDAQ short interest table.

Chapter 19

1. Shah Gilani, "The Trend Is Your Best Friend in the Stock Market," *Money Morning*, February 29, 2012.
2. Staff Writer, *Investopedia Dictionary*, "Short Sale," http://www.investopedia.com/terms/s/shortsale.asp#ixzz1pHzKqWkF.

Chapter 20

1. Alexandra Zendrian, "4 Stocks Hitting 52-Week Highs: MSFT, NKE, MAT, BWLD," *The Street*, March 1, 2012.
2. Ibid.

Chapter 21

1. Dr. Terry F. Allen, "How to Trade Rumors of Takeovers," *Terry's Tips for Stock Options Success*, July 7, 2011. Available at http://www.terrystips.com/blog.
2. Shira Ovide, "No One Knows Anything about Sears," *Wall Street Journal*, January 17, 2012.

Chapter 22

1. Lori Spechler, "Reverse Stock Splits Are Usually Good for Investors: Report," CNBC, March 22, 2011.

Chapter 23

1. Staff Writer, "Six Dividend Stocks to Hold Forever," *Dividend Growth Investor*, May 4, 2011.

2. David Sterman, "5 More 'Forever' Stocks on Sale," *Investing, Investing Ideas*, September 29, 2011, available at http://community.nasdaq.com /News/2011-10/5-more-forever-stocks-on-sale.aspx?storyid=96643#ixzz1px7 9Vt00.

Chapter 24

1. Ken Little, "Averaging Down—Good Idea or Foolish Risk?" April 11, 2006, *About.com Guide*. Available at http://stocks.about.com/b/2006/04/11 /averaging-down-good-idea-or-foolish-risk.htm.

Chapter 25

1. Alexandra Twin, "Wall Street: Sell What in May and Go Away?" *CNN Money*, May 1, 2008, http://money.cnn.com/2008/05/01/markets/sellmay _markets/index.htm.

2. Linda Stern, "Sell in May and Go Away? Stock Strategists Not So Sure," Reuters Money, April 27, 2011, http://blogs.reuters.com/reuters-money /2011/04/27/sell-in-may-and-go-away-stock-strategists-not-so-sure.

Chapter 26

1. "Dollar Cost Averaging," Wikipedia, en.wikipedia.org/Dollar _cost_averaging.

2. Gregg S. Fisher, "Does Dollar Cost Averaging Make Sense?" Personal Finance, Forbes.com. October 3, 2011.

3. Ibid.

Chapter 27

1. Read more at http://www.investopedia.com/terms/s/sellagainstthebox .asp#ixzz1kUjwwjC5.

2. Data source: Yahoo! Finance, Quotes, COH.

Chapter 28

1. Harry M. Markowitz, "Portfolio Selection," *Journal of Finance* (1952) 7/1: 77–91, http: //doi:10.2307/2975974 or JSTOR, http://www.jstor.org .stable/2975974.

2. See http://www.investopedia.com/articles/01/051601.asp#ixzz
1o0Ix7VLd.

3. Wikipedia, "Exchange-Traded Funds," http://en.wikipedia.org/wiki
/Exchange-traded_funds. Article cites ETFConnect, "Index ETFs—Know
Your Funds" and "American Stock Exchange, ETFs—Individual Investor."

Part 4

Chapter 29

1. Barry Popik, "Never Sell a Dull Market (Short)," quoting a March 31,
1905, *New York Times*, p. 14 article, October 9, 2008, http://www.barrypopik.
com/index.php/new_york_city/entry/never_sell_a_dull_market_short
_wall_street_proverb/.

2. "Eugene Peroni—Market Pullback Will Wait a While," MarketWatch
Morning, *Stock Talk Archives*, March 16, 2012. Eugene E. Peroni, Jr., is a senior
vice president at Advisors Asset Management, Inc. He joined the firm in 2007
and is responsible for Unit Investment Trust (UIT) product development as
well as equity portfolio management. Prior to this, he was a senior managing director of equity research at Claymore Advisors, LLC and Claymore
Securities, Inc. and managed portfolios across several platforms. Previously,
he served as a managing director of equity research at Nuveen Investments.
Prior to that, Mr. Peroni was the director of technical research at Janney
Montgomery Scott, LLC. He is a recognized market strategist with over 30
years of investment management and analysis experience. *Bloomberg Businessweek*, August 5, 2012 by staff writer. Available at http://www.marketwatch.
com/story/peroni-market-pullback-will-wait-a-while-2012-03-16.

Chapter 30

1. Staff Writer, "Market Order," U.S. Securities and Exchange Commission, http://www.sec.gov/answers/mktord.htm.

Chapter 31

1. Staff Writer, "What Does a Low Stock Price Mean?" Smart Stock
Research, 2012, http://www.smartstockresearch.com/InvestingBasics
/Articles/~tm2AFD.html.

Chapter 32

1. James Cramer, "Stick With the Dips," *Time Magazine*, Monday, October 20, 1997.

2. Jason Zweig, "Why Buying on the Dips Isn't All It's Cracked Up to Be," *The Intelligent Investor*, September 24, 2011.

Chapter 34

1. Staff Writer, "General Rules and Regulations Promulgated under the Securities Act of 1933," Marx Law Library, University of Cincinnati College of Law, http://www.law.uc.edu/CCL/33ActRls/rule501.html.
2. Teo Lasarte, "An Introduction to Hedge Fund Strategy," *The London School of Economics and Political Science*, March 17, 2011, International Asset Management, http://www.iam.uk.com/press/lse-publications /An-Introduction-to-Hedge-Fund-Strategies.pdf.
3. Michael Bartolo, "Hedge Fund Strategies Guide," Goizueta Business School, Emory University, September 2008, http://www.cai.emory.edu /documents/HF_Strategies.pdf; BarclayHedge, "Understanding Event-Driven Investing," available at http://www.barclayhedge.com/research /educational-articles/hedge-fund-strategy-definition/hedge-fund-strategy -event-driven.html.
4. Alexander Ineichen, *Absolute Returns: The Risks and Opportunities of Hedge Fund Investing*, Hoboken, NJ: John Wiley, 2002, p. 181.
5. Gretchen Morgenson, "Surveys Give Big Investors an Early View from Analysts," *New York Times*, July 15, 2012, http://www.nytimes.com/2012/07/16 /business/in-surveys-hedge-funds-see-early-views-of-stock-analysts.html.

Part 5

1. S. A. Nelson, *The ABC of Stock Speculation*, New York: A. Nelson, 1902.

Chapter 35

1. Peter Lynch and John Rothchild, *One Up On Wall Street*, second edition, New York: Simon & Schuster, 2000.
2. Staff Writer, "Markets Slightly Up in Anticipation of Positive Earnings Reports (AMZN, GM)," *Investor Guide*, January 9, 2012.
3. Rebecca Lipman, "Google Results Suck—What Does This Mean for Other Tech Stocks?" Yahoo! Finance, http://community.nasdaq.com /News/2012-01/google-results-suck-what-does-this-mean-for-other -tech-stocks.aspx?storyid=117186#ixzz1ksHyUteX.

Chapter 36

1. Data source: Yahoo! Finance, Quote, CYBI.
2. NASDAQ Staff Writer, "RiskMetrics, Risk Assessment Tool for Stocks," http://www.nasdaq.com/services/riskMetrics.stm.
3. After Quotes, http://www.afterquotes.com/great/quotes/risk.htm.

Chapter 37

1. Matthew Ericson, Elaine He, and Amy Schoenfeld, "Tracking the $700 Billion Bailout," *New York Times*, Business, 2009, nytimes.com/packages /html/national/200904_CREDITCRISIS/recipients.html.

Chapter 38

1. Staff Writer, "If All the Money in the U.S. Only Totals $6 Trillion, How Can the New York Stock Exchange Have Stocks Valued at $15 Trillion?" How Stuff Works, A Discovery Company. Available at http://money.howstuffworks. com/question241.htm.
2. Source: Yahoo! Finance, Get Quotes, PRFDX+Profile.
3. Source: Yahoo! Finance, Get Quotes, PRFDX.
4. Morningstar data through December 31, 2011.
5. Yahoo! Finance, Get Quotes, PRFDX, Holdings.
6. "Commission Guidance Regarding Client Commission Practices Under Section 28(e) of the Securities Exchange Act of 1934," Securities and Exchange Commission, 2006-07-18. Available at http://www.sec.gov/rules /interp/2006/34-54165.pdf.
7. "U.S. Securities and Exchange Commission Information on Mutual Funds," U.S. Securities and Exchange Commission (SEC), http://www.sec .gov/answers/mutfund.htm.
8. Ibid.
9. Ibid.

Chapter 39

1. Larry Swedroe, "Investing: 'Buy What You Know' Is a Bad Strategy," *CBS Money Watch*, February 15, 2012.
2. Peter Lynch and John Rothschild, *One Up on Wall Street*. New York: Simon & Schuster, 2000.

Part 6

Chapter 40

1. Hans E. Wagner, "Stop Orders vs. Protective Put Options," Trading Online Markets LLC, http://www.tradingonlinemarkets.com/Articles/Options/Stop_Loss_Orders_vs_Protective_Put_Options.htm.

Chapter 41

1. Ken Sweet, "Dow Plunges After S&P Downgrade," *CNN Money*, August 8, 2011.
2. Standard & Poor's, "S&P | About S&P | Americas—Key Statistics," http://www.standardandpoors.com/about-sp/key-statistics/en/us.
3. Damian Paletta and Matt Phillips, "S&P Strips U.S. of Top Credit Rating," *Wall Street Journal*, August 6, 2011, http://online.wsj.com/article/SB10001424053111903366504576490841235575386.html.

Chapter 42

1. U.S. Securities and Exchange Commission Staff Writer, "Penny Stock Rules," last modified April 4, 2008, available at http://www.sec.gov/answers/penny.htm.

Chapter 43

1. Stephanie Clifford and Jenny Anderson, "S.E.C. Warns Wall Street: Stop Spreading the False Rumors," *New York Times*, July 14, 2008.
2. Shayndi Raice, "Facebook Moves to Debunk Phone Number Rumor," Meredith Chin, a Facebook spokeswoman, comments. *Wall Street Journal*, August 10, 2011.

Chapter 44

1. Staff Writer, "About the Financial Industry Regulatory Authority," Financial Industry Regulatory Authority, Inc. (FINRA), http://www.finra.org/AboutFINRA.
2. Staff Writer, FINRA, "FINRA Rules, Interpretations of FINRA's Margin Rule," http://www.finra.org/.

Chapter 45

1. Mark Koba, "Market Circuit Breakers," *CNBC Explains*, August 10, 2011.

Part 7

Chapter 46

1. Securities and Exchange Commission, http://www.sec.gov/news/press/2012/2012-18.htm.

2. U.S. Securities and Exchange Commission, Litigation Release No. 22240, January 26, 2012, SEC v. First Resource Group LLC, and David H. Stern, Civil Action No. 0:12-CV-60137-KMW (S.D. Fla., filed January 26, 2012).

Chapter 47

1. "SEC Investor Beware," Securities and Exchange Commission, Office of Investor Education and Assistance, 1996.

Chapter 48

1. Jeff Macke, "The Santa Claus Rally Isn't What You Think: Hirsch," *Breakout, Yahoo! Finance Worldwide*, November 28, 2011.

2. Allan Roth, "Santa Claus Rally or Stocking Full of Coal?," *CBS Money Watch*, December 21, 2011.

3. James Brumley, "The January Effect: Fact or Fiction? Supposed Market Metronome Might Just Be a Myth," *InvestorPlace*, December 28, 2011.

Chapter 49

1. Yahoo!, Finance, Get Quotes ORCL, MSFT, INTC, EMC, GE, IBM, splits taken from the long-term charts.

2. Motley Fool Staff, "Why Companies Split Stock," Motley Fool, May 27, 2004.

3. Howard Silverblatt, "Where Have All The Stock Splits Gone, Long Time Passing," *Bloomberg Businessweek*, June 7, 2010, http://www.businessweek.com/investing/insights/blog/archives/2010/06/where_have_all_the_stock_splits_gone_long_time_passing.html.

Chapter 50

1. Mark Gongloff, "Where Are They Now: The Beardstown Ladies," *Wall Street Journal*, May 1, 2006, available at http://latrobefinancialmanagement.com.

2. Staff Writer, NAIC website; http://www.betterinvesting.org/.

INDEX

About the Author

Michael D. Sheimo has been an author of investing books for more than twenty years. He has a Bachelor of Science degree in English and Speech. Prior to writing about the stock market he was a Registered Representative and Registered Options Principal for several years. He was a Financial Consultant at Merrill-Lynch and Olde Financial Corp. His books have received positive reviews in publications around the world, from India to the United States, including *The Wall Street Journal*. He received the "Editor's Choice" award from the American Library Association in 1999. Michael D. Sheimo lives in Edina, Minnesota.

CPSIA information can be obtained
at www.ICGtesting.com
Printed in the USA
BVOW09s0240031117

499406BV00009B/75/P